DATE DUE

MAY 11 1979

Longman business studies

Edited by D. C. Hague

Forecasting for Business: Methods and Applications

Doug Wood
Robert Fildes

Longman
London and New York

Longman Group Limited London

*Associated companies, branches and representatives
throughout the world*

*Published in the United States of America
by Longman Inc., New York*

© Longman Group Limited 1976

First published 1976

Library of Congress Cataloging in Publication Data

Wood, Douglas.
    Forecasting for business.

    (Longman business series)
    Includes bibliographies and index.
    1. Business forecasting.   I. Fildes, Robert, joint author.   II. Title.
HB3730.W64   338.5'44   75–46513
ISBN 0 582 44059 9 pbk.

Set in IBM Journal 10 on 12pt
and printed in Great Britain by
William Clowes & Sons Ltd., London, Colchester and Beccles.

Contents

Preface

Forecasting is a managerial activity

Virtually every manager has to take decisions where the effects are dependent on the outcome of factors which are uncertain at the time the decisions are made. For many of these decisions, managers will be able to resolve the uncertainties by referring to their own previous experience, so that activities such as the preparation of annual budgets, setting sales targets or investments in new equipment can be performed without using any formal forecasting techniques.

This approach often works satisfactorily, but when an error does occur the absence of a formal forecasting method makes it almost impossible to check which of the many assumptions made in generating the forecast was unfounded. The manager therefore finds it difficult to learn from his mistakes. Similarly, without an explicit forecasting system it is difficult to learn from colleagues. The increasing complexity of modern organizations tends to require the integration of the opinion of more and more people in the formulation of each forecast. Without some degree of structure such integration becomes an impossible task.

However, few managers have much specific training in forecasting techniques. Even though his qualification might have included some mathematics and possibly some statistics and economics as well, finding the appropriate forecasting technique in a realistic situation remains far from easy. Before we can expect to see these more formal methods permeate practical forecasting it is necessary to translate the ideas of statistics and economics on which forecasting is based into a language accessible to the typical manager. It is no use expecting him to learn about advanced matrix algebra, the theory of consumer demand and statistical estimation. He has not the time, even if he had the inclination.

Our primary aim in this book is to provide the practising manager or student, studying for a degree in management, with the tools and the framework necessary to produce a good forecast. We hope the book can be used as a do-it-yourself guide so that a non-specialist may, by careful reading and use of the many references, produce an adequate forecast profitable to his organization. For many a manager this aim is unnecessarily ambitious. He only wishes to understand the possible methods and their limitations which are at the disposal of an economic/statistical/operational research department. We expect that a selective reading of the book will give an adequate overview.

Forecasting is a task all managers perform with varying degrees of success. We see the framework proposed here for understanding and projecting current information as extremely helpful in the management decision process, and the correct choice of forecasting method quite crucial in selecting the best of the many alternative strategies available to a firm.

D. Wood
R. Fildes

Acknowledgements

We are indebted to the following for permission to reproduce copyright material:

Prentice-Hall Inc. for Fig. 7.1 from *Smoothing, Forecasting and Prediction: of Discrete Time Series* © 1963 by Robert Goodell Brown. Reprinted by permission of Prentice-Hall Inc., Englewood Cliffs, New Jersey; The American Statistical Association for Figs. 8.10(*a*) and 8.10(*b*) taken from an article entitled 'An Economic Linear Programming Model of the U.S. Petroleum Refining Industry' by F. C. Adams and J. M. Griffin from Vol. 67 of the *Journal of the American Statistical Association*.

We regret that we have been unable to trace the copyright holder of a table showing *Total World Supply of Arable Land* published by Earth Island Publishers Ltd.

During the preparation of this book we have benefitted from the suggestions of our colleagues and students. In particular we would like to thank the series editor Professor Douglas Hague for his initial encouragement and continued interest. Stephen Lofthouse, Peter Fitzroy and John Westwood commented helpfully on various drafts and much of whatever clarity has been achieved is due to their efforts.

Our friends and family have fortunately had remarkably little to do with the project. However, their scepticism about our progress with the work did provide us with sufficient incentive to complete the book, albeit 1 year earlier than we expected though 2 years later than we forecast.

Part 1
Introduction

The demand for forecasts in business is a response to uncertainty. Without forecast information business decisions could only be related to current conditions and in a rapidly changing world this policy cannot in the long term generate acceptable results.

It is easy to suggest that decision makers should avoid this mistake and relate their decisions to future conditions, but putting this into practice is more difficult because forecasts are an integral part of the whole planning process and as such do not just alter the way in which choices are made between existing alternatives; they alter entirely the way in which alternatives are specified.

In the first part of this book we therefore think it important to reflect the close relationship between forecasting and the decision-making framework within which it is applied, if only to dispel the impression that forecasting is a statistical rather than a managerial activity.

It is argued that the quality of a forecast cannot be judged outside this managerial context except in a narrow, technical sense. The value of a forecast is derived as much from the way in which it relates to specific decisions as it is from being accurate, and in turn decision making in the firm should recognize and take advantage of the existence of forecasts.

1

Forecasting and managerial decisions

§ 1.1 Introduction

Businessmen, like everyone else, have to make decisions in an uncertain world. As a consequence most decisions have to be taken with incomplete information on some of the factors which influence the outcomes of those decisions. Information may be incomplete for two reasons. In many cases data may actually exist, but may be difficult, impossible or prohibitively expensive to obtain. For example, at any moment in time the state of wear on every moving part of each of the engines used by an airline are scientific facts, yet for the airline to establish those facts would require an enormous expenditure. Instead of collecting data on actual wear, an airline will invariably use its judgement and experience to make estimates of wear, and will then use these estimates as a basis for a planned maintenance schedule.

In contrast to the situation where data exists but is not readily obtainable there is the situation where data may be non-existent. This generally occurs when we are concerned about the future. For example, tomorrow's weather conditions can never be exactly predicted from today's, because today's weather is a historically unique combination of factors. Experts may look at past data and find conditions that are similar and use what happened then as the basis of judgements about what will happen tomorrow; but today's weather, and the way in which it will develop into tomorrow's is strictly a unique occurrence.

For the same reason future economic prospects are always uncertain, however much data we collect, because there is no historical comparison which would tell us exactly how to translate present conditions into future conditions. Instead estimates are made using relationships that applied on similar occasions in the past.

Thus most business decisions are taken in situations where relevant data is missing and where the process of change means that even with a complete set of data some aspects of the decision are different from anything that has previously been encountered.

The forecaster's contribution to business decision making is one of generating data about future conditions and also commenting on the reliability with which current relationships can be assumed to apply in the future. To do this the forecaster has to provide a set of assumptions and estimates by which he hopes to generate missing data from a basis of current knowledge.

Forecasting exists as a formalization of this process. Through forecasting, managers hope to obtain sufficient information about future conditions to anticipate the consequences of their existing policies and to evaluate the potential of alternative ones.

As we have seen, forecasts, whether they are made explicitly or not, are an essential element in decision making. For management decisions this is particularly true since a manager's performance is closely connected with the speed and accuracy with which he can respond to change. If forecasts can help to identify the likelihood and nature of changes, then responses that anticipate these changes can be made. Without such forecasts management actions would lag unprofitably behind events.

However, casual statements about the future do not generate these benefits; we have to be concerned about the quality of forecasts in relation to management needs.

§ 1.2 The quality of forecasts

It is a popular misconception that the more accurate a forecast turns out to be the better it is, and that the quality of a forecast can be measured purely on a statistical basis.

In fact, perfection in forecasting future conditions would often prompt the suspicion that the forecast itself was worthless as an aid to improved decision making. For example businessmen often congratulate themselves because their forecast of sales turned out exactly right (sometimes their modesty compels them to admit an error of ½ per cent) without realizing that they had set the production schedules on the basis of the sales forecast and then quoted a price that allowed them to sell all they produced. It would be far more profitable to have less accurate forecasts of potential sales at different price levels because this information would allow decisions about price and output to maximize expected profits.

In the situation just discussed the statistical accuracy occurred because the original forecast was self-justifying, and as a consequence the apparent accuracy of the forecast was spurious. However, even a genuinely accurate forecast may be inadequate if it fails to relate to specific management decisions.

As an example a forecaster could prepare an extremely accurate estimate of the country's Gross National Product (GNP) next year. To be useful to the firm, and to form the basis of effective action this prediction of GNP needs to be interpreted to show the effect on variables that directly affect the firm. The effect of the predicted change in GNP on consumer expenditure in relevant market sectors, for example, would help the firm to plan production schedules. The effect of the national rate of growth on the price and availability of purchased materials and labour would also provide the information needed in planning the pattern of resource usage and in pricing output. By combining the forecast changes in costs and sales revenue it becomes possible to estimate the total effect on the profitability of the company, and with this information it is possible to judge whether the existing plans and policies of the firm provide an acceptable basis for future viability.

If it is impossible to relate the forecasts of GNP to factors of some immediate concern to the enterprise, either because no such relationship has been established, or else because none exists, then it follows that the forecast, however accurate it may turn out to be, is essentially irrelevant to the firm's information needs.

Exactly the same problems may arise with even quite detailed forecasts if these do not recognize the specific information needs of decision takers. A forecast of future demand for detergent may seem highly relevant to a detergent company, yet if marketing decisions are made by brand managers, it follows that less accurate forecasts of demand by brand categories — for instance into soap-based products, foaming detergents and non-foaming detergents — would be more useful.

It is also possible that a regional breakdown of a forecast is required if it is to be useful in decision making. While a total market may be growing rapidly, some geographical regions in the market could quite easily be declining, perhaps because of demographic changes or alterations in the economic activity of those areas. It is important, therefore, that if these distinctions are relevant to decision making they should be reflected in the degree of detail and disaggregation provided in the forecasts.

Another factor contributing to the quality of a forecast over and above its statistical accuracy is the degree of lead time before the change it predicts is expected to occur. An inaccurate forecast with sufficient lead time to allow appropriate action to be taken may be quite valuable, whereas an accurate forecast allowing inadequate lead time to take corrective action would be useless. Thus a somewhat inaccurate forecast that there will be an unsatisfied demand for houses in three years' time may be useful, because it allows time for appropriate action in terms of stepping up the building programme to be taken before the forecast conditions arise. An accurate forecast that unsatisfied demand will emerge in three months' time would not be useful, since managers would be unable to adjust their building programme to offset this prospective shortage within such a short period.

Finally, and only when taken in conjunction with the two other factors already discussed, the accuracy of forecasts in a statistical sense is an important factor in contributing to improved decision making.

At this stage then it is possible to summarize the previous discussion and list the factors that contribute to the quality of forecasts:

1. The degree to which forecasts can be related to specific decisions.
2. The adequacy of the lead time generated by the forecast in relation to the time needed to make desired changes in policy.
3. The statistical accuracy of forecasts.

Improving the quality of forecasts in any of these three ways generally involves increasing the cost of the forecasting effort. Detailed forecasts, for example, absorb more effort than aggregate forecasts, and improving the lead time or the accuracy of a forecast generally demands an increase in sophistication in the forecasting model employed.

This increase of cost can only be justified where clear benefits ensue over and above the additional forecasting costs incurred. In many cases even a perfect forecast, which matches information needs exactly, would generate little benefit because the resulting improvement in the decision contributes only an insignificant part to the overall performance of the organization. Thus in applications such as detailed production scheduling or routine stock reorder policies, a very simple extrapolative forecasting technique generating low-quality forecasts would be adequate (appropriate methods are discussed in Chapters 4 and 7). By contrast, where decisions are of crucial significance to the future operation and profitability of an organization — for example, the addition of new production capacity, the issue of new capital or the introduction of a new product — the expense of a high-quality forecast that reduced uncertainty to an unavoidable minimum is likely to be justified.

§ 1.3 Forecasting as a source of information

Forecasting is an attempt to create a bridge that links data that we currently have with data that we would like to have but cannot obtain directly. If we decide that a given decision requires information about the level of cash flowing into the firm next month, then the forecaster must provide the required information by describing future cash flow in terms of variables whose levels are already known at the time the forecast is made.

In some situations such a description may be simple. The firm's cash flow next month, for example, could be almost exactly determined by the total invoices currently outstanding less the amount the firm itself owes to suppliers. This would be true if we could assume that there is a direct and almost perfect causal relationship between the issue of an invoice and the subsequent exchange of cash. If there were, cash flow next month is virtually defined by the levels of variables that are already known, and we can show in Fig. 1.1 the simple forecasting model that arises from the assumption. If we need to know cash flow 3 months ahead however, the forecast is not quite so simple, since we have no direct observation on the level of outstanding invoices 2 months ahead. As a result, it is necessary to build a model to connect the desired output, the forecast of cash flow in 3 months time, to variables that can currently be observed.

The obvious inputs to the model are those factors which tend to explain the company's future purchase and sales, for example the production plans of the company and the size of the current order book.

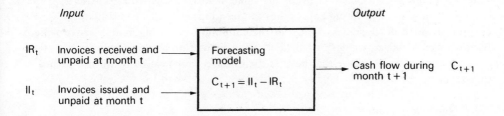

Input

IR_t — Invoices received and unpaid at month t

II_t — Invoices issued and unpaid at month t

Forecasting model

$C_{t+1} = II_t - IR_t$

Output

Cash flow during month t + 1 — C_{t+1}

Fig. 1.1 Cash flow projection — 1 month ahead

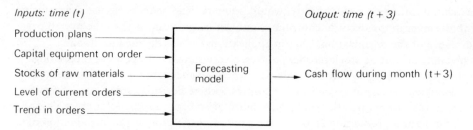

Fig. 1.2 Cash flow projection — 3 months ahead

The forecasting model in Fig. 1.2 consists as before of a set of assumptions and relationships that link the input data with the output data. It is necessarily a much more complicated model than that used for the short-run prediction, because it is far more susceptible to change. An order, for example, could be cancelled, a strike may invalidate the production plan, or a new production method which reduces the consumption of raw materials might be adopted. For the forecast to work, either all of these factors have to be taken into account, or else if these possibilities have been ignored, the forecast should be appropriately qualified by specifying the accuracy of the forecast and the situations in which it applies.

In making use of the forecasting model to define future cash flows on the basis of the current information, the forecaster should spell out each of the assumptions he has made in the forecasting model. For example, for orders to be translated into sales, it may have been assumed that there would be no change in price competition in the industry, and in converting sales into cash flow at the normal rate a similar 'no-change' assumption would be made for financial variables such as credit availability or interest rates which could otherwise affect the timing of such transactions. In the same way the forecaster may have assumed that the capital equipment ordered to fulfil existing production plans would be delivered (and invoiced on time). All these routine assumptions are as important a part of the forecasting model as is the numerical value of the forecast itself.

§ 1.4 Forecasting models

In the previous sections we defined forecasting as an activity which estimated the value of unknown variables in terms of the value of variables which are currently known. A number of differing approaches can be adopted to this end. In later chapters detailed descriptions of most of the common forecasting models are provided. At this stage, however, we wish to make a major distinction between two distinct types of forecasting model — those that have as their basis a set of causal relationships and those that have not.

1.4.1 Non-causal models
Non-causal forecasting models rely on the assumption that it is not necessary to describe or understand the factors which determine the level of any variable in order

to predict it — the level of a variable is simply explained as a single step in a process of organic development. Therefore, if the organic process has been correctly observed it is possible to predict its continued progress without requiring any separate consideration of the factors generating that process. The only operational problem then becomes one of identifying an organic pattern from a series of observations that are subject to a good deal of temporary and random disturbance.

One example of non-causal forecasting is the use of chart analysis in stock exchange transactions. Chart analysts, using no other information than the past history of a share price, see in this pattern an organic development so pronounced that they talk of shares bursting through their trend curve or describe them as trapped in a box.

In other applications too, non-causal models have an honourable history. Both marine and aviation engineering rely extensively on testing a new design in wind tunnel or water tank. The tests allow them to predict that a 'plane will fly or a boat will float, even though the full aerodynamic or hydrodynamic principles involved have neither been isolated or understood.

In management too, because causal models are expensive, non-causal models are widely used either because the benefits of a causal model, as measured by the contribution it can make to improved decision making, do not justify the substantial development costs involved in building it, or else they may be used where the underlying causal structure cannot be identified because of lack of knowledge or an inadequate data base.

In the first case we are looking for a low-cost forecasting model to provide relatively well specified information. A model relying on the extrapolation of past history may be quite adequate. A number of the models enjoying widespread use throughout industry are described later in the book. (Chapter 7 provides a full discussion of a particular type of non-causal model, in which the variable to be forecast is related to its historical values. Such models are called *naive*.) In the second situation too, where the existing state of knowledge is incapable of providing a full causal explanation, forecasting models are used which rely on survey or panel techniques. (Chapter 9 contains a brief discussion of the available models.) These techniques are used extensively in situations where the impossibility of establishing a causal basis from which to measure and predict human response is recognized. Instead, panel and survey procedures rely on the assumption that the panel participants can be used in experiments to simulate the behaviour of the population at large.

We are by now all familiar with the pre-election public opinion polls — exactly the same approach is used to try and predict, for example, the acceptability of a new product, or whether there is a need for a new bus service. Survey or panel techniques are particularly useful for forecasting in those circumstances where the causal relationships involved are imperfectly understood or else are non-quantifiable. For example, market response to a product with a new flavour could be tested by experimenting with a tasting panel. The result of this exercise would provide information for a decision on whether to develop the new product further. However the testing procedure would not have described the underlying motivations leading the members of the panel to accept or reject the product. Nor would the process lead to any useful predictions of the future response that the same panel would make to any other new product alternative that was offered. Each new product would have to be tested in exactly the same way.

Survey techniques may also be used for purposes that are not directly related to specific decisions, but may provide a valuable input into further forecasting activities. In this category surveys of consumer and business intentions (e.g. Confederation of British Industry survey of Business Opinion) are useful in establishing information on variables such as the level of business confidence which would be difficult to define let alone measure objectively.

1.4.2 Causal models

We have argued that the value of a forecasting model can be measured in terms of the additional payoff from improved decision making. If the potential payoff seems high enough to justify the additional expense, a causal model can be developed. This type of model, because it is based on establishing the relationships that determine the forecast variable, tends to be more general in its application than a naive model relying on extrapolation.

A multiple regression model (described in Chapters 6 and 8) used to predict sales, for example, would seek to isolate the independent effects of the principal determinants of the level of sales. A model designed to predict sales through supermarkets might take into account the level of competitive prices, the growth of consumer expenditure, the number of sales outlets and perhaps the increase in consumer mobility brought about by the growth in car ownership. Once this model is in operation it can be used to predict the consequences of a change in any of the explanatory factors used. Thus the implications of extending the number of supermarkets, or of their achieving further competitive price advantage, could be directly estimated without any need of a change in the model. A further benefit of the causal approach is that it becomes possible to monitor the continued relevance of the forecasting model as conditions change and to form some idea of the errors associated with its continued use.

The introduction of parking controls, for example, might affect the level of supermarket sales to the extent that it made access by car more difficult. While the forecasting model was not general enough to include parking regulations directly, it did contain a term measuring the part of supermarket sales directly attributable to the growth in car ownership. By reducing the level of the car ownership variable by an arbitrary amount, perhaps in line with the reduction of parking capacity under the new regulations, and comparing the results of the forecast made using the forecast with the result obtained using the unadjusted model, we can obtain some idea of the sensitivity of the model to changes in regulations. We also obtain some idea of the possible error if the unadjusted model continued in use for forecasting.

The causal model is thus more general than the naive model that relies substantially on extrapolation, since extrapolation depends on the stability of underlying trends. Any alteration in the trend causes the model to generate biased or unreliable results. On the other hand a causal model relies on the identification of a stable set of relationships. This causal structure is likely to remain stable precisely because it has been constructed to explain changes in the underlying behaviour of the series.

§ 1.5 The use of forecast information — prediction and control

The generation of forecasts is not an end in itself. The forecast information has to be used to aid decision making. However, the kind of decision activity incorporating the forecast can be of two types. The decision taker can accept that the predicted future will in fact occur and seek to make decisions that will be optimal under these antici-pated circumstances. Alternatively if he can influence any of the factors which deter-mine forecast outcome, he may use his power to do this in order to produce a new forecast outcome more to his liking.

The distinction can be illustrated by considering the response of a householder to a weather-forecast that it will be cold tomorrow. Since he cannot influence nature, in general he adapts to the forecast by wearing a heavy coat to work. Inside his own house, however, he has control of his micro-climate, and can choose between sitting in discomfort and allowing the forecast to come true, or turning up the heating so that the house temperature remains unchanged. In the latter case the forecast temperature as it affected his house, would be 'untrue', but not misleading.

In business decision making exactly the same distinction can be made. Given fore-casts of large aggregate variables, the decision maker accepts that the probability of that predicted future in fact occurring is independent of anything he might do. He therefore takes decisions that will be optimal under the anticipated conditions. A factory manager reading a forecast of a world shortage of petroleum products might switch to alternative fuels for his power and heat. He would not, however, expect his action to alleviate the world shortage. In the same way, if a forecast that future wage rates will expand at 15 per cent per annum is made available to an employer of 100 people, no decision he can take will have any discernible effect on the level of future wage rates. The forecast, if it was a good one, will be realized in due course.

However, a firm may forecast that its sales are likely to be sluggish over the next few months. The mere existence of this prediction may be sufficient to generate action — special discounts, price cuts, sales promotions and so on — with the effect that the forecast down-trend is reversed. In these circumstances, the forecast outcome would tend to bear little resemblance to the actual outcome, although the forecast itself was certainly acceptable as an input to the decision-making process.

The distinction between forecasts that can be influenced by decision makers and those that cannot, raise difficult questions in assessing forecasts. The accepted statistical measures of forecasting accuracy is the degree of fit that can historically be observed between the predicted and actual values of a series. However, the very provision of a good forecast — one that would produce a true prediction of future events if anticipated conditions remained unchanged — tends to produce a situation in which conditions are changed by deliberate decision. In these circumstances a direct measure of forecasting accuracy would be misleading. Instead of comparing the out-come with the forecast directly we should compare it with the recalculated forecast in which the levels of all the variables, altered by the provision of the initial forecast, are set at their new value.

§ 1.6 Forecasting and planning

In the firm the structure, ordering and relationship between tasks, and the creation and dissemination of information are all arranged to allow the firm to steer towards its agreed objectives against a background of continuous change. The benefit of forecasting is that it allows policies to be coordinated with change rather than lag behind it.

Forecasting and planning are often, misleadingly, discussed as identical activities. The distinction is that forecasting is value free; it is an attempt to arrive at an objective view of the future using given assumptions. It is then a managerial activity to assess how the impact of forecast future conditions on the internal and external operations of the firm will alter the firm's ability to achieve desired objectives. Managers then devise suitable policies and actions to respond to this impact in a way that restores the firm's progress towards its objectives. This translation of forecasts into actual or intended action is the process of planning.

When reaction to forecast changes does occur it is necessary to consider whether this alters the assumptions made in the original forecast. If the forecast provided purely predictive information this would not be a problem. However, if it provided control information there would necessarily be a feedback from the revised policy that would mean the old forecast no longer provided an objective view of expected outcome. To restore this status, forecasts would have to be reworked. To illustrate this, a firm's forecast cash flow may be negative under the assumption that existing policies are to remain in force. Faced with this prospect it would be a mistake to assume that a price increase would generate a proportionate increase in cash flow. A price increase changes one of the assumptions made in determining the original forecast of sales. Consequently the old forecast no longer provides an indication of the most likely expected outcome. Before implementing the price increase, forecasts of sales based on the new assumption of a higher price should be made, and the cash flow effects resulting from the new price should then be calculated to see if an improvement has occurred. We see that before a decision on pricing is taken the forecast should be revised to take into account both the increased price *and* the expected lower sales that will result.

The role of forecasting in an integrated planning and control system is illustrated in Fig. 1.3. In this figure the activities of the system are represented by the flow of production resources through a production process that transforms them into saleable products. Observations on this process are collected and compared with planned performance. Any significant deviation between the two would result in a feedback adjustment being made to current activities. For example, if the rate of growth in sales was falling below planned growth because of inadequate sales management, the control response might be to introduce more marketing skills into the company.

At the same time the relationship with the environment is continuously monitored by a forecasting sub-system. A forecast might show that marketing skills are generally

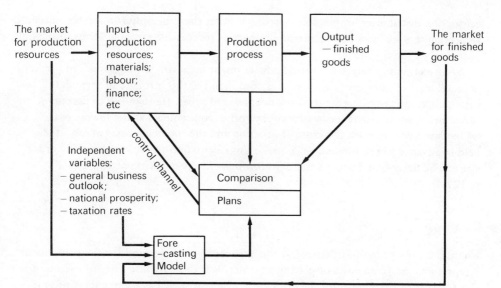

Fig. 1.3 Forecasting and planning: a schematic representation

becoming scarce. This is a change in the environment which makes planned growth more difficult to achieve than was expected when the initial forecasts were made. As a consequence planned growth would be reduced to conform to the rate of growth in sales forecast under the revised conditions. The continuing performance of the company is therefore evaluated against the new plans.

§ 1.7 Sensitivity testing in forecasting systems

One advantage of operating a formal forecasting procedure is that it sets out clearly the assumptions made in arriving at the forecast. Unlike a subjective forecast where different individuals would produce different forecasts from identical data, a formal forecasting system using the same data should always produce similar results or else should permit rapid identification of sources of difference.

A similar result, however, is in no sense a proof that the forecast is right. In fact any single valued forecast estimate is almost invariably wrong. This is because a forecast while intended as the most likely value of a forecast variable is by no means the only possible value that could arise, given the incompleteness of the data and model being used. There is therefore, a substantial possibility that the actual outcome may differ considerably from the forecast value. In general when a forecast is made it is advisable to specify the likely range of error associated with the forecast and specific methods to do this are discussed in the latter part of the book when we consider various forecasting models in detail.

However, even without formal estimates of the errors associated with a given forecast it is still possible to investigate what happens if we regard the forecast as the

11

centre of a distribution of possible outcomes rather than the only foreseeable outcome. Accepting this we need to consider the impact of forecasting errors in terms of possible outcomes of the decisions.

As an example, a television manufacturer might use a forecasting model to predict his total level of sales over the next year, and then use this estimate in formulating his total procurement requirements for subcontracted tubes. He then has to determine an economic order size that secures his overall tube requirements at the lowest cost, taking into account both the costs of ordering and the financing costs of any stocks held in advance of requirements. To make this calculation the cost-minimizing order size can be determined using a standard formula (Levin and Kirkpatrick, 1965, p. 122)†

$$n = \sqrt{\frac{2AP}{RC}}$$

where n is the optimum order size, A the expected yearly demand for the component, P represents the fixed costs of placing an order, R is the purchase price of each unit and C is the cost of carrying a unit in stock for a year, expressed as a percentage of unit price.

If carrying costs, C are 20 per cent of the price of £25 and the costs of placing each order amount to £30 it is possible to examine the costs of any error in the forecast level of sales. Suppose the forecasting model indicated next year's demand at 20,000 units, the optimum order size would be:

$$n = \sqrt{\frac{2 * 30 * 20,000}{0.20 * 25}}$$
$$= 490,$$

and total expected purchase costs would be given by:

$$\frac{AP}{n} + \frac{RCn}{2}$$

(ordering costs) + (stockholding costs where n/2 is the average stockholding)

$$= £\frac{20,000 * 30}{490} + \frac{25 * 0.2 * 490}{2}$$
$$= £2,449.$$

Suppose, however, that the forecast of 20,000 sales does not mean that sales will be exactly 20,000, but that sales will be distributed between 18,000 and 22,000 with an average value of 20,000. Are the costs of procurement particularly sensitive to forecasting error? If sales turned out to be 22,000 then the manufacturer, had he had an

† References are listed at the end of chapters.

accurate forecast, could have achieved his resourcing objectives by buying in lot sizes of 514 with annual procurement costs of £2,569:

$$n = \sqrt{\frac{2 * 30 * 22,000}{0.20 * 25}} = 514.$$

$$\text{Total costs} = \frac{£22,000 * 30}{514} + \frac{514 * 0.2 * 25}{2} = £2,569.$$

However, operating on the basis of the incorrect forecast of 20,000 units, and still buying in lot sizes of 490 his total costs would still only have been

$$\frac{£22,000 * 30}{490} + \frac{490 * 0.2 * 25}{2} = £2,572.$$

In this case a 10 per cent error in the forecast produces a cost increase of only £3. The results, in terms of procurement costs are not, therefore, particularly sensitive to forecast error. However, the results are determined by a solution — the economic order size — which is more sensitive to forecasting error, since the optimum order is 514 while the actual order was 490. This is a difference of 5.5 per cent.

The distinction between the sensitivity of a result to forecasting error and the sensitivity of a solution to the same error is a fundamental one in considering problem solving structure, because many business problems require a choice between two or more alternatives. In such a situation a sensitivity study may show that while the quantitative outcome of the decision procedure may be sensitive to forecasting error, the choice between alternatives is not.

The example illustrates the general point that purely statistical accuracy in forecasts is not always essential. Firms can and do adapt their business so that even unreliable forecasts can help to illuminate a specific choice between alternatives. In seeking, perhaps at considerable expense, to improve a forecasting model there is always the possibility that the same objective could be achieved at lower cost by structuring the firm's operations in a way that makes them relatively insensitive to forecasting error.

§ 1.8 Conclusion

In this chapter we have presented a number of the themes that recur in the rest of the book. The most important of these is the emphasis on the close relationship between forecasting and decision making. It is only by considering the context within which forecast information is used that we can make any valid deduction about the required or actual quality of that forecast.

Reference

Levin, I. L. and **Kirkpatrick, C. A.** (1965) *Quantitative Approaches to Management*, McGraw-Hill, New York.

2
The value of forecasts as decision inputs

§ 2.1 Introduction

Forecasters can draw from a wide range of alternative approaches in their efforts to use current knowledge to provide information about the future. However, because forecasting is an expensive activity, the choice of approach cannot be made on purely statistical grounds. Instead alternative methods have to be considered in relation to economic criteria — what improvement in decision making does the provision of forecast information make possible, and what are the costs incurred in operating the forecasting system to provide that information? In this chapter we discuss methods for evaluating the cost effectiveness of forecast information where it serves as an input to a decision-making system.

§ 2.2 Forecasts as an information source

Forecasts are only of overall benefit when the extra profit arising from the improved decision making at least covers the additional costs of preparing the forecast. In this, forecasts are no different from any other procedure adopted to gain additional information. To illustrate this similarity consider a situation in which a firm is sustaining a regular level of bad debts because of insolvencies among its customers. To reduce this loss it is decided that orders will not be accepted from new customers until a commercial credit rating agency has approved them.

As experience is built up with this new policy the reduction in bad debts, if any, should become apparent. By comparing the savings resulting from the information provided by the credit agency with the costs of using the agency, the costs and benefits of three possible courses of action can be considered:

1. Ceasing to use the agency.
2. Continuing to use the agency for all customers.
3. Using the agency for only certain classes of customer who had characteristics marking them out as possible bad risks.

From this evaluation a rational choice can then be made between the three actions.

In exactly the same way the preparation of a forecast can be seen as 'buying' information about the future, and to justify the activity the benefits should exceed the costs.

In practical terms, however, the estimation of the value of forecast information is complicated by the delay between the forecast becoming available and the time at which a judgement on its effectiveness can be made. Current resources are being spent in order to obtain hypothetical future benefits that may arise from improved decision making. The problem is thus transformed into an attempt to balance the *certain costs* of gathering forecast information against the *expected future benefits* that would result from adjusting operations to take account of the forecast.

§2.3 The value of perfect information

The maximum benefit obtainable from a forecast can be estimated by considering the situation where a perfect forecast — one that always predicted future events with total accuracy — becomes available. Performance making use of the forecast can then be compared with expected performance if any such perfect forecast were available. This would establish the maximum cost it would be worth incurring to obtain perfect forecasts.

2.3.1 The value of perfect information — an example
The new products committee of a food manufacturer meets regularly to consider the advisability of launching particular new food lines. They have to iron out a large number of problems that arise in introducing new products. These range from the technical issues posed by scaling up pilot operations to a commercial scale and setting up a new production line to the problems of training new personnel, deciding the form and extent of the initial promotion budget and ensuring the product is going to be available to the consumer at an adequate number of retail outlets.

With all these matters to consider the committee feels that they have neither the time nor competence to make satisfactory assessments of the other factors which typically play a major part in determining the eventual success of new products. One factor of particular interest to the committee is the level of consumers' disposable income 3 to 6 months ahead because growth in consumers' income is considered important in the reception of new products. Only when incomes increase do consumers start to have a residue of income, over and above their normal expenditures, to cover purchase of new products.

The committee decided that the best procedure would be to subscribe to a specialist economic forecasting service that would provide regular expert forecasts of the way in which consumers' disposable income was likely to change. This would free the committee to concentrate on the problem of considering the relative merits of different product launches under the forecast economic conditions. Before taking a decision on this, however, the committee felt that they should try to work out how much the commercial forecasts were likely to be worth as an aid to their decision making. As an exercise they thought it would be interesting to examine the implications for decision making of the three possible alternative forecasts of the annual rate of growth in consumers' disposable income — low growth, medium growth and high growth. These three possibilities are defined in Table 2.1.

Table 2.1
Possible changes in consumers' disposable income

		Per cent	
State of growth in	1	0—2	Low growth
consumers' disposable	2	2—4	Medium growth
income	3	4—6	High growth

As a further simplification the committee chose to consider only a restricted set of policy alternatives available in launching a new product. The policy alternatives chosen were the following:

1. To launch the product nationally with extensive national consumer advertising.
2. To launch regionally with limited retailer advertising.
3. To launch the product through encouraging retailers to cooperate by offering special discounts and providing point of sales support, but with no advertising.

Taking a product that had already been evaluated for its likely consumer acceptability, a schedule of anticipated returns for each type of launch under any of the possible economic conditions could be prepared. The data obtained is shown in Table 2.2

Table 2.2
Payoffs for a new product launch

	State of economic growth (£)		
Policy alternatives	*Low growth* 1	*Medium growth* 2	*High growth* 3
Policy 1	20,000	60,000	120,000
Policy 2	40,000	70,000	90,000
Policy 3	50,000	60,000	70,000

In order to be sure that all possible outcomes have been considered the information in Table 2.2 can be set out in the form of a decision tree.† In the decision tree shown in

† Decision theory, from which the 'decision tree' is derived, forms an increasingly important part of management, statistical, economic and psychological theory. Two useful references for the reader who wishes to explore the ideas used here with a view to their application are: Raiffa, 1968, and Miller and Starr, 1969, Chapters 4 and 5.

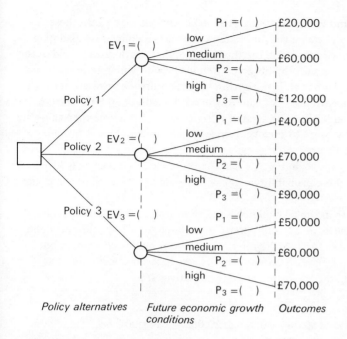

Fig. 2.1 Product launch decision tree

Fig. 2.1 the three policy alternatives that are available are shown as radiating from the square initial decision point.

Each of these three alternatives then has three possible outcomes, depending on whether low, medium or high growth conditions apply at the time the decision is implemented. These three sets of outcomes are shown as radiating from a circle, a device which serves to distinguish the chance event from a decision point. Since there are three policy alternatives and three possible states of growth there are nine possible outcomes, represented by the nine terminal branches at the right of the decision tree. For each of these consequences we can attach a monetary outcome derived from the data in Table 2.2.

In using a decision tree similar to Fig. 2.1 the approach is to calculate the expected value (EV) (see Appendix 1, p. 264, for an extended explanation of EV) of each policy alternative. This is done by adding the possible outcomes radiating from each policy alternative, after multiplying each of them by the probability (P), that it will occur. By definition, because the outcomes are an exhaustive and mutually exclusive set of events their combined probabilities for each and every policy alternative must sum to one.

An inspection of the outcomes shows that all policy alternatives generate some profits whatever economic conditions happen to apply, although these profits vary widely — from only £20,000 to as high as £120,000, so that potential returns to effective decision making are quite high. Suppose we look at the best policy decision that

17

could be made where no indication of future growth conditions existed. In these circumstances we can only evaluate the outcome of alternative policies by assuming that the expected frequency with which the three economic growth rates would occur in the future would be in line with the observed frequency with which they occurred in the past. On this assumption if an investigation of recent history showed that high growth (growth state 3) occurred 10 per cent of the time, medium growth (state 2) 60 per cent of the time and low growth (state 1) 30 per cent of the time then these are the probabilities we would assign to the occurrence of each of the three economic growth possibilities in the future.

The probabilities P_1, P_2 and P_3 in Fig. 2.1 can therefore be designated as 0.3, 0.6 and 0.1. We can then use these probabilities to calculate the EV for each of the policy decisions.

If policy 1 is adopted then the probability is 0.3 that low growth would occur and the outcome would be profits of £20,000; 0.6 that medium growth would occur and £60,000 would result; and 0.1 that high growth would be experienced with an outcome of £120,000. Multiplying each outcome by its associated probability and summing, policy by policy the EV of the policy alternatives are:

For Policy 1
$EV_1 = 0.3 * £20,000 + 0.6 * £60,000 + 0.1 * £120,000 = £54,000$

For Policy 2
$EV_2 = 0.3 * £40,000 + 0.6 * £70,000 + 0.1 * £90,000 \quad = £63,000$

For Policy 3
$EV_3 = 0.3 * £50,000 + 0.6 * £60,000 + 0.1 * £70,000 \quad = £58,000.$

The probabilities and EVs can now be filled in the decision tree and the results are shown in Fig. 2.2. In comparing these EVs, the committee, without any further information about future growth rates, can do no better than pick the policy showing the highest returns using the historic relative frequency of occurrence of the three growth rates. The preferred policy would thus be policy 2 — a regional product launch with limited retailer advertising. This policy promises an expected return of £63,000 against policy 3's £58,000 and policy 1's £54,000.

Of course, in retrospect, the committee would normally find that their decision to use policy 2 was not the best choice. For example, if they have just enjoyed a period of rapid growth they know, with the benefit of hindsight, that it would have been much better to have chosen policy 1 which would have yielded £120,000, instead of using policy 2, which generated actual profits of only £90,000. However, this does not help them decide what to do in the future. Unless the committee has access to a forecast that provides some information about future developments of the economy they are powerless to improve on the results attained by simply using policy 2.

Suppose, though, that the committee were suddenly offered forecasts of future growth rates that were invariably accurate. They would then be able to improve their decision making considerably. If the committee knew from the forecasts exactly what

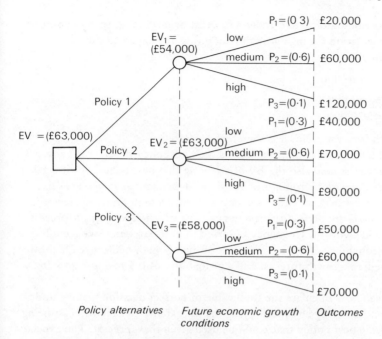

$P_1 = (0.3)$ £20,000

$EV_1 =$
(£54,000)

low

medium $P_2 = (0.6)$ £60,000

high

Policy 1

$P_3 = (0.1)$ £120,000

$P_1 = (0.3)$ £40,000

low

$EV_2 = (£63,000)$

EV = (£63,000)

Policy 2

medium $P_2 = (0.6)$ £70,000

high

£90,000

$P_3 = (0.1)$

Policy 3

$EV_3 = (£58,000)$

$P_1 = (0.3)$ £50,000

low

medium $P_2 = (0.6)$ £60,000

$P_3 = (0.1)$

high

£70,000

Policy alternatives   *Future economic growth*   *Outcomes*
conditions

Fig. 2.2 Product launch decision tree, evaluated

economic conditions were going to develop in the immediate future, they would naturally be able to select the policy that offered the highest payoff under the specific forecast conditions.

The forecast might, for example, be one of low growth. Because this forecast is perfectly reliable there is no chance of any other growth outcome, so that the EV from each policy is given by the payoff it achieves under low growth conditions.

EV_1 (low growth) = 1.0 * £20,000 + 0 * £60,000 + 0 * £120,000
           = £20,000

EV_2 (low growth) = £40,000

EV_3 (low growth) = £50,000.

An inspection of the EVs shows that with a correct forecast of low growth, policy 3 has the highest EV at £50,000, compared with the £20,000 produced by policy 1 and the £40,000 of policy 2.

Under a forecast of medium growth the position changes. Then the probability of medium growth, because the forecast is perfectly accurate, rises to 1, and for high or low growth the probability is 0. Recalculating the EVs for each policy we have:

EV_1 (medium growth) = 0 * £20,000 + 1.0 * £60,000 + 0 * £120,000 = £60,000

and similarly,

EV_2 (medium growth) = £70,000   and EV_3 (medium growth) = £60,000.

19

Clearly policy 2 is the best alternative under a forecast of medium growth conditions.

Repeating the calculation for high growth conditions, the expected values of the three policies become:

EV_1 (high growth) = £120,000

EV_2 (high growth) = £90,000

EV_3 (high growth) = £70,000.

Under a high growth forecast policy 1 is therefore preferred.

From these calculations the committee knows the best policy to select for any perfectly accurate forecast, and also the EV of selecting that best policy. All it needs to know to calculate the payoff from those decisions, dependent as they were on perfect forecasts, is an estimate of the frequency with which each type of forecast is given. Since the forecasts are perfect the frequency with which each type of forecast is given should coincide with the frequency observed in past outcomes. We would therefore attach a probability of 0.1 to a forecast of high growth being given, a probability of 0.6 to a medium growth forecast and a probability of 0.3 to a low growth forecast.

The committee can now calculate the total value of correct decision making under conditions of perfect knowledge by multiplying the probability of each forecast being made by the EV of the best policy that could be used given that forecast. The expected payoff with perfect forecasting information is therefore:

£120,000 * 0.1 + £70,000 * 0.6 + £50,000 * 0.3 = £69,000.

That is:

EV_1 (high growth) * (probability of high growth being forecast) +
+ EV_2 (medium growth) * (probability of medium growth being forecast) +
+ EV_3 (low growth) * (probability of low growth being forecast) = £69,000.

Thus provided the committee used the accurate forecast in order to select the best policy they could expect a profit of £69,000 from a new product launch.

This represents a considerable improvement in the expected performance that could be achieved when no such perfect forecast of future conditions was available. Then the group would have had to use policy 2 continuously, and would only have been able to obtain expected returns of £63,000. Obviously, the addition of forecast information permits an improvement in decision making that makes a direct contribution of £69,000 − £63,000 or £6,000, to the expected returns from a new product launch.

Since the extra information leads to an expected improvement in the decision making of the firm of £6,000, it would follow that it would be worth paying anything up to £6,000 in order to obtain the perfect information. In any decision situation where forecast information is available at additional cost the calculation of the payoff obtainable using perfect information, in comparison with the payoff when no forecast information at all is available, is a useful first step.

This is not because we actually expect to encounter either perfect or zero information forecasts because we know that both these types of forecast are extremely rare.

(Construction of a zero information forecast is quite difficult, since it requires that there is no association of any kind between predicted and actual outcomes; a consistently wrong forecast is just as valuable as a consistently right one.) The value arises because in making the calculation we determine the bounds within which the additional payoff from a less than perfect forecast must fall. While we show in the next section that it is possible to calculate the payoff from an imperfect forecast, this may not be necessary if we can see that the cost of acquiring such a forecast is above the maximum additional payoff obtainable using a perfect forecast. In this situation we can decide confidently against the proposed forecast on grounds of cost without further analysis.

§ 2.4 The value of imperfect information

In the previous example we saw how the addition of forecast information had enabled the decision makers to become much more selective in the choices they made. Under conditions of complete uncertainty the most attractive policy is one that offers similar payoffs whatever the conditions. As forecast information improves and we gain knowledge of the probability distribution of future events, it becomes less risky to select a policy that is particularly effective under the forecast conditions but less effective in other conditions. The more certain the future environment becomes as forecast knowledge is improved, the more specific the decision making becomes, as it relates more and more to the opportunities of a particular expected future.

The value of forecast information is at its maximum when the decision maker has perfect information about future conditions. The policy which is most profitable under the forecast conditions can be selected without regard to possible consequences if the forecast future does not occur.

In practice, of course, perfect forecasts do not exist, and while estimating the value of policy making under them provides a useful definition of the maximum possible gain from forecast information, the normal situation is where forecasts indicate something about the future environment but stop a good deal short of providing perfect information. In dealing with a less than perfect forecast the decision maker has to take into account the possibility that what is the best policy on the assumption that the forecast is right may be disastrous if the forecast turns out to be in error. A method for evaluating the payoff from forecasts of this type is developed in a continuation of the example.

2.4.1 The value of imperfect information − an example
Suppose the committee considering the best strategy for introducing a new product is reviewing its policies for a new product launch, but this time they do not have access to a perfect forecast of future conditions. Instead they have been offered a commercial forecasting service at a cost of £2,000. In order to find out whether this service would improve their policy making, the committee asked the forecasting service to provide details of its previous performance. The committee, when provided with this information about past forecasts, made a comparison of the outcome that actually transpired

Table 2.3
Economic growth forecasts — predictions and outcomes

	Actual outcomes			
Forecast outcomes	*High growth*	*Medium growth*	*Low growth*	*Total*
High growth	2	2	1	5
Medium growth	1	13	3	17
Low growth	0	3	5	8
Total	3	18	9	30

for each type of forecast, and were able to collect the information shown in Table 2.3. From the information in the table, it is apparent, for example, that five forecasts of high growth have been given. Of these five forecasts of high growth, two were actually followed by high growth, two preceded medium growth and one was followed by low growth.

Given this forecasting record how should the committee proceed? As we said earlier, without any forecast the committee could adopt a policy with an expected payoff of £63,000. With perfect information the payoff would increase to £69,000. Since the cost of the forecast at £2,000 does not exceed the maximum potential gain from improved information of £6,000, the new service cannot be dismissed on cost grounds alone. We have to consider if the improved decision making that the service allows more than covers the cost of the service.

The first stage in the evaluation of the new forecasting service is to analyse the actual distribution of growth outcomes following each type of forecast. Using the data presented in Table 2.3 we can for example, consider the distribution of outcomes which have followed when a forecast of low growth has been made.

In all, eight forecasts of low growth were given and in no case was this forecast actually followed by high growth. On this evidence the probability of high growth occurring following a forecast of low growth is 0/8, or 0. However, in three of the eight cases the forecast of low growth was followed by a medium growth rate. We can assign a probability of 3/8 or 0.38 to this occurrence. On the remaining five occasions on which a low growth forecast was made, low growth actually followed. The probability of low growth, following a low growth forecast is thus 5/8, or 0.62. Repeating this procedure for the other two forecast conditions the distribution of eventual outcomes following each forecast can be calculated, the results being shown in Table 2.4.†

Using the probabilities in Table 2.4, together with the payoff values in that table, we can now evaluate the expected payoff from each policy, given each one of the alternative forecasts.

† Given two events, A and B, the conditional probability that A will occur, given B has occurred, is: Prob $(A:B) = \dfrac{\text{Prob (A and B)}}{\text{Prob (B)}}$. The values calculated above are the conditional probabilities of each economic outcome given a forecast outcome.

Table 2.4

The distribution of actual outcomes conditional on a particular forecast

Forecast outcomes	Actual outcomes for given forecasts						Total
	High growth		Medium growth		Low growth		
	No.	Probability	No.	Probability	No.	Probability	
High growth	2	0.40 = 2/5	2	0.40 = 2/5	1	0.20 = 1/5	5
Medium growth	1	0.06 = 1/17	13	0.76 = 13/17	3	0.18 = 3/17	17
Low growth	0	0 = 0/8	3	0.38 = 3/8	5	0.62 = 5/8	8
Total	3		18		9		30

For example, suppose the forecasting service predicts conditions of high growth; we know from Table 2.4 that a prediction of high growth is followed 0.2 of the time by low growth, 0.4 of the time by medium growth and only 0.4 of the time by high growth. Using this distribution of actual outcomes from a forecast of fast growth the payoff from each policy can be evaluated as shown in the following three processes.

1. Forecast of high growth

EV_1 (forecast : high growth) $= 0.2 * £20,000 + 0.4 * £60,000 + 0.4 * £120,000$
$= £76,000$

EV_2 (forecast : high growth) $= 0.2 * £40,000 + 0.4 * £70,000 + 0.4 * £90,000$
$= £72,000$

EV_3 (forecast : high growth) $= 0.2 * £50,000 + 0.4 * £60,000 + 0.4 * £70,000$
$= £62,000.$

An inspection of these results leads to a conclusion that in the event of a forecast of high growth being given then policy 1 should always be followed since it offers the highest payoff − £76,000.

Repeating the calculations for a forecast of medium growth, we know from Table 2.4 that there is: a probability of 0.18 that this forecast will be followed by low growth; a probability of 0.76 that medium growth will follow; and a probability of 0.06 that high growth will result. Using this probability distribution the EV of the alternative policies, given a forecast of medium growth, can be evaluated.

2. Forecast of medium growth

EV_1 (forecast : medium growth) $= 0.18 * £20,000 + 0.76 * £60,000 + 0.06 * £120,000$
$= £56,400$

EV_2 (forecast : medium growth) $= £65,800$

EV_3 (forecast : medium growth) $= £58,800.$

Here the best policy given a forecast of medium growth is policy 2, yielding £65,800.

For a forecast of low growth the process is repeated:

3. *Forecast of low growth*

EV_1 (forecast: low growth) = 0.62 * £20,000 + 0.38 * £60,000 + 0.00 * £120,000
$$= £35,000$$

EV_2 (forecast: low growth) = £51,400

EV_3 (forecast: low growth) = £53,800.

Reviewing these results, the committee can now pinpoint the best policy to adopt, given any of the three possible forecasts. If a forecast of high growth is given, then policy 1, yielding an expected gain of £76,000, is the best policy; if medium growth is forecast then policy 2, yielding £65,800 is preferred; while if low growth is forecast then the best that can be done is to select policy 3, to produce £53,800.

Now that we know which is the best policy for given forecasts it only remains to consider what would be the overall returns that could be achieved using the forecasts. This depends on the frequency with which each forecast is given. Looking at the breakdown of previous forecasts shown in Table 2.4 high growth forecasts constituted 5/30 of the total forecasts, medium growth forecasts 17/30 of the total, and low growth forecasts the remaining 8/30. Weighting the payoff of the best policy possible for each forecast by the relative frequency with which each of the forecasts has been given in the past gives an estimated overall payoff of:

£76,000 * 5/30 + £65,800 * 17/30 + £53,800 * 8/30 = £64,300.

The expected earnings of £64,300 that could be earned using the forecast are thus greater than the expected earnings of £63,000 that would follow the consistent use of policy 2 under conditions of complete uncertainty. Average performance would be improved by £1,300 by using the forecast. However, since the forecast service costs £2,000 this expected gain would be insufficient to cover the cost of the forecasts, and the committee maximizes profits by choosing to continue with policy 2 without buying in the additional information. The decision, of course, would be different if there were two or more products to be launched at about the same time, because then we could expect the increased payoff from improved information to apply to each of the products while subscription costs would remain unchanged.

§2.5 Forecasting the distribution of possible outcomes

In the discussion so far, the value of forecast information has been estimated by calculating the increase in expected payoff that is generated by the improvement in decision making made possible by the forecast.

However, the objective of most business decisions will rarely be as simple as maximizing expected payoff. This will be particularly true where decisions start to have a major impact on the viability of the firm. Then it becomes important to consider the distribution of possible outcomes as well as the expected value that will result from them before making any decision.

We could, as Table 2.5 illustrates, have two policy alternatives that gave identical expected outcomes. However, if we look at the possible outcomes which make up the

Table 2.5
The distribution of outcomes for two policy decisions

Policy 1			Policy 2		
Outcome (£)	Probability	Expected value (£)	Outcome (£)	Probability	Expected value (£)
70,000	0.2	14,000	−40,000	0.2	−8,000
90,000	0.4	36,000	0	0.1	0
120,000	0.3	36,000	75,000	0.4	30,000
140,000	0.1	14,000	260,000	0.3	78,000
−	1.0	100,000	−	1.0	100,000

expected outcome for each alternative we see there are marked differences between the policies. Policy 1 and policy 2 both have expected values of £100,000. However, a casual inspection shows that if policy 1 is adopted all possible outcomes will lie reasonably close to £100,000. The total spread of outcomes is only between £70,000 and £140,000, and the outcome would be either £90,000 or £120,000 70 per cent of the time. In the case of policy 2 the outcome would never be within £20,000 of the expected outcome.

Since the expected value is identical for the two policies it follows that there would be little point in being exposed to the greater uncertainties inherent in following policy 2. Policy 1 would thus be preferred. This preference for a less risky alternative would probably exist even if the expected value of the less risky policy was somewhat less than the expected value of the higher risk policy and in general this arises because people are risk averse. This assumption of risk aversion should be qualified to take into account situations in which only the highest outcomes are enough to meet the decision maker's financial requirements. In such a situation a decision taker would select a policy that at least offered some chance, however small, of the required return, even though such a policy offered a lower expected value than alternatives.

In forecasting the probability attached to each possible outcome the forecaster thus has a wider brief than simply pointing out the policy which he estimates has the highest expected value, because the relative advantages of decisions do not depend solely on this one measure. The distribution of outcomes in relation to requirements is also of importance.

§ 2.6 Forecasting and the distribution of possible outcomes – an illustration

A contract engineering firm with the capacity to handle approximately £130,000 worth of work at any one time obtains most of its work by competitive tender. The firm experiences a persistent problem in deciding how many jobs to bid for. If it bids only for the exact amount of work it needs to fill the factory it has to ensure the success of all these bids by quoting almost at a loss. On the other hand if the firm bids for a workload above capacity, relying on the higher prices it quotes to lose some of this work, it runs the risk of gaining more than the expected amount of work and having to subcontract, often at a loss, to avoid penalty payments. In an attempt to minimize these difficulties the firm decides on a policy of matching the expected value of work out at tender to its available capacity.

Currently the firm has been invited to tender for three jobs, A, B and C. After costing these jobs it is estimated that tender prices of £120,000 for Job A, £80,000 for Job B and £93,000 for Job C should be quoted. The marketing department then forecast that on the basis of these tenders and given their estimates of the strength of expected competition there was an 0.3 chance of obtaining Job A, an 0.6 chance of obtaining Job B and an 0.4 chance of being successful with Job C. The expected workload generated by these three tenders is therefore:

$$0.3 * £120,000 + 0.6 * £80,000 + 0.4 * £93,000 \quad \text{or} \quad £121,200$$

which seemed comfortably within available capacity.

However, before the tenders were submitted it was thought desirable to calculate how likely it was that the workload would be anywhere near the capacity of £130,000. To do this an analysis of the possible distribution of workload was made by considering all the possible outcomes that could result from the bids.

Since each bid must result either in a success (S) or failure (F) it follows that where, as for contract A, a probability of success of 0.3 is estimated we can calculate the probability of failure as $1 - 0.3$ or 0.7. Similarly the failure probability for Jobs B and C are $1 - 0.6$, or 0.4 and $1 - 0.4$, or 0.6 respectively. Setting down all outcomes and assigning probabilities of both success and failure using the estimates above produces the data in Table 2.6.

In arriving at the value shown for each possible bid outcome we simply add the values of all successful bids included in that possibility. Thus possibility 4 occurs if bid A fails but bids B and C succeed. Therefore, the workload generated by possibility 4, if it occurred, would consist of the £80,000 of Job B plus the £93,000 of Job C, a total of £173,000.

We also have to calculate the probability of such an outcome occurring. It is calculated as the product of the probabilities attached to the occurrence of each of the three events that make up that outcome, provided we are able to assume that these three events are independent.†

In this case as each of the contracts were with separate organizations the contract

---

† If two events A and B are independent then knowledge that B happens tells us nothing about whether or not A happens. Consequently Prob.(A : B) (the probability of A occurring, given that B has occurred), is just the probability that A will occur (Prob.(A)). For two independent events the probability of both A and B occurring (Prob.(A and B)) is simply the product of the probabilities that they will occur separately, or: Prob.(A and B) = Prob.(A) * Prob.(B).

Table 2.6
Distribution of bid outcomes

Possi-bility	Possible bid outcome	Value (£)	Contract A		Contract B		Contract C		Joint proba-bility	Expected value
			Outcome	Proba-bility	Outcome	Proba-bility	Outcome	Proba-bility		
1	All successful	293,000	S	0.3	S	0.6	S	0.4	0.072	21,096
2	2 successful, 1 fails	200,000	S	0.3	S	0.6	F	0.6	0.108	21,600
3		213,000	S	0.3	F	0.4	S	0.4	0.048	10,224
4		173,000	F	0.7	S	0.6	S	0.4	0.168	29,064
5	1 successful, 2 fail	120,000	S	0.3	F	0.4	F	0.6	0.072	8,640
6		80,000	F	0.7	S	0.6	F	0.6	0.252	20,160
7		93,000	F	0.7	F	0.4	S	0.4	0.112	10,416
8	All 3 fail	0	F	0.7	F	0.4	F	0.4	0.168	0
									1.000	121,200

Contract A is worth £120,000, Contract B £80,000, and Contract C £93,000.

outcomes could be assumed to be independent. This allows us to calculate the joint probability that, for example, outcome 4 would occur as:

Prob.(F_A and S_B and S_C) = Prob.(F_A) * Prob.(S_B) * Prob.(S_C)

$$= 0.7 * 0.6 * 0.4 = 0.168,$$

where: F_A represents the failure of contract A; S_B the success of B etc.
We now multiply the value of outcome 4 if it occurs, by the joint probability we calculated for its occurrence to find the expected value of this outcome:

£173,000 * 0.168 = £29,064.

To calculate the probability of overloading the firm's capacity we first plot the probability distribution of all possible outcomes (Fig. 2.3). In plotting this, probabilities have been calculated by including all outcomes within a given range of workload. Thus in the interval above £200,000 but less than £250,000, we have outcome 2 with a value of £200,000 and outcome 3 with value £213,000 and these occur with probability:

0.108 + 0.048 = 0.156.

On inspecting the distribution of outcomes it becomes obvious that despite the expected value of the workload being £121,000 there is a very low probability of getting a workload between £100,000 and £150,000 — in fact we have as much chance of getting one in the range £250,000–£300,000. Clearly with a capacity of only £130,000 this would be extremely embarrassing and possibly expensive.

The set of bids submitted, far from producing the desired workload, achieve almost the contrary result. Instead of a prospective workload that corresponds to capacity we

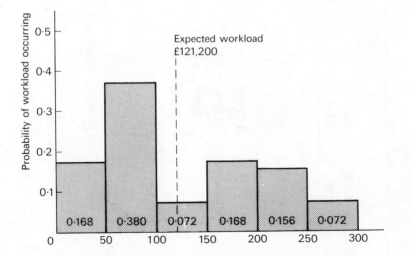

Fig. 2.3 The distribution of possible workloads

have a distribution of possible outcomes in which the probability of obtaining a work-load close to capacity is low compared with the alternatives of working far below capacity or well above it. The reason for this is that the company initially considered that a calculation of expected workload would show up any potential under utilization or overload situation. In fact this is an inadequate procedure because it does not reflect the high level of risk that actual outcomes could be much greater or much less than the expected outcome.

Simply using the forecasts to calculate an expected outcome does not make use of their full value in each situation. By using them to measure the risk of getting a result somewhat different from the expected one a method for actually increasing the consistent utilization of the plant can be developed.

It would not be possible to estimate the benefit from such an approach from the data presented here because this would only emerge once the ability to forecast the distribution of outcomes as well as their most likely value had been translated into management actions. Specific actions suggested by the analysis here might include:

1. Bidding with a lower profit margin to increase the probability of success for each job.
2. Bidding for jobs that are smaller in relation to available capacity.
3. Bidding for interdependent jobs, so that the acceptance of one makes the rejection of another more likely.

All these modifications would result in the value of forecast information increasing without any alteration in the basic activity of forecasting success probabilities.

§2.7 Summary

In this chapter we have considered how the provision of forecast information can lead to an improvement in decision making. The benefits of this changed decision making, rather than the statistical accuracy of the forecast, provide the only realistic basis on which the value of forecasting information can be judged. In measuring the value of forecast information in this way the discussion moved from the preliminary step of valuing the benefits to decision making of perfect information to the more realistic situation in which less than perfect forecasts were used.

Finally the concept that knowledge of the distribution of possible error round a forecast could have important consequences in decision making was introduced, together with the view that again a statistical measure of this error was useless in calculating the value of a forecast unless it was accompanied by some indication of the tolerance of the decision making situation to variability in forecast outcomes. This tolerance depends on the particular circumstances of each case. In the example of the engineering contractor the large size of contracts relative to available capacity contributed to an extremely low tolerance to variability which could only be handled by pursuing cautious policies. In other circumstances forecast error could be far less important.

References

Miller, David and Starr, Martin (1969) *Executive Decisions and Operational Research* (2 edn), Prentice-Hall, New Jersey.

Raiffa, H. (1968) *Decision Analysis*, Addison-Wesley, Reading, Mass.

3

Forecast timing and structure for management decisions

§3.1 Forecasting and business objectives

In choosing from the wide range of available forecasting models (many of them described in other chapters of the book) there is a temptation to give low priority to the ultimate purpose of model building, which is to contribute to the effectiveness with which decision making achieves desired objectives. Thus, an over-preoccupation with the complexities of demand or cost forecasting or with predictions of the techno-logical or economic environment of the firm, may be at the expense of effort more properly devoted to integrating the forecast into the activities of the organization. Naturally this process of integration is a two-way one, because not only must the forecast relate to the decision making and organization of the firm, but in turn the type of decision making and organizational structure adopted should be modified to take maximum advantage of the forecasts available.

The considerations affecting the two-way integration process can be illustrated by considering two general requirements that have to be met for successful forecasting.

1. Structural requirements. Forecasts should relate to specific decisions. Problems should be structured to show what alternatives are to be considered and where the major areas of uncertainty arise.

2. Timing. Forecasts should be available at the time when decisions are taken and should predict far enough ahead to provide information on conditions that are likely to apply when the decision becomes fully operationalized.

§3.2 Forecast structure and decision trees

One way in which decisions can be usefully broken down into their component parts is by the use of decision trees. The decision tree approach developed in §2.3.1 was used to represent the range of choices facing a decision maker at any particular point in time. Because the decision tree specifies all alternative strategies it provides con-siderable guidance as to the type and amount of forecast information that is required.

31

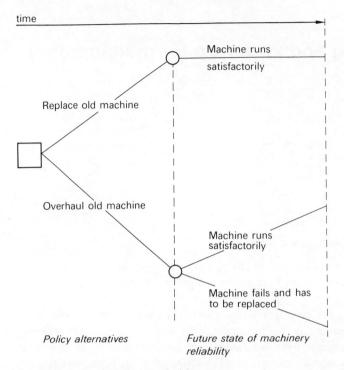

time

Machine runs
satisfactorily

Replace old machine

Overhaul old machine

Machine runs
satisfactorily

Machine fails and has
to be replaced

Policy alternatives   *Future state of machinery
reliability*

Fig. 3.1 Machine replacement decision tree

As an illustration of the way these alternatives are displayed, suppose a manager is deciding at the start of the year whether to replace a machine or to overhaul it and accept the risk that it might break down later and need to be replaced anyway. The decision tree in Fig. 3.1 shows the situation in terms of his decision and its possible outcomes.

The choice the manager makes now depends on the cost of each of the alternative outcomes, together with the associated chance of their occurrence. The costs in this situation are known accurately, since the manager knows that an overhaul costs £2,000 while the increased capital charges that would be incurred if a new machine were bought would amount to £4,000.

He now requires a forecast of the probability of a machine failure if the machine is overhauled instead of replaced. This may be done either by studying previous experience with similar machines, or by predicting the effects of another year's wear on the critical parts of the machine. If he estimates that there is a probability of 0.4 that the machine will run for the year, it follows that there is an 0.6 chance of a breakdown during the year, since the two events are exclusive and exhaustive. We can now enter these costs and the associated probabilities that then will be incurred on the decision tree in Fig. 3.2.

Looking forward from the decision point, the manager's objective is to select the alternative that has the lowest expected cost. If the manager chooses to replace the

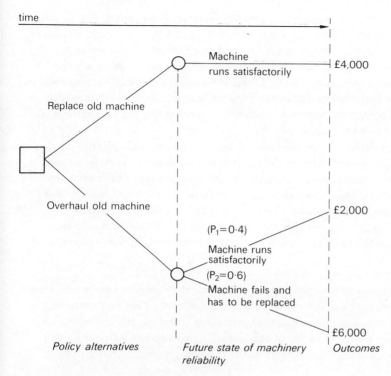

Fig. 3.2 Machine replacement decision tree

machine he faces a certain cost of £4,000. On the other hand if he chooses to overhaul the machine he expects to pay £2,000 in the event that the machine continues to run satisfactorily, and that £2,000, plus £4,000 extra for a new machine if he has trouble. Since he has forecast probabilities of 0.4 and 0.6 for these two events then his expected total cost amounts to £2,000 * 0.4 + £(2,000 + 4,000) * 0.6 = £4,400. Unless the decision maker places a high value on deferring cash expenditure till the last possible moment he would normally prefer to replace his existing machine with a new one.

From this example it is apparent that formulating the admittedly simple strategic alternatives in the situation as a decision tree has helped to structure the problem. In particular we have pinpointed the need for forecast information on the probability of machine breakdown following overhaul. Having done this it is comparatively simple to ask the question — how important is accuracy in this forecast in relation to the decision that has to be taken? A simple answer to this is given by calculating the probability of machine failure, P, which would result in expected costs following an overhaul equal to the £4,000 spent on a new machine. This value is given by:

$$£P * (2,000 + 4,000) + £(1 - P) * 2,000 = £4,000$$

and therefore

$$P = 0.5.$$

33

In this particular case the manager knows that in calculating the probability of machine survival following overhaul his esimate would have to be 25 per cent in error (a true probability of 0.5 instead of the forecast 0.4) before his decision to buy a new machine became wrong. From past experience it would be easy to check whether such a wide margin of error in forecasting machine survival has occurred frequently in the past. Given the technical nature of the problem it would be unlikely that such errors would have been made and as a consequence the manager can be confident that the decision he took was the right one.

In reviewing this example, the role that the decision tree plays in structuring the problem is a useful one. Not only are the alternatives inherent in the problem clearly specified but at the same time we are provided with an indication of the accuracy required from the forecast in order that the chosen strategy remains optimal. In the absence of such a problem structure we might be tempted to authorize research efforts at substantial cost to provide an exact forecast of machine survival, when such accuracy is not required to choose between the alternatives facing the decision taker.

3.2.1 A further decision tree example

A manufacturer intends to produce a new product for the domestic equipment market, but he is uncertain about the size of the immediate market and the continued rate of market growth he can expect after the new product is launched. His immediate problem is to decide on the capacity of the factory he sets up to manufacture this product. The technological requirements of the product give him a choice of two factory sizes:

1. A large-output factory involving heavy capital costs but offering low costs at its capacity of 55,000 units.
2. A smaller volume plant requiring less investment but incurring slightly higher unit costs at its capacity of 29,500 units.

To decide between these two alternatives the manufacturer needs to obtain forecasts of the demand for his product. At this stage he is less interested in the exact size of the future market than in information that helps him to choose between his available strategies which are:

Decision point 1
{ 1. He can build a large plant initially.
{ 2. He can build a small plant initially.

Decision point 2
{ 3. If he builds the small plant and demand appears likely to exceed
{   capacity he can add another small plant.

These strategies are shown in the form of a decision tree in Fig. 3.3, where e_1 and e_2 are variables representing the initial choice at decision point 1 between a large factory and a small one, while a_1 and a_2 similarly represent the choice between adding a second small factory and not adding it at decision point 2. $P_1 \ldots P_5$ represent the probabilities of demand falling within each of the class intervals shown in Table 3.1, and $O_1 \ldots O_{15}$ represent the values of all the possible outcomes which are also shown in the same table.

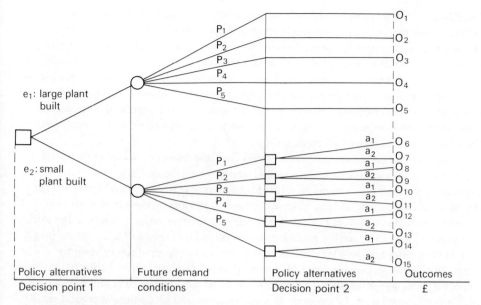

Fig. 3.3 Plant investment decision tree

Inspection of the decision tree in Fig. 3.3 shows that the decision at point 1 cannot be taken without considering the possible choices available at decision point 2, since in choosing to build the small plant, one of the benefits is the flexibility granted by the subsequent opportunity to expand production capacity by adding a second small plant if market opportunities seem favourable.

The next step is to consider the alternatives in the light of forecast demand and to estimate the total value of expected outcomes for each decision. Suppose that a demand forecast predicting sales of 50,000 units was available. As it stands this forecast is not particularly helpful because, in view of the original problem, interpreted

Table 3.1
Distribution of expected demand and associated profitabilities for factory alternatives

Demand	Probability distribution of forecast	Profitability large factory (£)	Profitability 2 small factories (£)	Profitability 1 small factory (£)
55,000 and above	$P_1 = 0.16$	$O_1 =$ 250,000	$O_6 = 180,000$	$O_7 = 90,000$
50,000–55,000	$P_2 = 0.34$	$O_2 =$ 185,000	$O_8 = 150,000$	$O_9 = 90,000$
45,000–50,000	$P_3 = 0.34$	$O_3 =$ 100,000	$O_{10} = 120,000$	$O_{11} = 90,000$
40,000–45,000	$P_4 = 0.14$	$O_4 =$ −50,000	$O_{12} =$ 60,000	$O_{13} = 90,000$
35,000–40,000	$P_5 = 0.02$	$O_5 =$ −200,000	$O_{14} = −30,000$	$O_{15} = 90,000$
	1.00			

35

literally it would leave us either with an under utilized large factory, two under utilized small factories or else a single small factory unable to cope with demand. However, as with any forecast we have to take into account the possibility of error, since this often has a critical bearing on decision taking. If the standard deviation† of the forecast of 50,000 units was 5,000 units we could use this to assign the probability distribution (shown in Table 3.1) to the single forecast of demand. Using this probability distribution we can now evaluate the discounted costs and revenues for each demand range and for each alternative policy, thus allowing us to calculate the overall profitability of all three policies.

Before we calculate expected values from the data, however, we need to consider the fact that if we decide to build a small factory we retain an option to double capacity if demand warrants it. In effect this means that once demand is known the decision taker would be able to choose the best of the alternatives in the last two columns, provided he chose the smaller factory at decision point 1. Thus, if the initial decision was made to install a small factory he would be certain of a minimum profit of £90,000, since any level of demand is sufficient to keep the factory running profitably. However, where demand is more than 45,000 (and from Table 3.1 we expect it to be above 45,000, 0.16 + 0.34 + 0.34 or 0.84 of the time and below only 0.14 + 0.02, or 0.16 of the time) profits can be increased by opening a second small factory.

To estimate the total expected value of an initial small factory we thus need to add the expected value on the occasions when demand falls below 45,000 and only one small factory is operated:

£90,000 * 0.14 + £90,000 * 0.02 = £14,400

to the expected value when demand is above 45,000 and two small factories are operated:

£180,000 * 0.16 + £150,000 * 0.34 + £120,000 * 0.34 = £120,600

to give an overall expected profit of:

£14,400 + £120,600 = £135,000.

Against this the expected value if a large factory is selected initially is:

£250,000 * 0.16 + £180,000 * 0.34 + £100,000 * 0.34 − £50,000 * 0.14 −
$$£200,000 * 0.02$$

= £124,900.

From this it can be concluded that the forecast results in a decision to commission a single small factory and to open a second small factory if demand actually builds up to a level of 45,000.

In this example the decision tree structure focusses the attention of the forecaster

---

† The meaning of standard deviation is discussed in §4.5 at greater length. It is plausible to assume that the forecast will be less than one standard error above the true demand about 34 per cent of the time and less than two standard errors above about 48 per cent of the time.

on two particular aspects of the decision problem. Firstly, by systematically considering all available decisions the forecaster defines the alternatives between which his forecast should be able to discriminate. Secondly, the forecaster recognizes that being right on average is not enough because he cannot assume that profit opportunities are symmetrically distributed round the expected profit generated when his forecast turns out to be exactly right. By quoting a standard deviation for his forecast, he allows the decision taker to evaluate alternative decisions on the well-founded assumption that the forecast is not going to be exactly right.

§ 3.3 Structuring requirements for forecast information

In the previous section we have illustrated the use of decision trees as part of a deliberate attempt to simplify problems to the point at which the required forecast information can be specified fairly precisely.

In many strategic decisions there will be a host of technological, administrative and behavioural factors which reduce a seemingly infinite set of options to a relatively small number. In structuring the problem with a decision tree and asking simply for guidance between a small number of exclusive possibilities we are carefully defining the accuracy we require from the forecasting activity. This has the effect of setting the forecaster a more manageable problem than if he had been asked to pick the best from a limitless set of possibilities.

In many cases it may seem arbitrary to restrict the number of possible decisions to a handful of significantly different versions but this procedure can be justified because we are not usually faced with a situation of total inflexibility once a decision is made. Thus we might talk about a large or small factory at the time a decision is made to commence work on it, but during the process of construction actual specifications will be altered to take account of new information. The actual factory which we end up with may not be the one we chose initially, but because modifications were made in the light of information flowing in after the initial choice was made, it is difficult to argue that even if we had considered every conceivable factory size at the outset we would have been able to select the best one.

Problem structuring thus should not only reflect the reality of actual business decisions but should also tend to reduce the complexity of forecasting, to allow the use of simpler and less accurate forecast information than would otherwise be the case. Of course it is important that the simplification should not involve a decrease in the reliability of the decision process.

§ 3.4 The timing of forecast information

Most business decisions are made in the knowledge that their implementation will only be completed at some future date. For any decision, therefore, there will be a characteristic lag between the time the decision is taken and the time it becomes fully effective. For example, a decision to reduce prices would require new price lists to be prepared; perhaps the rate of production would have to be stepped up, and more salesmen would be needed to support a higher sales level; inventories throughout the distributive system would need to be increased and so on. Perhaps one or two months would be required between the time the price decision was taken and the time it came into operation. Delays may be much longer than this. At the other end of the spectrum a Mediterranean olive farmer deciding to expand production would have to wait more than a decade before his new trees bore their first commercial crop.

Given, then, that there is this characteristic lag between a decision being taken and its consequences becoming fully operational, it follows that the decision taker, in making a decision, should assess it, not in relation to current conditions, but in relation to the conditions that he thinks are going to exist by the time the effects of the decision are fully realized. In order to do this the decision taker involved perhaps in selecting a new product must be able to draw on currently available forecasts which predict market conditions at least up to, and preferably beyond, the time at which the product is to be launched. In other words the forecast, to be of value, must refer to a period far enough ahead to generate an adequate lead time for a decision to be implemented. Thus, in Fig. 3.4 if we take a decision at time t_m that requires a delay of d_1 before full operational status is achieved it follows that the decision maker, to make a correct decision at t_m, would like at that time to have available forecasts of likely operating conditions as far ahead as t_n.

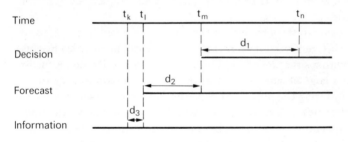

Fig. 3.4 Lead time and delay in forecasting and decision

However, forecasts cannot be generated instantaneously. Suppose a period equal to d_2 was required to prepare forecasts. It follows that the forecaster, in order to place his advice about conditions at period t_n in front of the decision maker at t_m has to start work at t_l. Naturally, he can only work with data available at time t_l and we will normally find that the collection and publication of data will generate a third delay, d_3. This means that the latest data used to forecast conditions at time t_n refer to time t_k. Adding all the delays it follows that to support decision making the forecasting technique has to be capable of predicting events for a period $d_1 + d_2 + d_3$ ahead. While this may seem an obvious and somewhat elementary point, an identification of this lead time is an essential preliminary to setting up a forecasting model. Unless it is done there is the danger that a forecasting model developed on historical data to provide the decision maker with a 12 months lead time may utilize, for example, September data to forecast events 12 months ahead in the next September. When the model is actually used to forecast, and it transpires that September data is not available until October, the forecast would then only provide 11 months, not 12 months of lead time. This interval would not be sufficient for a full response to the indicated conditions to be made and therefore, the value of the forecast would be much less than was initially expected. To be of maximum value the forecast therefore should provide at least the lead time required to make a full response to indicated future conditions. At the same time, if the forecast provides more lead time than is strictly necessary we immediately run into the problem that the further ahead we project, the less accurate the forecast is likely to be.

§3.5 Forecasting and network analysis (critical path methods)

If forecasts are regarded as a resource input into a firm's activities it follows that, as with any other resources, the forecast is required at the appropriate time. Network methods can monitor this function because they are concerned principally with dis-aggregating and ordering the sequence of events triggered off by a given strategic decision. They are thus a useful complement to decision trees which are basically concerned with the way in which strategic decisions are structured and taken. Given that such a decision has been made, critical path methods provide a useful basis by which the implementation of a decision can be monitored against the initial assumptions about how it should have progressed. Network methods also provide the basis of a planning and control system in the organization whose goal is to compare those forecasts instrumental in the initial decision with developing external events. This permits the initial decision to be modified where possible to incorporate revised forecasts and estimates as they arise, and also provides a timetable for the provision or re-estimation of forecast information.

§3.6 Critical path methods

The details of Critical Path Methods and PERT procedures are available in most operations research textbooks (see, e.g., Staffurth, 1969; Price, 1971; Miller and Starr, 1969, pp. 289–302). Here we are not concerned with developing the detailed methods in order to represent every complex situation. Instead we will outline the approach in sufficient detail to illustrate how it can be integrated into an ongoing forecasting, planning and decision system.

There are two basic components in any network representation — events and activities. An *activity* occupies time and usually requires additional resources — factory space, labour, materials, and so on. The other components in the network are *events*, which mark either the start or the completion of all contributory activities. Connecting all the activities and events in a logical and sequential way forms a network. If the network is properly constructed it follows that activities using the same resources and equipment or manpower, or activities based on the performance of earlier activities must display a characteristic set of dependency relationships. This pattern of depend-ence may be established by a variety of reasons. Technical constraints mean that foundation laying must precede brickwork in building a house. Commercial usage requires that finance must be available to cover construction costs before work starts on building ships. Even legal reasons may establish a pattern of precedence. It is, for example, illegal to operate an airliner without first obtaining an appropriate airworthiness certificate.

Before considering how network methods can contribute to integrating forecasts into the management process we will demonstrate the mechanics of the network method with a simple example.

3.6.1 An illustration of critical path methods

A project is split into the set of activities represented in the network shown in Fig. 3.5. Estimates for the time required for each activity to be completed are then entered on the network. The end of each activity is an event indicated in the network by a numbered circle. Such an event can only occur when all contributing activities have been completed. Consequently the network gives a clear indication of the logical sequence of events that must occur between the start of the project (event ①), and its completion (event ⑥).

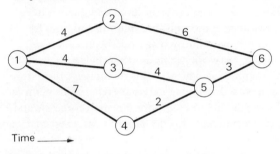

Fig. 3.5 *A simple network*

The network can then be analysed to provide estimates of the overall time that is required for the project to reach completion. This is done, starting from event ① by entering at each successive event the earliest cumulative elapsed time by which it is possible to complete all contributory activities.

In the example shown in Fig. 3.5, event ② for instance, can be reached after a delay of 4 periods, as can event ③. Where two or more contributory activities have to be completed prior to a merge event such as event ⑤ however, it is evident that completion necessarily depends on completing all preceding contributing activities. Clearly the activity between events ① and ③, and between ③ and ⑤ could be completed in 8 periods, but the earliest event ⑤ can occur is after the activities between ① and ④ and between ④ and ⑤ have also been completed. This takes a minimum of 7 + 2, or 9 periods. Therefore it is expected that 9 periods will have to elapse before event ⑤ could take place, and a further 3 periods – 12 altogether – before event ⑥ could be reached.

Event ⑥ itself is a merge event, and cannot occur until the activities between ① and ② and ② and ⑥ have also been completed. The times entered on the network for these activities occupy a total of only 10 periods, or 2 periods less than was required to arrive at event ⑥ on the path through events ①, ④ and ⑤. However, since both contributing paths have to be completed before event ⑥ can occur it follows that it is the longest route through the network that dictates the earliest possible completion time − in this case 12 time periods. This longest route is called the *critical path* because any delay along it will delay completion of the network. An off-critical path delay simply reduces slack time. In Fig. 3.6 we show the expected completion times against each event and indicate the critical path with a dotted line. The earliest elapsed time at which each event could occur is shown against it in parentheses.

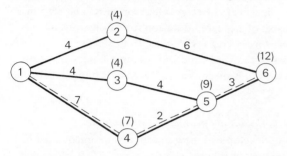

Fig. 3.6 A simple network − the completion time

The direct application of network methods in breaking down complex operations are varied. Construction jobs, engineering contracts, defence work and assembly jobs are all extensively organized on the basis of network methods. By using these methods potential bottlenecks can be forecast, resource requirements can be predicted and scheduled, and the progress of the project evaluated against forecast progress. The details of the often elaborate techniques devised for these applications are, however, of specialist interest − here we are interested in the forecasting implications of the technique.

§ 3.7 Forecasting activity in networks

The basic inputs to the network model are a set of technological or economic dependencies among the activities forming a project, together with estimates of the time required to complete each activity in the network. For many projects activity times are simply based on historical data − the time needed to complete a given amount of steel erection is easily estimated by considering the time required in the past for an equivalent amount of work. On the other hand, one of the areas where network techniques are widely used is in advanced technology projects, where new equipment or a new process has to be developed. Clearly without any historical precedent the estimates of activity time have to be set on a purely subjective basis and are subject to a considerable degree of uncertainty.

The basic network developed so far takes no account of the likelihood of inaccuracies in the time estimates for completing each activity. In practice the predictive powers of the network techniques under conditions of uncertainty are improved by considering the range of uncertainty associated with estimated activity times. One accepted approach to this problem is to estimate activity times on an optimistic and pessimistic basis, as well as estimating the most likely completion time. The optimistic time estimate predicts the shortest possible time in which an activity can be completed in ideal circumstances, while the pessimistic estimate is made on the assumption that all possible problems and setbacks are encountered in completing the activity.

For existing activities that are small in scale, relative to the overall uncertainty and requirements of a project, forecasts of activity times are often left to the judgement of the manager concerned. If the project is still at the stage where activities and responsibilities have yet to be defined, estimates of expected duration for subsections of the network can be made, using statistical forecasting techniques. In this case estimates of the accuracy associated with forecasts of required time and resource inputs are useful in predicting the range of outcomes for the project as a whole. (An example is provided in §10.10.1.)

3.7.1 A network approach to a product planning problem — an example

A food-processing firm is interested in developing a new product to be introduced in 2–3 years' time as the demand for existing products begins to taper off. It is decided that a network approach is the sensible way to integrate all the necessary decisions and define the deadline for each decision. A simplified version of the resulting network showing activity times, earliest dates of completion and the critical path is given in Fig. 3.7. The estimated times shown in the figure are given in months of elapsed time. Analysis of the critical path through the network (indicated by the dotted line) shows the necessary lead time to develop a suitable new product is about 30 months. This information has important forecasting implications. When the estimates of market requirements are being made (activity ①⟶②) it follows that it is market conditions at a time at least 2½ years in the future that are important to the current product selection decisions rather than current market conditions. If current demand is used as a test of suitability for each product it would follow that the product is being assessed on a basis that would be already 2½ years obsolete when it was first launched. To avoid this we need a forecast, giving at least 2½ years lead time, of both market demand and the social climate of which it forms a part. Similarly, further along the network, we know that forecasts of competitors' strategies have to be completed after an elapsed time of 20 months (event ⑦), in order to allow the product to be efficiently launched at 30 months (event ⑩). Therefore the forecasts of competitors' market strength, cash flow position, spare productive capacity and progress with new products should refer to their strategies 10 months ahead, in order to forecast the competitive environment in which our new product is to be launched. Again the network defines the relevant lead time.

3.7.2 Networks and forecast timing

The use of a network has thus enabled us to specify both the timing of forecasts in relation to the decisions of which they form a part, and also to alter the timing of

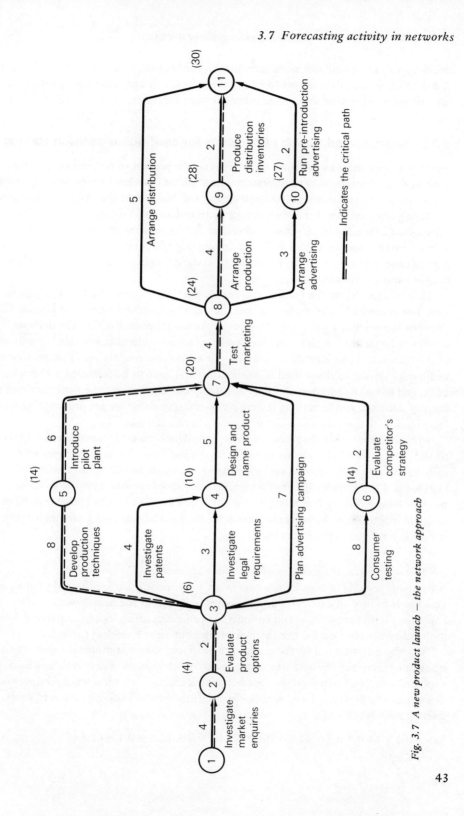

Fig. 3.7 A new product launch – the network approach

decisions to use all available slack to minimize the lead time we require from forecasts. A reduction of lead time normally allows the use of a cheaper forecasting model, or else the same expenditure results in more accurate forecasts.

§3.8 Structure and timing of forecasts for continuous decision making

In the previous sections the close links between the process of forecasting and the process of decision making have been emphasized, and methods have been suggested to ensure that forecasts relate both to the timing and content of the decisions they serve.

Having rejected the idea of forecasting as an isolated and independent activity and substituted a concept of an integrated system for forecasting and decision making, we create a further problem. This is that in an ongoing system we cannot fix a decision at a given time, nor can we draw watertight boundaries within which we can isolate a decision and its consequences.

Thus in considering the factory size problem in §3.2 we assumed that at a given time a decision had to be made and that the decision involved a clear-cut choice between factories of a given size. In practice we would normally find the decision could not be isolated in this way. For instance: some equipment suitable for only one of the factories might already be ordered; the workforce might already be proficient in techniques similar to those used in one factory and have to be retrained if the other is built, and so on. In addition all kinds of subsequent events might be contingent on the factory decision, and in making it we have to recognize that we are pre-empting many later choices that would still exist if we postponed a decision.

While it is inevitable that most of these considerations are ignored because analysis must stop somewhere, there are dynamic programming techniques that can reflect the continuous nature of decision making where it seems important to do so. (Bellman (1954, pp. 37–48) provides what is regarded as a simple introduction to dynamic programming.) Although it is not within the scope of this book to consider dynamic programming as such, some of the flavour of the class of sequential problems it can handle is provided in the following example.

3.8.1 A sequential decision problem — share acquisition
A company seeking to acquire the control of a competitor before the end of the tax-year needs to buy an extra 10,000 ordinary shares within the next 5 weeks. After analysing market conditions and commercial prospects forecasts are prepared for the probability distribution for the share price over the next 5 weeks (Table 3.2).

Now the question is how to acquire the proposed shares at minimum cost. Initially it might appear that the best strategy is to buy all the shares in the week in which expected cost (EC) based on the forecast probabilities is at its lowest. By inspection this appears to be Week 1 and this can be confirmed by calculating expected costs, starting with Week 1 (EC_1).

$EC_1 = 0.1 * £1.0 + 0.3 * £1.2 + 0.3 * £1.4 + 0.2 * £1.6 + 0.1 * £1.8$

$\qquad = £1.38,$

Table 3.2
Forecast probability distribution of share prices

Share price (£)	Forecast of probabilities for each of the next 5 weeks				
	(1)	(2)	(3)	(4)	(5)
1.0	0.1	0.1	0.1	0.1	0.0
1.2	0.3	0.2	0.1	0.1	0.1
1.4	0.3	0.3	0.2	0.1	0.2
1.6	0.2	0.3	0.3	0.3	0.3
1.8	0.1	0.1	0.2	0.3	0.2
2.0	0.0	0.0	0.1	0.1	0.2

and similarly

$$EC_2 = £1.42, \quad EC_3 = £1.54, \quad EC_4 = £1.58 \quad \text{and} \quad EC_5 = £1.64.$$

Thus Week 1 is the week when expected cost is lowest. Buying then should cost the company only an estimated £1.38 per share.

However, taking a decision on this basis does not reflect the full situation, because by buying in Week 1 we have pre-empted the opportunities to buy in Week 2 if the price was only £1. On the other hand if the shares had not been bought in Week 1 there is no guarantee that the price in Week 2 would be £1.20 − it could be £1.80.

The realization gradually dawns that we cannot take any decision unless we have analysed all the other expected purchasing opportunities. The problem is how to do this. By restructuring the problem we can arrive at a simple method. The one certain thing we know is that if the take-over is to go through the shares have to be bought at the end of Week 5, and this makes a firm starting point.

If we had not bought our shares before the start of Week 5, then the price we would expect to pay would be the expected cost of £1.64 already calculated. From this it follows that we should buy in Week 4 if we have the opportunity to do so at a price less than £1.64. From the forecasts we expect that there will be an 0.1 probability of a price of £1.0, an 0.1 probability of a price of £1.2, an 0.1 probability of a price of £1.4 and an 0.3 probability of a price of £1.6. Purchasing at any of these prices would be preferable to delaying purchase till Week 5, when £1.64 is the expected price. However, we only expect to purchase at a price below £1.64 with a total probability of 0.1 + 0.1 + 0.1 + 0.3, or 0.6, while the chance that the price will be £1.8 or higher, making it preferable to delay purchase till Week 5 is thus 1 − 0.6, or 0.4.

The expected cost of buying in Week 4, given a further opportunity exists to buy in Week 5 and that the purchase has not been made earlier can be represented by $EC_{4:5}$ and is calculated below:

$$EC_{4:5} = 0.1 * £1 + 0.1 * £1.2 + 0.1 * £1.4 + 0.3 * £1.6 + (0.4 * £1.64)$$
$$= £1.494.$$

If we expect to pay £1.494 to purchase in Weeks 4 or 5 it follows that we should buy in Week 3 if the price is below £1.494 — that is if the price is £1.0 (P = 0.1), £1.2 (P = 0.1) or £1.4 (P = 0.2).

The expected cost of buying in Week 3, given a further opportunity exists to buy in Weeks 4 or 5 and that the purchase has not been made earlier is thus:

$$EC_{3:4} = 0.1 * £1.0 + 0.1 * £1.2 + 0.2 * £1.4 + (0.6 * £1.494)$$
$$= £1.396.$$

On a similar basis the expected cost at Week 2, buying if the price is £1.20 or less is:

$$EC_{2:3} = £0.1 * £1.0 + 0.2 * £1.2 + (0.7 * £1.396),$$
$$= £1.317$$

and for Week 1, buying at a price of £1.20 or less is:

$$EC_{1:2} = 0.1 * £1.0 + 0.3 * £1.2 + (0.6 * £1.317)$$
$$= £1.25.$$

Thus by representing the continuous nature of the decision process, and reflecting the opportunities to defer a decision to a later date if conditions are unfavourable we end up with an expected cost of £1.25 per share rather than £1.38.

In making this calculation we have been able to translate a set of static forecasts into inputs to an ongoing decision process, in which current decisions necessarily reflect past history as well as the existence of future options.

The example shows that forecasts need not be regarded as contributing to one off decisions. In many instances decision making is a process of continuous adaption. By taking a multi-period view of the problem the example shows that forecasts which on first sight, because of their wide spread, were almost useless could be transformed into valuable inputs simply by viewing them as part of a process of getting to B rather than an aid to deciding exactly how we should leave A.

§3.9 Summary

In this chapter two complementary methods of integrating forecasts with ongoing decision making have been presented.

The decision tree approach was recommended as an aid to structuring forecasting problems while network methods seemed more appropriate for judging the timing of forecast requirements. If requirements for forecast information are generated within the framework of these methods, then the forecast can be fed into a decision on a basis that maximizes its expected profitability.

There is the additional advantage in using these models that they permit a systematic approach to both problem structuring and forecast timing. In many situations this means that comprehensive data requirements can be identified and provided at an appropriate time. This avoids the typical problem that arises when a number of excellent forecasting methods exist but they cannot be used because the data which would be required to estimate them no longer exists. For example a network model for product planning which contains an activity in which market strategy is derived might well convince a forecaster that it would be a good idea to record current information on market share, relative price and advertising because by the time he is formally asked to prepare a forecasting model these basic items of data may no longer be recoverable.

References

Bellman, R. (1954) 'Some problems in the theory of dynamic programming', *Econometrica*, vol. 22.
Miller, D. W. and Starr, M. K. (1969) *Executive Decisions and Operations Research*, 2nd edn, Prentice-Hall, New Jersey.
Price, W. L. (1971) *Graphs and Network, An Introduction*, Butterworth, London.
Staffurth, C. (ed.) (1969) *Project Cost Control Using Networks*, O.R. Society and Institute of Cost and Works Accountants, London.

Progression — Part 1

In Chapter 1 we sketched the relationship between forecasting and decision making and argued that the specifications of a forecast in terms of timing, detail and accuracy arose from the problem in which it would be used rather than from statistical considerations.

Two general surveys which offer a marketing perspective to the integration of forecasting with decision making are:

Pearce, Colin (1971) *Prediction Techniques for Marketing Planners*, Associated Business Programmes, London;
Bolt, Gordon J. (1971) *Marketing and Sales Forecasting*, Kogan Page, London.

They offer an intuitive description of forecasting seen as a part of the firm's marketing system and are helpful in setting the forecasting scene. However, they do little more than sketch out the various alternative methods available to the forecaster and do not provide the reader with any means of evaluating the results.

A more structured introduction which gives the reader a framework for understanding the different forecasting methods described later in the book is given in:

Clark, John J. (ed.) (1969) *The Management of Forecasting*, St Johns University Press, New York

while:

Benton, William K. (1972) *Forecasting for Management*, Addison-Wesley, Reading, Mass.

provides a clear and basic introduction to the forecasting system, and some of the best tested methods used by management.

Pearce's book proposes a decision theory framework as a means of evaluating the information contained in forecast. It is the topic we discuss in Chapter 2. However, we are only able to touch the surface of the subject which is, from both a theoretical and practical viewpoint as highly developed as forecasting. Two excellent books which are fascinating and very clear are **Raiffa** (1968) (*see Ch. 2 References*) and **Miller and Starr** (1969) Chs 4 and 5 (*see Chs 2/3 References*).

For a simple clear review of decision analysis:

Lindley, D. V. (1971) *Decision Making*, Wiley—Interscience, New York.

Four articles all of which clearly present these quite complicated ideas in the framework of management decision making are:

Magee, J. F. (1964) 'Decision trees for decision making', *Harvard Business Review*, vol. 42:4;
Magee, J. F. (1964) 'How to use decision trees in capital investment', *Harvard Business Review*, vol. 42:5;
Swalm, R. D. (1965) 'Utility theory — insights into risk taking', *Harvard Business Review*, vol. 44:6;
Hammond III, J. S. (1967) 'Better decisions through preference theory', *Harvard Business Review*, vol. 45:6.

Three books which, with **Raiffa**, give a thorough grounding in the subject area, are:
(*a*) At a simple mathematical level:

Thomas, Howard (1972) *Decision Theory and the Manager*, Pitman, London;
Coyle, R. G. (1972) *Decision Analysis*, Nelson, London.

(*b*) At a level demanding familiarity with calculus:

Moore, P. G. (1972) *Risk in Business Decisions*, Longman, London.

This last book is more complete with many interesting examples.

In Chapter 3 we argued that the forecast's relation with the structure and the time dependence of a decision situation were important in deciding on the necessary forecasting accuracy as well as the forecasting time horizon. While decision theory provided the structure, critical path methods provided information on the timing, **Miller** and **Starr** (1969) (*see Chs 2/3 References*) provides a brief introduction, while **Staffurth** (1969), **Price, W. L.** (1971) (*see Ch. 3 References*) and:

Lockyer, K. G. (1964) *An Introduction to Critical Path Analysis*, Pitman, London

are simple introductory texts to the subject. A fuller description of critical path and some of its variations is given in:

Moder, J. and **Phillips, C.** (1970) *Project Management with CPM and PERT*, 2nd edn, Van Rostrand Rheinhold, New York.

Part 2
Methodology of forecasting

In a sense the next three chapters form the core of the book. Without a thorough understanding of the methodology of forecasting the analyst is forced to rely on either his own intuition, or the methods which historically have been used by the organization. He is unable to evaluate the adequacy of current practice without some knowledge of the alternative methods available to him, and their likely effectiveness. He is unable to improve the forecasting system without a careful guide showing how to develop and implement a number of the many models available. We therefore aim to discuss forecasting methodology at two levels. The first is concerned with giving insight into the two basic ideas on which most forecasting models are based: the decomposition of the history of a time series into a number of stable components; and the identification of systems which explain the movements of components. The second level of our argument, an expansion of this second point, is concerned with showing exactly how to build such models of covarying systems.

Although we have tried to avoid formal explanation of phenomena, preferring a less rigorous approach, we have sometimes been forced to use a formula without explaining its derivation. This omission we have tried to alleviate by extensive use of references and footnotes: sometimes to expand an explanation, sometimes to make a more advanced point and sometimes, in the usual academic tradition, to reference our sources.

Our aim throughout then is to give our own somewhat idiosyncratic view of the nature of time series and to sufficiently develop ideas concerning their statistical base so that the reader will be able to take a real situation and describe it by using these formal modelling techniques. If he is familiar with the basic ideas of statistics most of Chapter 4 on 'Smoothing and interpreting information flows' and Chapter 5 on 'Linear regression' will prove superfluous, while Chapter 6 contains much material new to an elementary text. The pace of presentation therefore has been chosen to meet the non-specialist's need for each logical step to be carefully described. With these basic ideas understood he will then be in a position to develop an appropriate forecasting system for his organization.

4

Smoothing and interpreting information flows

§ 4.1 Introduction

Information is the raw material of the decision-making process. It provides the data by which the direction and effectiveness of a firm's current activities are monitored and is used to assess the relative benefits to be derived from alternative future strategies.

Because the structure of decision making is determined by the information inputs decision makers receive, the effectiveness of each decision is directly related to the quality of that information. It follows that the quality of an information system should not be judged by the frequency and accuracy with which it reports events, without also considering the possible bias transmitted by taking observations over short, often non-representative time intervals.

§ 4.2 Errors in data series

A forecaster makes the assumption that he can use past observations on a data series to predict its future behaviour. This assumption rests on a belief that past observations are accurate and are relevant to the series to be forecast.

Both these beliefs of accuracy and relevance need to be tested before undertaking a forecasting exercise. For observations to give an accurate representation of the past behaviour of a series the data should be checked for possible arithmetic and recording errors. Since errors in observation, transmission, aggregation and copying are all likely sources of otherwise inexplicable variation the origin of a data series should be checked and its basic accuracy established.

The relevance of a data series also needs to be checked. A sales forecast based on past sales data would not be successful if over the observed period a waiting list for the product had existed. The sales data in those circumstances reflect production decisions and not the level of demand.

Comparability is also required in the data series. An attempt to forecast television sales from historic data sales would run into difficulties unless specific account was taken of environmental changes (increased broadcasting, altered transmission standards) and technical improvements (colour, set size) which produced an untypically high rate of product obsolescence and replacement.

In theory, whatever adjustments are made, no two observations in a data series can ever be completely comparable since each observation is influenced by a unique combination of a thousand-and-one separate factors. In practice however, the forecaster attempts to overcome this problem of comparability by smoothing or averaging his data over a sufficiently long period for random disturbances to cancel out.

§ 4.3 Components of a time series

If a set of observations have been checked for relevance and comparability the next step is to analyse such a time series into its 'true' component (i.e. that part to which it is desirable to react) and its random component. Freund and Williams (1970) have compared a time series to the haphazard scrawlings of a 3-year old child yet this data provides the raw material that the analyst uses in producing forecasts.

In analysing time series data it is helpful to think of the series as made up of four main components:

1. Long-term trend.
2. Cyclical variation.
3. Seasonal variation.
4. Irregular variation.

1. Long-term trend. The trend in a time series is the long-term movement after the observations have been transformed to remove short-term fluctuations. Trends tend to be produced by long-term influences such as changing real incomes, population changes, changes in taste and changes in technology.

2. Cyclical variation. For a variety of reasons, principally because of the leads and lags inherent in responding to change, most series tend to fluctuate round rather than converge on their long-term trend. Periodic swings in business confidence from optimism to pessimism produce corresponding changes in investment expenditures. The UK Government's stop—go economic policies during the 1960s produced pronounced cyclical patterns in the unemployment and balance of payments figures. Wheat production and prices exhibits one of the most persistent cycles, the movement from peak to trough taking about 7 years.

3. Seasonal variation. In a time series this is caused by such short-term changes in behaviour that reoccur on a weekly, monthly or seasonal basis. Retail sales, for example, tend to be higher on Fridays and Saturdays than on Mondays or Tuesdays. Unemployment among building and catering workers tends to be at its highest each winter.

4. Irregular variation (or residual error). This is that part of a time series that is unexplained after the three types of systematic variation have been removed. If this were reduced to zero we could predict the future exactly from knowledge of the three systematic components.

In isolating the four components, T (trend), C (cyclical), S (seasonal) and I (irregular) we need to decide on the form of their inter-relationship. The main alternatives are an additive relationship:

$$Y = T + C + S + I$$

where Y is the variable we wish to forecast and a multiplicative relationship (for a further discussion of the problems of specifying the appropriate model, see Freund and Williams, 1970, pp. 432—5):

$$Y = T * C * S * I.$$

While the methodology to be employed in isolating and recombining the components of a time series will be discussed in more detail in §4.7, we can illustrate the use of the concepts introduced in this section by considering the unemployment data illustrated in Fig. 4.1.

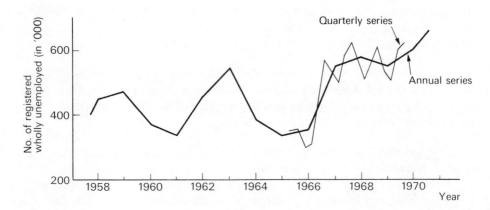

Fig. 4.1 *Annual and quarterly unemployment in the UK. Source: OECD Main Economic Indicators: 1955 to 1971*

An inspection of the annual unemployment data over the period 1959—71 reveals an upward trend. However, unemployment does not increase smoothly. Instead unemployment tends to rise steeply for 2 successive years then falls by a smaller amount over the next 2 years. This is evidence of a 4-year cycle in the series.

The quarterly data also shows signs of seasonal variation. Unemployment tends to be higher at the beginning and end of the year (the winter months) than in the middle of the year. Using a multiplicative model these seasonal effects result in unemployment being 10 per cent above trend in the first quarter, 2 per cent below trend in the second quarter, 7 per cent below in the third and 2 per cent above in the fourth.

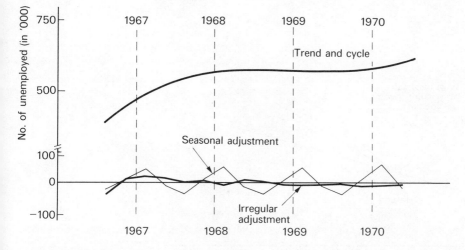

Fig. 4.2 Components of the unemployment figures

In Fig. 4.2 the quarterly observations for 1966—70 are decomposed into its basic elements. We can see that trend, cyclic and seasonal components explain almost the whole of the variation in unemployment.

§4.4 Necessity of smoothing information flows

We have seen that information reaching the decision maker is rarely completely reliable. Ideally we would like to be able to take each piece of information and split it into two parts, one part containing the disturbances arising for the reasons examined in previous sections and the other part containing information on permanent and significant changes that demand a response from the decision maker. In practice this can never be done, except with the benefit of hindsight. The decision maker, in using any technique, is making a choice about the proportion of valid information he is choosing to ignore and the proportion of random variation he responds to with unnecessary activity.

The dilemma posed by the choice is illustrated in Fig. 4.3 where over the years a long-term trend line has been used to describe the sales data for a product. A new sales total for the year 1973 (point N in the diagram) now becomes available that is considerably above the existing trend line (which passes through point M in 1972). Three alternatives present themselves.

1. The decision maker can assume that the value of 'N' is quite compatible with the existing trend line. On this interpretation the 'true' component of N, the component that indicates a permanent irreversible change in sales, is measured by the distance a while the rest of the apparent change (b + c) consists of random, non-recurrent variation. On this assumption the forecast for 1974 would be given by X.

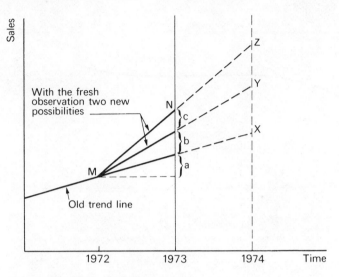

Fig. 4.3 The effect of a fresh observation

2. At the other extreme the value 'N' can be assumed to provide a completely 'true' guide to future events. In this case the whole of the change indicated by the new observation (a + b + c) is 'true' and there is no random variation. Also the new trend line, if N is an accurate observation, must pass through point N as well as M. This new trend line can be extended to provide an estimate of Z for the sales in 1974.
3. An intermediate assumption is that a certain amount of the change indicated by the new observation must be random, distance c in the diagram, and hence should not influence expectations of future conditions, but that the 'true' change (a + b) is larger than is compatible with what had previously been considered the trend line. This assumption produces a new trend line, and therefore a new forecast Y.

All techniques of smoothing and interpreting information flows are attempting to reduce the 'false' or random component without eliminating too much of the 'true'. In the next section we will consider some typical changes that occur in a time series that require the analyst to find some means of operationalizing this concept.

§ 4.5 The concept of distribution in time series observations

(The reader who is totally unfamiliar with the concepts developed in this section is recommended to read the first five chapters of Mendenhall and Reinmuth, 1974.)

The distinction between 'true' and 'false' information in time series observations is one that cannot be made with certainty. Instead we are forced to use a probabilistic model to discriminate between the two.

Suppose we have a set of time series observations, covering twenty periods, and that examination of these observations suggests a hypothesis that there is no significant trend or seasonal effects, with all variation round the calculated mean† $\bar{X}$, being generated apparently at random.

Suppose we now obtain a twenty-first observation on the series larger than any of the previous observations. We want to assess whether the information suggesting an increase in the level of the series is 'false' because such an increase appears incompatible with the hypothesis of a random fluctuation round the mean. Alternatively we may consider whether the indicated increase is 'true' information, indicating the existence of a change in the time series behaviour which will invalidate the original hypothesis of no trend or seasonal effects. A casual inspection of the data, shown in Fig. 4.4 suggests that the twenty-first observation on X, with a value of 1.9, is so out of line with the mean ($\bar{X}$ = 1.41) of the preceding twenty observations as to put in doubt the existing hypothesis that all variation in the value of X is random.

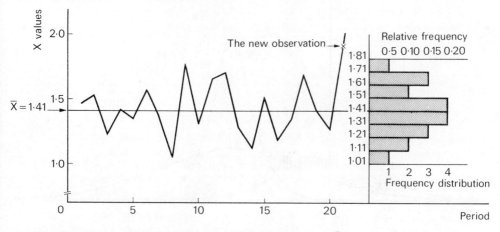

Fig. 4.4 A probability distribution of time series observation

This impression is reinforced by examining the frequency with which the original observations fall into class intervals progressively more remote from the sample mean. For example, there are four observations with values within the range 1.41 to 1.51. Viewing the complete distribution, 80 per cent of all observations (16 out of 20) fall between 1.11 and 1.71, so that under the hypothesis 'no trend and seasonal variation' a value as high as 1.90 occurs very rarely. How unusual an occurrence it is can be estimated statistically if we make an additional assumption that the population from which our sample of observations is drawn conforms to a known probability distribution. In this case we will assume a normal distribution‡. Using the available data we

---

† The mean of a sample of n observations $X_1, X_2, \ldots X_n$ will be denoted by $\bar{X}$, where $\bar{X} = (\sum\limits_{i=1}^{n} X_i/n)$. This summation notation is explained in Appendix 2 (p. 265).

‡ There are a large number of different probability distributions, from the normal and t with which the reader is perhaps familiar, to the β (beta) and γ (gamma) distribution. They vary both in their shape and the possible range of the observations which they are used to describe. For example, the normal distribution is symmetric and can take any value between $-\infty$ and $+\infty$. The γ distribution is skewed and only takes positive values. The β distribution has a finite range.

can estimate the parameters of such a distribution and then use this distribution to test whether the new observation can be reasonably assumed to have been drawn from it.

Any normal distribution can be described by just two parameters. The mean of the distribution μ (mu) locates its centre while its dispersion is measured by the variance σ^2 (sigma squared) or its square root σ, the standard deviation. The characteristic shape of the normal distribution with different assumed parameters is shown in Fig. 4.5. In estimating the parameters of the normal distribution from which our observations are assumed to have been drawn, we use the sample mean, $\overline{X}$, as an estimate of the unknown population mean μ, while the sample variance, s^2, is used to estimate the population variance σ^2.

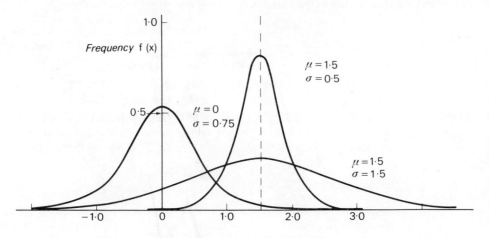

Fig. 4.5 *The changing shape and position of the normal distribution as its parameters alter*

The mean value of the observations, $\overline{X}$, is 1.41, and the sample variance s^2 can be calculated by the formula:

$$s^2 = \frac{1}{(n-1)} . \sum_{i=1}^{n} (X_i - \overline{X})^2.$$

The data in our example provides an estimate of sample variance of 0.04, leading to an estimated standard deviation of $\sqrt{0.04}$, or 0.20. The sample mean and standard deviation are now used as estimates of the parameters of the normal distribution. Reference to standard tables of the normal distribution (given in most statistics texts or e.g. CUP, 1964, p. 4; Mendenhall and Reinmuth, 1974, p. 528) gives the proportion of all observations that fall within a specified number of standard deviation of the mean. For example, 97.7 per cent of all observations would have values less than the mean (1.41) plus two standard deviations, i.e. 1.41 + 2 * 0.20 or 1.81, and that 84.1 per cent of all observations have values less than the mean plus one standard deviation, i.e. 1.61.

Using these standard tables we can graph the normal distribution resulting from our

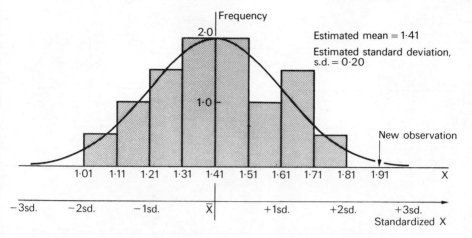

Fig. 4.6 Actual and normal probability distributions

estimated parameters and compare it with the distribution shown in Fig. 4.4. This is done in Fig. 4.6.

We can now consider the position of the new observation with a value of 1.9. The normal distribution shows that occasionally we would expect an observation of 1.9 or higher to arise even when the model is correct. However, the vast majority of observations would have values much below this. In fact, a value of 1.9 when standardized† is 2.5 standard deviations above the mean and this level of variation or greater would occur only 0.6 per cent of the time. We would therefore expect to be right 99.4 times out of 100 if we judged that the new observation was not a point of the earlier observed probability distribution but conveyed some true information about a change in the basic behaviour of the series.

§4.6 Changes in time series

Whatever model we use to explain a series of observations — random variation, seasonal variation, trend and so on — the appearance of any new observation showing a large deviation from the value predicted by the model in use calls for further investigation. In Fig. 4.7(*a–d*) we show a situation in which a set of observations is assumed to fluctuate randomly round a mean level of α (alpha). Using the methods developed in the previous section we may estimate the parameters of the probability distribution from which the time series observations are drawn. Suppose now that at time t_0 a further observation is recorded. Some of the problems arising from the availability of this new observation have already been discussed in §4.4 but with the vocabulary developed in the last section it is possible to state them more precisely. The question to be answered is whether or not the new observation obeys the same probability law as the earlier data.

† A standardized score for an observation X is equal to the number of standard deviations it lies away from the mean, i.e. the standardized score of X (which we will call Z) is equal to $Z = (X - \bar{X})/s$. The twenty-first observation 1.9 has a standard score of $(1.90 - 1.41)/0.20 = 2.50$.

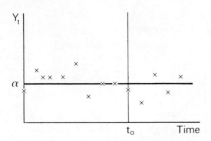

Fig. 4.7(a) Random time series

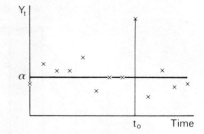

Fig. 4.7(b) An impulse at t_0

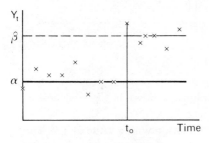
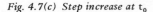

Fig. 4.7(c) Step increase at t_0

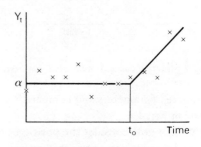

Fig. 4.7(d) A trend change at t_0

Now at time t_0 we will suppose a change takes place in the underlying probabilistic model. Figure 4.7(*b*) illustrates the curious phenomenon of an impulse, which is identified by a very large deviation (positive or negative) from the expected value of the previous observation. The errant observation at t_0 is followed by a return to a series of observations consistent with the original model. Such an observation could be generated by many causes — an expectation that taxes might go up on a product, an interruption to a competitor's output or even a clerical error in obtaining or processing data. Needless to say a check for these or similar factors should be the first reaction to unexpected information.

A more common situation is shown in Fig. 4.7(*c*) where the observation at t_0 is followed by a series of observations which suggest that variation is still random but at a new and higher level of sales — round a mean of β rather than α. Such a situation might occur where a new use for a product was discovered, or where a new market opened up.

Another possibility, shown in Fig. 4.7(*d*) is that the observation at t_0 is the start of a change in trend, and that it will be confirmed by further observations. This new trend could arise perhaps from a change in market acceptance of a product. Perhaps a brand of cigarettes has been re-launched or a major competitor has experienced supply restrictions which do not allow him to compete for any growth in the market.

The forecaster at time t_0 would find the identification of exactly what was going to happen to the series very difficult, and of course, there are other possibilities for him to consider, including the entry of seasonal effects. Unless he is aware of the strike in a major consumer's plant, the situation in Figs 4.7(*b*) and 4.7(*c*) would appear identical. Similarly, in Fig. 4.7(*d*) it is only with the fourth observation after the change has occurred that the analyst will recognize what has happened.

In the previous section we illustrated the dilemma posed by a new observation: which part is true, which part is random? More accurately phrased the problem becomes one of devising a system which quickly identifies when the model changes, but is not so responsive as to confuse a particular random observation with a change in the underlying model. What is desirable is a system which sorts out the two elements, the random and the 'true' and is only responsive to changes in the latter.

§ 4.7 Smoothing

4.7.1 Simple averaging and totalling

Most of the information available to the decision maker will be normally either in the form of totals or averages. It therefore reflects a cumulative set of observations made over some specific time period. Different time periods may be used for different information flows. A company may prepare a profit and loss account covering its trading activities for a period of a year, but on the other hand report production and sales figures weekly. In each case the aggregate figures are composed of hundreds of distinct events. In averaging or totalling these events over a period, a conscious decision has been made that the chosen interval is long enough to allow most of the random variation associated with a large number of small events to cancel out, while still showing up significant changes in the underlying behaviour of the time series. Some of the implications of this decision are set out using the data illustrated in Fig. 4.8. In the graph the average quarterly sales of a product are compared with the weekly sales on which the averages are based. An inspection of the weekly figures reveals a considerable amount of variation, a very low proportion of which corresponds to any long-term change in the true level of sales. Averaging the figures for the longer period of 3 months allows time for these short-run effects to cancel out.

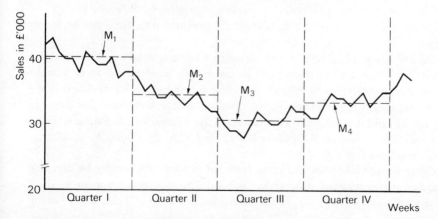

Fig. 4.8 Weekly sales of a consumer product

However, the 3-month period is by no means ideal. In the first two quarters the trend estimated by computing the quarterly averages follows the trend of the week to week sales quite successfully. In the third quarter, though, the average becomes quite misleading, since it indicates a continued fall in the series, while an inspection of the weekly figures suggests a gentle recovery during the later part of this period. Forecasts of future sales arrived at by continuing the trend shown in the first three quarterly averages would, therefore, be underestimates and this is borne out by considering the actual sharp improvement of average sales in the fourth quarter.

From this example we may deduce that while weekly sales figures are too unstable to provide satisfactory information about future events, average sales figures based on total sales for the 3 months are averaged over too long a period, and because they only start to give accurate information sometime after the event they provide a poor base from which to forecast. Ideally, figures should be based on a shorter period, perhaps of only 1 or 2 months.

In general, then, it appears that where averaging or totalling operations are used, there is some fairly specific time base over which minor fluctuations are ironed out but major changes are transmitted. Selecting a longer or shorter time base introduces problems for both the decision taker and the forecaster. This runs somewhat against the conventional wisdom that assumes that speed and fullness of data transmission to the decision maker is automatically a good thing. On the contrary, over-frequent reporting can lead to overactive decision making, with decisions made unnecessarily to adjust to random fluctuations that would have been self-cancelling over a slightly longer period. What is needed is some method of reporting by exception which distinguishes between a true change and a random fluctuation, and yet responds quickly when necessary. These two facets of the forecasting problem act in opposite directions, the first towards less hyperactive data reporting and the second towards a constant vigilance. Any information system needs to resolve this conflict.

4.7.2 The moving average

One solution adopted to the problem of providing continuous and representative information not subject to short-term, random disturbances is to use a moving average technique.

A moving average is constructed by maintaining a running total of all observations over the last, say one-and-a-half months. If we use weekly observations there would be seven figures in the moving total. When a new observation becomes available this is added to the running total, and the value of the observation that is now just over one-and-a-half months old is subtracted, thus restoring the number of observations used to seven. The mechanism for this is illustrated in Table 4.1 the data being on product sales, shown earlier in Fig. 4.8.

The moving average is obtained directly from the moving total simply by dividing by the number of observations included in the total. The moving average, or total, relates to the midpoint of the data used in its estimation. Thus in Table 4.1 we calculate average sales for the period Week 22 to Week 28 inclusive as 32.7. The midpoint of this series is Week 25, so the moving average for these weeks must refer to Week 25.

Table 4.1

Moving averages, weekly sales of a consumer product

Week	22	23	24	25	26	27	28	29	30	31	32	33	34
Sales in £'000	33	34	35	33	32	32	30	29	29	28	30	32	31
7-period moving total					229	225	220	213	210	210	209		
7-period moving average					32.7	32.1	31.4	30.4	30.0	30.0	29.9		
4-period moving total			135	134	132	127	123	120	116	116	118	120	
4-period moving average				33.6	33.2	32.4	31.2	30.4	29.5	29.0	29.2	27.2	

A four-period moving average is calculated by computing the totals $\sum_{i=1}^{4} X_i$ and $\sum_{i=2}^{5} X_i$, summing the results and dividing by the total number of observations, in this case 8. This method is necessary because with an even number of periods over which the data is to be smoothed, the moving total is not associated with a particular time period, 135 falling between Week 23 and Week 24, 134 between 24 and 25. Averaging the sum of these two totals overcomes this difficulty. Note that both the four-period and five-period moving average contain exactly the same observations, although they are weighted differently, i.e.:

four-period average $= (X_1 + 2(X_2 + X_3 + X_4) + X_5)/8$;
while the five-period average $= (X_1 + X_2 + X_3 + X_4 + X_5)/5$.

The central measurements in the four-period average are weighted more heavily than those in the five-period.

In forecasting from the moving average one drawback arises from the loss of observations implicit in its calculation. For example, in the seven-period moving average although we have observations on sales until Week 34 we can only calculate the average up to Week 31. The last three data points, perhaps the most important in the time series, are being under utilized, and the forecast has to be made by projecting ahead from Week 31 (not 34).

Now as we have pointed out before, the forecaster is mostly concerned with recognizing when the behaviour of the time series alters. The point at which a series, previously increasing, starts to decrease (and vice·versa) is called a turning point, and a good forecasting method will identify such turning points quickly. Moving average methods are a relatively poor guide because of the lag we have just mentioned. For example, by referring to Fig. 4.8 we note that in Week 31 sales were at the minimum level for the year. To forecast, the trend, identified by the moving average, has to be extrapolated. However, if we used the seven-period average as a basis, the forecast for Weeks 31 onward would be one of decreasing sales, but a glance at the graph (Fig. 4.8) will show how inaccurate this is. The warning signals lying in observations 32, 33 and

34 are ignored because of the time lag inherent in the method. On the other hand, a four-period average correctly identifies the change in trend. Nevertheless, with so few observations included it is too responsive to temporary, random fluctuations which very often have the effect of disguising the underlying trend.

However, moving averages are fairly effective in damping the random fluctuations in a time series and they are easy to calculate on a continuous basis. While they cannot predict trend changes with any accuracy they are useful in dealing with seasonal and cyclical disturbance patterns in the data, and for this reason fitting a moving average is often a useful first step employed in more elaborate forecasting procedures.

4.7.3 Forecasting periodic variation in time series

As we mentioned earlier, most economic series display some regular pattern of variation associated with the passage of time. Almost all series are affected by the progress of the international business cycle, which produces noticeable swings over a 4- or 5-year period. Industries particularly prone to variation from this source are usually manufacturing investment goods, where sales are more closely related to a change in the level of prosperity rather than to the absolute level of prosperity itself. In Fig. 4.1 we illustrated the cyclic component using the British unemployment figures. Pronounced cyclical disturbances are also common in agricultural production, where many of the products have long delays before production can be increased. Thus the coffee and olive-oil markets, for example, are subject to alternate shortages and surpluses that make planning particularly difficult for the developing economies that tend to depend heavily on these crops. Similarly most products are affected in the shorter run by recurring seasonal patterns. The yield of a chemical process, for instance, is often dependent on the ambient temperature. Each year the warmer months produce an upward deviation in production, the colder months a downward deviation.

A simple method of detecting cyclical disturbances is by visual inspection of the data plotted against time. In Table 4.2 we give data on the daily turnover in a supermarket which depends, as we would expect, on daily shopping habits. In the early part of the week sales are low but they increase in the middle of the week, rise to a peak at the weekend and then drop back to the starting level at the beginning of the next week. The raw data and the corresponding moving averages are shown in Fig. 4.9.

If we suppose the store manager is interested in monitoring the level of sales to see whether there is any upward or downward trend, he will find this difficult to do because trends are small relative to the disturbances due to random and day-to-day variability. In analysing the problem he will need to explain the pattern of sales in terms of three components — changes due to trend, changes caused by day of the week variations and, finally, residual variation. The cycle can be neglected because in the short term it is included with the trend.

The first step is to eliminate the effect of the day of the week variations from the series. Since from inspection we believe the seasonal effect has a period of 6 days, if we take our moving average over that period most of the seasonal and irregular fluctuations should be removed. Using Table 4.2, column (4) has been used to track the basic six-period averages, used in calculating the centred moving averages of column (5).

Table 4.2
Estimating the seasonal variation

Observa-tion	Day	Sales in £'000 Y	Weekly moving average (6-period)	Centred moving average T * C	Sales as a % of moving average S * I
(1)	(2)	(3)	(4)	(5)	(6)
1	Monday	1.94			
2	Tuesday	3.06			
3	Wednesday	3.54			
			4.38		
4	Thursday	4.25		4.39	96.81
			4.40		
5	Friday	6.51		4.40	147.95
			4.40		
6	Saturday	6.97		4.41	158.05
			4.41		
7	Monday	2.06		4.41	46.71
			4.40		
8	Tuesday	3.04		4.40	69.09
			4.39		
9	Wednesday	3.62		4.40	82.27
			4.40		
10	Thursday	4.22		4.38	96.34
			4.36		
11	Friday	6.43		4.36	147.48
			4.35		
12	Saturday	7.00		4.34	161.29
			4.33		
13	Monday	1.85		4.34	42.63
			4.35		
14	Tuesday	2.95		4.35	67.82
			4.35		
15	Wednesday	3.48		4.34	80.18
			4.33		
16	Thursday	4.34		4.33	100.23
			4.33		
17	Friday	6.45			
18	Saturday	6.88			
19	Monday	1.89			

N.B. The model used above is multiplicative: $Y = T * C * S * I$ where T is trend, C cycle, S seasonal and I irregular.

Column (5) then is just $T * C$ (in the multiplicative time series model). The entries in column (6) are the sales as a percentage of the moving average, calculated in column (5). Consequently, the first entry in column (6) is calculated according to the procedure:

$$96.81 = \frac{4.25}{4.39} * 100.$$

Symbolically $(6) = Y_t/(5) = S * I$.

From the symbolic representation we see that the entries in column (6) are the seasonal and irregular parts of the series. To complete the isolation of the seasonal

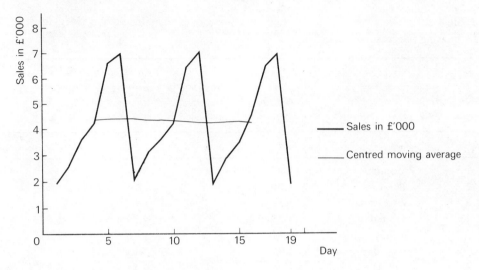

Fig. 4.9 Supermarket sales: raw data and moving averages

effect, the irregular component has to be removed. Table 4.3 gives the S * I entries by day.

We have shown that the irregular component in a time series may be removed by averaging. This is exactly how we choose to extract the seasonal from the S * I entries in Table 4.3. Each column, however, contains only a few entries and consequently the average will still include too much of the irregular component, and we will be left with a poor estimate of the seasonal indices. An alternative method, described in Freund and Williams (1970, pp. 440—6) is to use the median of the observations. (The median of a set of n measurements is the 'middle' measurement when they are placed in order of size. If n is even it is the average of the two 'middle' measurements. Like the mean it measures the location of a frequency distribution.) For example, the index for Thursday would be 96.81 measured using the median, while it is 97.79 using the mean. Either method leaves us with an estimate of the seasonal (here daily) indices.

Adjusting the average daily seasonal components so that their total is 600 gives us a

Table 4.3
Tabulation of S * I components

	Monday	Tuesday	Wednesday	Thursday	Friday	Saturday
				96.81	147.95	158.05
	46.71	69.09	82.27	96.34	147.48	161.29
	42.63	67.82	80.18	100.23		
Average	44.67	68.45	81.23	97.79	147.71	159.67
Adjusted average	44.70	68.50	81.30	97.87	147.83	159.80

convenient interpretation of the daily sales indices; the index for each day is defined as the percentage of the average daily sales sold on that particular day of the week when the overall trend has been removed from the data. Thus:

(Daily index) = 100 * (Sales on that day)/(Average sales)

where the trend has been removed from both sales figures. Because the average daily sales is just the average of the six daily sales figures, the sum of the indices for each of those days should total to 600.

We have shown the first estimates of each seasonal index in Table 4.3 in the row labelled 'Average'. They total 599.52. If we are to think of each index as the percentage of the average daily sales that week sold on that particular day, their sum should be adjusted to 600. This is brought about by multiplying the estimated seasonals by 600/599.52 and these final daily indices are shown in the last row of Table 4.3, 'Adjusted average'.

Since we have now broken the original pattern of sales down into trend/cycle, seasonal and irregular variation it is possible to set up a scheme to monitor the sales level. An inspection of the trend shown in column (5) of Table 4.2 shows a slight decline over the period investigated. Since the decline is minor it may not be important, but the analysis of the daily variation permits a continuous check of new data against the estimated trend to see if any noticeable deterioration has taken place. For example, the sales achieved on the last Monday observed amounted to £1,890, a considerable drop on the preceding Saturday's sales of £6,880. The question is whether this drop corresponds to a deterioration in the underlying position or is solely due to the day-of-the-week effect. From Table 4.3 we know that seasonal influences make Saturday observations 59.8 per cent above an average day's sales. To seasonally adjust our observation of £6,880 we therefore multiply it by 100/158.9 to give £4,305. Similarly, Monday's sales of £1,890 should be increased by 100/44.17 to £4,228, a figure consistent with a long-term decline being maintained. Therefore the calculation of a trend and an appropriate set of adjustments for seasonal disturbances allows the store manager to check actual sales against expected sales and allows him to modify his cash control and stock control decisions if necessary.

Supermarket sales are likely to depend on the season of the year as well as the day of the week. Similarly, when discussing seasonal variation we argued that, for example, quarterly unemployment figures contain both a seasonal and a cyclic component. The technique of decomposition of a time series just described can be used to remove consistent disturbances associated with monthly, quarterly or annual time periods.

The analyst first specifies the number of periods to be used in a moving average to get rid of the seasonal, and irregular components (typically four in quarterly data), and will then isolate the seasonal indices using the methods just illustrated. With the components of the time series known, the forecaster is now able to complete the development of a forecasting model.

4.7.4 A forecasting model
In separating the seasonal influences from the trend we assumed that the moving

average represented the trend. But unfortunately before we can forecast the super-market sales we need to extrapolate the trend into the future. In fact when we were discussing the year's sales of a particular consumer product we noted that a seven-period moving average terminated three periods before the final observation, and therefore the forecaster will have to project the trend for a time period including these points as well. It is a weakness of the method described here, because the longer the time period the forecast covers, the less likely it is to be accurate.

Let us suppose that we are convinced that the trend in sales, as represented by the moving averages, is going to continue. To forecast on the basis of this trend in the moving averages we need to choose a trend line which fits the calculated averages as well as possible. Let M_t be the moving average on day t for the supermarket sales of Table 4.2. The values of M_t are given in column (5) and the corresponding values of t in column (1). Obviously no straight line can pass through all the observations,† however the fit provided by the line:

$$M_t = 4.420 - 0.005t,$$

gives an acceptable approximation. If the first Monday is at time 1, while the last Friday is at time 17, we can use the equation to predict the moving average value for sales on that last Friday:

$$M_{17} = 4.420 - 0.005 * 17 = 4.335.$$

Remember that we have already calculated the seasonal indices for each day. Friday's was 147.83, so in order to convert the deseasonalized sales to actual sales the trend estimate of 4.335 needs to be increased by 47.83 per cent to 6.408. Of course, we can compare this forecast with the observed value of 6.45, to see that this method has slightly underestimated the observed supermarket sales.

Table 4.4 shows the forecast sales for the next week. The trend values are calculated using the above equation. Multiplying by the appropriate seasonal index gives us a forecast in terms of actual sales.

Table 4.4
The forecast for sales in the coming week

Day	t	Trend	Seasonal	Forecast
Monday	19	4.325	44.70	1.933
Tuesday	20	4.320	68.50	2.959
Wednesday	21	4.315	81.30	3.508
Thursday	22	4.310	97.87	4.218
Friday	23	4.305	147.83	6.364
Saturday	24	4.300	159.80	6.871

† The reader familiar with regression analysis will recall that the line is chosen using the method of least squares. The method is described at length in the next chapter.

4.7.5 Summary: moving averages

It should be stressed that the moving averge methods described here are not recommended as appropriate for forecasting other than in the simplest applications. In §4.3 we discussed the four components of a time series. Here we have developed a simple method for isolating three of them (not the cyclic), and this has then been used to produce a forecast, which is the product of the extrapolated trend (a line fitted to the observed moving averages) and the seasonal indices. The method is intuitive, and is useful as a basis for understanding the more advanced techniques described later.

§4.8 Exponential smoothing techniques

Averaging or even moving average techniques are not always ideal. As we described in the last sections they are effective only under stable conditions. Unfortunately, time series observations are often subject to other kinds of variation, and the moving average technique, because it gives as much weight to some of the past observations as to the most recent, is rather insensitive to what may be quite radical changes in the trend of the series being forecast. And it is exactly these most recent observations that are representative of the current behaviour of the time series.

A possible solution to this problem is to use a weighted moving average, where the more recent observations are given greater weight in forecasting future events than the historically more remote. The difference between the straightforward moving average of the last section and a weighted moving average is illustrated in the following two equations. In both cases the average of the series which we will call S_t is calculated using the last r observations $Y_t, Y_{t-1}, \ldots Y_{t-r+1}$. The moving average equation, (i), assigns equal weight to each of the r observations, while the weighted average, equation (ii), assigns the weights $a_1, a_2 \ldots a_r$.

(i) $S_t = \dfrac{1}{r}(Y_t + Y_{t-1} + \cdots + Y_{t-r+1})$;

(ii) $S_t = a_1 Y_t + a_2 Y_{t-1} + \cdots + a_r Y_{t-r+1}$.

In principle, the weights $a_1, a_2, \ldots a_r$ in the weighted average could have any value, provided all those used sum to 1 to maintain the arithmetic consistency of the forecast. Usually the coefficients are arranged so that data points are given less weight as they become historically more remote. This implies that:

$a_1 > a_2 > a_3 > a_4 > \cdots > a_r,$

and that

$a_1 + a_2 + \cdots + a_r = 1.$

One of the more usual methods of choosing the weights $a_1, a_2 \ldots a_r$ is so that the $(i + 1)$th weight is a constant proportion of the ith, the proportion being less than 1, i.e. $a_{i+1} = \alpha a_i$, for each value of i. This is called an *exponential* (or geometric) weighting.

69

For example, suppose the weights decrease by a proportion of 0.7, i.e. $\alpha = 0.7$, then $S_t = a_1(Y_t + 0.7\,Y_{t-1} \ldots (0.7)^{r-1}Y_{t-r+1})$ and a_1 is now chosen to make the weights add to 1. A slightly different approach leads us in the same direction. If S_t is the (exponentially) smoothed average of the latest observation Y_t and the previous smoothed average S_{t-1} and we use the weights p and $1 - p$ in smoothing these two values we obtain an equation:

$$S_t = pY_t + (1 - p)S_{t-1}$$

Since we obtained S_{t-1} by a similar process:

$$S_{t-1} = pY_{t-1} + (1 - p)S_{t-2}$$

we can substitute for S_{t-1} in the first equation to get:

$$S_t = pY_t + (1 - p)(pY_{t-1} + (1 - p)S_{t-2})$$

or multiplying out:

$$S_t = pY_t + p(1 - p)Y_{t-1} + (1 - p)^2 S_{t-2}$$

and by repeating this process we can finally define S_t in terms of the original Y observations and S_0, the initial smoothed average

$$S_t = pY_t + p(1 - p)Y_{t-1} + p(1 - p)^2 Y_{t-2} + \cdots + p(1 - p)^{t-1}Y_1 + (1 - p)^t S_0$$

By setting S_0 equal to Y_0, a typical Y observation we see that S_t is simply a linear sum of all the original observations and since the weights used in the calculation sum to one† it is also comparable with them.

Suppose we select $p = 0.3$ then

$$S_t = 0.3(Y_t + 0.7Y_{t-1} + (0.7)^2 Y_{t-2} \cdots + (0.7)^{t-1}Y_1) + (0.7)^t S_0$$

which we may compare with the equation derived above using the first approach:

$$S_t = a_1(Y_t + 0.7Y_{t-1} \ldots (0.7)^{r-1}Y_{t-r+1})$$

The two intuitive derivations produce almost identical equations. As r is increased, so the two equations become closer and closer, and when $r = t$ the only difference lies in the inclusion of the last term $(0.7)^t S_0$, though this term hardly matters at all because the coefficient $(0.7)^t$ decreases quickly with t; after ten periods it takes the value of only 0.028, and after twenty the value is less than 0.001.

The equation $S_t = pY_t + (1 - p)S_{t-1}$, is called the *basic equation of exponential smoothing* and p is called the smoothing constant. Table 4.5 shows the original observations for the sales of a consumer product, first shown in Fig. 4.8, the four-period moving average, and the exponentially smoothed moving average for two different smoothing constants, $p = 0.2$ and $p = 0.4$ while in Fig. 4.10 the exponentially smoothed series are plotted for comparison with the original data.

---

† The weights $p, p(1 - p), p(1 - p)^2$ etc., form a geometric series and the formula for the sum of such a series shows it sums to one.

Table 4.5

Exponential smoothing: weekly sales of a consumer product

Week	22	23	24	25	26	27	28	29	30	31	32	33	34
Sales in £'000	33	34	35	33	32	32	30	29	29	28	30	32	31
4-period moving average			33.6	33.2	32.4	31.2	30.4	29.5	29.0	29.2	29.7		
Exponential average, p = 0.2	33.0	33.2	33.6	33.5	33.2	33.0	32.4	31.7	31.2	30.6	30.5	30.8	30.8
Exponential average, p = 0.4	33.0	33.4	34.0	33.6	33.0	32.6	31.6	30.6	30.0	29.2	29.5	30.5	30.7

It is apparent from Fig. 4.10 that the smaller the chosen value of p, the more the fluctuations in the original series are smoothed out. In the extreme case of p = 1 the basic equation of exponential smoothing simplifies to the equation $S_t = Y_t$; the smoothed series is identical to the original series and none of the variation in the original observation would have disappeared. At the other extreme of p = 0, the smoothed series is constant and equal to S_0, the initial smoothed value. None of the subsequent observations would affect the smoothed series. But since one of our criteria for smoothing was to recognize when a true change (step, trend or impulse) had taken place, such a choice of smoothing constant would be pointless. The choice of smoothing constant is in practice set by a compromise between two opposing objectives:

1. The elimination of random fluctuation.
2. A fast response to true changes.

Surprisingly enough, given the complexity of the exponential average, one of its main advantages lies in ease of calculation. Despite the fact that large numbers of previous

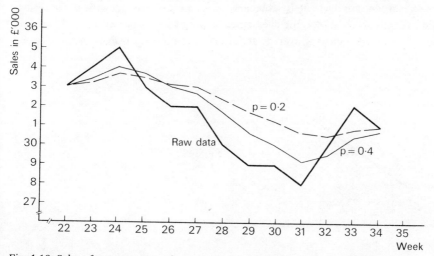

Fig. 4.10 Sales of a consumer product per week in £'000: exponential smoothing

observations are incorporated into the forecast, the current moving average can be obtained by using only two figures — the previous exponential average and the new observation. This arises from the constant proportionality inherent in the exponential weighting approach. Thus the working equation:

$$S_t = pY_t + (1 - p)S_{t-1}$$

can be used with only three items of information:

1. The new observation at time t, Y_t;
2. The value of the previous moving average, S_{t-1};
3. A value of p, the decay factor;

although, potentially, we are allowing an infinite number of observations to influence the outcome.

In operation, therefore, the exponential average can be used with great ease. Not only is the exponential average easy to calculate, producing a forecast from it is also simple. Appropriate methods will be discussed in Chapter 7. However, it is worth adding here that it is unnecessary to extrapolate as in the moving average method. For a process without seasonal or trend factors the forecast made at time t, k periods into the future $\hat{Y}_{t+k}$ is just S_t, the exponentially smoothed value of the series at time t.

§4.9 Smoothing techniques and information delay

While almost all information reaching decision makers has been smoothed by means ranging from the informal, through exponential smoothing to statistical trend fitting, it is seldom appreciated that the smoothing process introduces a significant delay into the information flow.

Consider the position in Fig. 4.11, where observations are made on a variable Y_t. Over the interval MN this variable is subject to constant, uniform growth. If the series is averaged over the interval MN, the average calculated for this period at time N would be $\overline{Y}_N$. Quite clearly this moving average at time N is exactly equivalent to the true

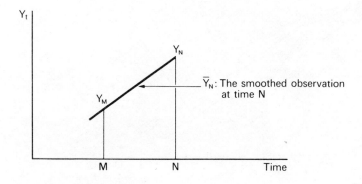

Fig. 4.11 Information delay

value of Y half a period earlier. The averaging process thus automatically delays information about the true level of the series by half the averaging period.

Exponential smoothing will produce a similar delaying effect. In this case, however, the delay is somewhat less, decreasing as the weight attached to the most recent observation, p, increases. The significance of a delay in either system is, of course, related to the length of time between each observation, and the length of time the organization takes to respond. The problem is particularly serious at the level of the national economy, where many figures are collected annually, or at best, quarterly. In these circumstances it is quite likely that a trend has reversed itself long before the averaged evidence starts to show this so for example one of the effects of such a delay in information is a recurrent tendency to over-shoot as decision makers respond to this 'old' data.

Delay as we have seen, is inherent in all processes of collection, aggregation and smoothing of data. It is particularly dangerous when the variable in question is close to a turning point. It is quite likely that the system will be analysed as in a state of growth when decline has set in, or vice versa. Together with appropriate smoothing methods, more frequent reporting of observations is most helpful in minimizing this problem, with advanced on-line computing systems being used to transmit and collate the data immediately.

§ 4.10 Summary

In this chapter we have discussed the nature of a typical data flow. Before a set of observations can be used as a basis for a forecast they must be comparable. There are often hidden changes in the series which account for much of its variability. There may well be errors of observation in measurement.

When a series of comparable observations is being considered it is often helpful to consider it as being made up of four components; the trend, the seasonal, the cyclical and the random. In § §4.3, 4.5 and 4.6, we discussed these factors in detail, in particular in relation to the types of change often seen in a time series. A series can be thought of as partially deterministic, and partially random, and in §4.4 we illustrated the necessity of decomposing a new observation into these two parts, responding only to the deterministic changes in the series. Moving averages or exponential smoothing are suitable methods for assessing the deterministic element in the series and removing the random. Nevertheless using any smoothing method increases the delay implicit in the forecasting system, a problem noted in the last section.

References

Cambridge University Press (1964) *Cambridge Elementary Statistical Tables.*
Freund, John E. and **Williams, J.** (1970) *Modern Business Statistics*, 2nd edn, Pitman, London.
Mendenhall, W. and **Reinmuth, J. E.** (1974) *Statistics for Management and Economics*, 2nd edn, Duxbury, Calif.

5
An introduction to linear regression

§5.1 Introduction

In Chapter 1 a forecasting model was defined as a set of assumptions that linked information inputs with forecast outputs. Such a model could test hypotheses, describe processes such as production or sales generation, and predict future outcomes from current information. A forecasting model can also form the basis of a system of control, where current decisions are altered in order to select the most preferred of all possible outcomes.

   Where the prospective benefits from forecasting information are high, more sophisticated models have been developed than those discussed in Chapter 4. Regression analysis forms the basis of most of these models. Instead of building a forecasting model using only the historical behaviour of the time series under consideration, as with smoothing methods, the model builder will attempt to find a general law connecting an input X and the corresponding output, Y. The pairing of the variables is done using what previous knowledge the analyst has of the causal system in which X and Y co-vary. We may illustrate the relationships between a single input X, and the output Y by Fig. 5.1, the 'black box' forecasting model. The term 'black-box' arises because the mechanism connecting variations in input and variations in output is unknown — the box is opaque. The scientist faced with such a situation would seek to break into the box to examine the mechanism, and to understand how it works. The forecaster's concern is not primarily with the mechanisms that connect the variables so much as with the ability of those mechanisms to generate reliable and accurate forecasts from input data. He is satisfied when he can determine the parameters and the extent of a

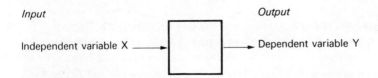

Fig. 5.1 The black box forecasting model

forecasting relationship. By 'extent' we mean both the strength of a relationship and also the range of situations within which the relationship holds good.

As an example, consider a well-known marketing relationship connecting the percentage of surveyed consumers who intend to buy a particular brand (I) with the percentage who claim to use it already (U):

$$I = K\sqrt{U},$$

where K is a constant related to the product field. This relationship and its parameter K have been empirically derived, and hold good across a wide range of established products. However, the forecaster using the relationship as part of a predictive model of future sales would not be able to explain why it worked; or what exactly was happening in the 'black box'. He would nevertheless be satisfied if the relationship was in his experience a reliable one, in that it provided a profitable input into decision making.

§5.2 The relationship between two variables

If for every value of the independent variable (X) there is just one value of the dependent variable (Y), then it follows that if we know the value of X we know the associated value of Y. Y is then said to be a function of X and the relation is written Y = f(X). For example, the simplest model connecting input with output is the straight line, $Y = \beta_0 + \beta_1 X$ (β_0 and β_1 are the parameters of the line, the intercept and the slope); a second example is† $Y = \beta_0 + \beta_1 \log X$, where the value of Y is linearly related to log X, rather than to X.

5.2.1 The choice of relationship
If the forecaster thought that total product sales (or unemployment for that matter) co-varied with time as the input variable, he would have a vast choice of possible relationships to consider, each of which could describe the time-series data he had collected. The choice of the appropriate relationship to use is often difficult. Nevertheless, such a choice has important consequences as the following example illustrates.

Suppose the demand for a new product is 1,000 units in the first year, and 2,500 in the second. Using just this information we might wish to calculate the expected demand in the third year. If D_t is the demand in the t th year of production, then the two available sales observations can be exactly described by the equation:

$$D_t = 1,500 * t - 500.$$

Unfortunately we can fit the same data by choosing a quadratic equation instead:

$$D_t = 500(1 + t^2)$$

which again passes through both observations. The two equations have completely different forecasting implications. In Fig. 5.2 the two curves are used to forecast the

† All logarithms are to the base e, where e = 2.71828 . . ., unless otherwise specified.

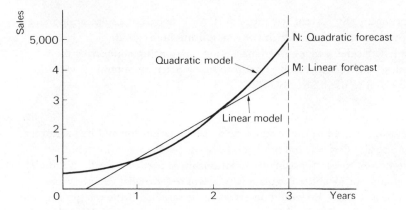

Fig. 5.2 A comparison of predicted sales volume when both a quadratic and a linear equation are fitted to the sales data

sales in year 3. Using the linear model sales in year 3 would be estimated as $D_3 = 1,500 * 3 - 500$ or 4,000, while the quadratic model predicts sales at $500(1 + 3^2) = 5,000$. The difference between the two forecasts is thus substantial.

The example illustrates two important concepts in regression. The first is the danger in extrapolating from very few observations. It is difficult to identify what, if any, underlying consistency there is in the observations when only a few are available. The decision maker is forced to rely completely on his own judgement and the advice of people closely identified with the problem. There is no comparison he can make between his own subjective feelings about the way things are going and the hard facts of a numerical forecast. The second, more subtle concept is concerned with deciding which (if any) of the forecasts to use. In later sections methods of analysing the usefulness of a forecast will be described. It may often happen that there is little to choose between the two models if only a mathematical basis is used. In the example discussed above there is no mathematical difference at all. The decision has to be made using all the available information, however subjective this process may be. What is important is that where there is a distinction between forecaster and forecast user, it is the user who finally decides which of the models he accepts.

5.2.2 A linear relationship

As we have mentioned, the simplest relationship between output and input is linear: $Y = \beta_0 + \beta_1 X$, and we will spend the remainder of the chapter discussing this model alone, leaving discussion of more complicated models until Chapter 6. To illustrate the basic concepts of regression, consider the data shown in Table 5.1 produced by a preliminary survey designed to investigate the factors determining the pattern of holiday-making. Using this data suppose we wish to establish whether a family's income level has any influence on the length of holiday that family takes. In other words, we wish to establish the nature of the relationship between family income and holiday-making.

Table 5.1

Family income and number of weeks holiday for ten families

Observation number	Weeks of holiday taken away from home	(Y)	Family income (£)	(X)
1	0.2	Y_1	482	X_1
2	0.8	Y_2	1,300	X_2
3	2.1	Y_3	2,400	X_3
4	1.2	Y_4	1,400	X_4
5	2.2	Y_5	3,100	X_5
6	1.4	Y_6	2,150	X_6
7	0.8	Y_7	1,500	X_7
8	1.6	Y_8	1,925	X_8
9	0.6	Y_9	1,200	X_9
10	1.7	Y_{10}	2,350	X_{10}
Total	12.6		17,807	

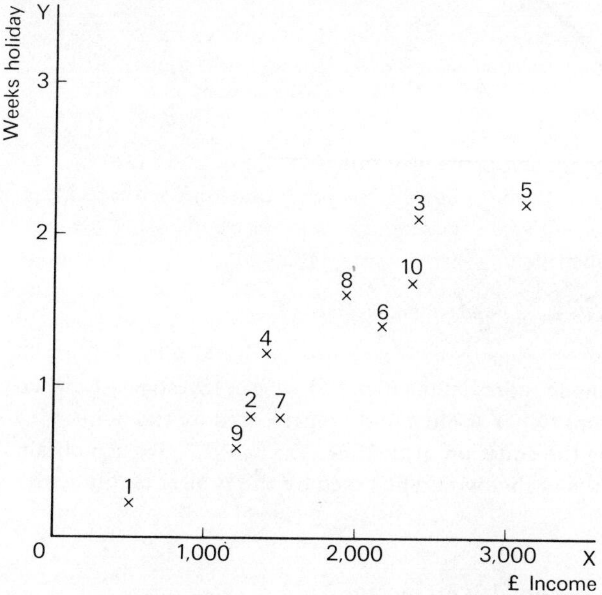

Fig. 5.3 A scatter diagram of the holiday–income data in Table 5.1

As a first step the data can be plotted graphically, in a scatter diagram (Fig. 5.3) and visually inspected for any association. We would hypothesize before looking at the data that the higher a family's income, the longer the holidays taken. We can therefore assume that there is a positive relationship between the variables. The next step is to look for an appropriate function to describe this relationship. A linear function, in the absence of any contradictory evidence provides the simplest departure point in the search for a good model.

As before, we will use β_0 to represent the intercept and β_1 the slope of the straight-line relationship which we write as:

$$Y = \beta_0 + \beta_1 X.$$

Simply by inspecting the scatter diagram in Fig. 5.3 we could draw one or more lines which seemed, visually at least to provide a good fit to the data, and this is done in Fig. 5.4. Which of the lines in Fig. 5.4 is the correct one? It is not easy to tell; we could only be sure if one or the other of the lines went through all the observed points. As it is, whichever line we choose misses most of the points.

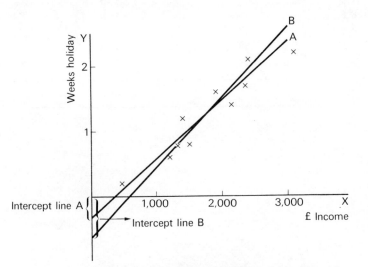

Fig. 5.4 Two possible relationships between holidays and income

If we consider a particular line in more detail (Fig. 5.5) we can investigate how well it predicts one of our observations (X_i, Y_i). The family represented by the point (X_i, Y_i) has an income X_i. Using the equation of the line, $Y = \beta_0 + \beta_1 X$, we can obtain a prediction of the length of holiday that would be taken by the typical family with an income of X_i:

$$Y_i^* = \beta_0 + \beta_1 X_i,$$

where Y_i^* is the predicted length of holiday for income X_i.

However, since Y_i weeks of holiday were taken by this particular family an error of $Y_i - Y_i^*$, or e_i has occurred. We can incorporate this error into a re-statement of the original model:

$$Y = \beta_0 + \beta_1 X + (error).$$

For any particular observation this equation implies that the line prediction $\beta_0 + \beta_1 X_i$

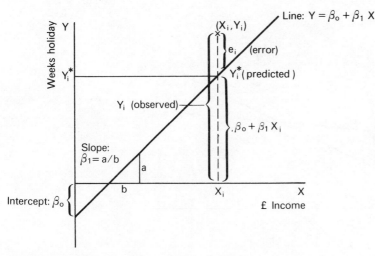

Fig. 5.5 Prediction and error in a linear relationship

explains some part of the level Y_i, but that an unexplained portion e_i exists, where $e_i = Y_i - \beta_0 - \beta_1 X_i$.

We can make a similar error calculation for each one of our original observations on families' incomes and their holiday habits. If this is repeated using the equations for lines A and B in Fig. 5.4 we will obtain two sets of 10 error terms reflecting the discrepancy between actual holiday-making and that predicted by using the two linear models. The question is how to judge from these sets of errors which of the many possible lines provides the best explanation of the relationship between family income and holiday-making.

5.2.3 The best line

In order to choose between lines to describe a given relationship we need a suitable criterion to define exactly what is meant by the 'best' line. Suppose the 'best' line according to some yet-to-be specified criterion is $Y = \hat{\beta}_0 + \hat{\beta}_1 X$. We can use such a best line to calculate a prediction $\hat{Y}_i$ for any given value of X, say X_i. In other words all predicted values for Y lie on the best line:

$$\hat{Y}_i = \hat{\beta}_0 + \hat{\beta}_1 X_i.$$

By subtracting the predicted value, $\hat{Y}_i$, from the actual observed value Y_i we can calculate the error made using this line for each of our observations on X and Y.

In fitting a line visually to such data the procedure adopted would be to adjust its position until positive error seemed in some way to balance the negative error. Formalizing this intuitive approach we might propose the criterion 'minimize the total observed error'. Now that total error is minimized when each predicted value Y_i is equal to each observed value $\hat{Y}_i$, i.e.:

$$\sum_{i=1}^{n} (Y_i - \hat{Y}_i) = 0.$$

79

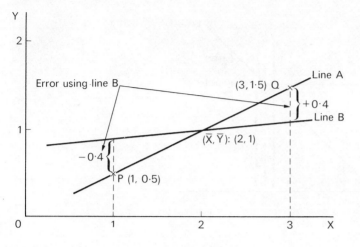

Fig. 5.6 Goodness of fit

Note that the quantities $Y_i - \hat{Y}_i$ are often called the *residuals*. However, every line that passes through the mean value of X and Y has a total observed error of zero,† as can be seen from Fig. 5.6. In the diagram we show two lines both of which pass through the mean value of the two observations. Line A passes through both observations P and Q and therefore the mean observation $(\overline{X}, \overline{Y})$ where $\overline{X} = 2$ and $\overline{Y} = 1$. Since $Y_i = \hat{Y}_i$ for each of the observations, total error around the joint mean $\sum\limits_{i=1}^{n} (Y_i - Y_i)$ is zero. Unfortunately despite this the calculated total error round line B is also zero:

$$Y_P - \hat{Y}_P = 0.5 - 0.9 = -0.4 \text{ and } Y_Q - \hat{Y}_Q = 0.4$$

and therefore

$$\sum_{i=1}^{2} (Y_i - \hat{Y}_i) = 0.$$

Even though visual inspection tells us that line B provides a much worse fit than line A the total error criterion cannot discriminate between them. Not only does it allow positive and negative errors to cancel rather than accumulate but it also fails to follow the intuitive visual fitting process by which large errors are also minimized. An alternative criterion which does overcome these difficulties can, however, be developed.

† Observed error $= \sum\limits_{i=1}^{n} (Y_i - \hat{\beta}_0 - \hat{\beta}_1 X_i)$

$= \sum\limits_{i=1}^{n} Y_i - n\hat{\beta}_0 - \hat{\beta}_1 \sum\limits_{i=1}^{n} X_i$

$= n(\overline{Y} - \hat{\beta}_0 - \hat{\beta}_1 \overline{X})$

but the expression in brackets is zero if $(\overline{X}, \overline{Y})$ lies on the line $Y - \hat{\beta}_0 - \hat{\beta}_1 X = 0$.

We will define the line of 'best' fit to be that line which minimizes the sum of the squares of the observed error:

$$\sum_{i=1}^{n} (Y_i - \hat{Y}_i)^2.$$

This is called the *principle of least squares*. It is certainly able to discriminate between lines A and B in the previous figure. Line A passes through both points and therefore has a total sum of squared observed errors of zero. Line B, on the other hand, gives a sum of squared errors equal to $(-0.4)^2 + (+0.4)^2$ or 0.32. Line A, as we know, is the better fit.

The rationale for choosing the square of each error is that squaring each error overcomes the problem caused by errors cancelling out rather than accumulating. Also small deviations are regarded as proportionately less important than large deviations. In terms of decision making, this choice makes sense, because you would expect the pay-off consequences of a major inaccuracy to be totally disproportionate to the consequences of a minor error.

To summarize the discussion of the preceding paragraphs we have assumed that the relationships between the dependant variable Y and the independent variable X may be written:

$$Y = \beta_0 + \beta_1 X + e,$$

where e is the error term. The line which 'best' fits the data we have called $Y = \hat{\beta}_0 + \hat{\beta}_1 X$ which can be used to predict the observed Y_i values by $\hat{Y}_i = \hat{\beta}_0 + \hat{\beta}_1 X_i$. After considering various possible ways of choosing the 'best' line we settled on the principle of least squares: the 'best' regression line is the line which minimizes:

$$\sum_{i=1}^{n} (Y_i - \hat{Y}_i)^2.$$

After all this preliminary explanation actually finding the line's parameters $\hat{\beta}_0$ and $\hat{\beta}_1$ is quite easy. (The proof is given in, e.g.: Frank, 1971.) They are given by the two equations†

$$\hat{\beta}_1 = \frac{\sum_{i=1}^{n} (X_i - \overline{X})(Y_i - \overline{Y})}{\sum_{i=1}^{n} (X_i - \overline{X})^2} \quad \text{and} \quad \hat{\beta}_0 = \overline{Y} - \hat{\beta}_1 \overline{X},$$

where $(\overline{X}, \overline{Y})$ is the joint mean of the observations. These two equations are called the *normal equations*. The second equation given above, which we use to estimate $\hat{\beta}_0$ also shows that because $\overline{Y} = \hat{\beta}_0 + \hat{\beta}_1 \overline{X}$, the 'best' line $Y = \hat{\beta}_0 + \hat{\beta}_1 X$ passes through the joint mean $(\overline{X}, \overline{Y})$.

† An alternative but computationally less accurate formula for $\hat{\beta}_1$ is:

$$\hat{\beta}_1 = \left(\sum_{i=1}^{n} X_i Y_i - n\overline{X}\,\overline{Y} \right) \Big/ \left(\sum_{i=1}^{n} X_i^2 - \overline{X}^2 \right)$$

5.2.4 *The error term*

In the previous section the normal equations were used to fit a linear relationship of the form

$$Y = \beta_0 + \beta_1 X + e$$

to the observations which had been collected on the variables X and Y. Now although the normal equations are designed to minimize total squared error round the fitted relationship, the choice of parameters cannot totally eliminate error unless all variation in Y is totally and completely explicable in terms of variation in X and every observation therefore lies on the line. For example, consider what might happen if we extended our sample survey of holiday habits discussed earlier in § 5.2.2. Sooner or later we would encounter a family with an identical income to one of the original families but with a different holiday-taking pattern. We might find a family with an income of £1,500 who took a week's holiday, while our original observation 7 was on a family with an income of £1,500 who took only 5½ days. Clearly no matter how much we sought to manipulate the relationship between income and holiday-making we would not be able to explain the fact that for a single level of income X, there are two observed levels of holiday-making.

This is not surprising since, intuitively, we would expect many factors other than just income to affect holiday-making. While two families have identical incomes they may have different numbers of dependent children, different holiday entitlements, different access to transport and entertainment facilities and so on. Differences in any or all of these characteristics could all play their part in explaining the differences in observed holiday-making habits. It would in practice be too time consuming and too expensive, even if it were possible, to collect and analyse data on every possible source of variation in family circumstances to see if it explained any of the variation in the length of holiday-making. Only a few of the variables considered are likely to have any consistent observable effect; the remainder will affect individual families in different non-predictable ways.

We will consider here the special case where only one factor, X, consistently affects Y and the relationship between the two is linear. Any remaining variables and any error made in measuring Y are included in the error term; and there is no observable systematic variation in the error. Such a model may be represented by the equation:

$$Y = \beta_0 + \beta_1 X + (\text{error}).$$

Because the error contains no systematic component we expect it to have certain properties:

1. A mean value of zero;
2. If e_i and e_j are two error random variables, corresponding to any two X values, then e_i and e_j are independent of each other;
3. The error random variable is independent of the observed values of X, with an identical probability distribution for every value of X: thus the error variance (which we will call σ^2) is constant.

We can understand this probabilistic model better by imagining what would happen if our sample of holiday-makers was infinite. Suppose we select any income level X_i and plot the probability distribution of actual holiday length for all families with that income. Because the error has zero mean and constant variance of σ^2 we would find that while the distribution of Y_i had a mean† of $\beta_0 + \beta_1 X_i$ it would have the same variance σ^2, as the error. Repeating the process for a different value of X_i, X_j say, would produce a probability distribution with an identical shape, but with a mean shifted to $\beta_0 + \beta_1 X_j$. The means of the probability distributions so obtained will all lie on the regression line $Y = \beta_0 + \beta_1 X$. This is illustrated in Fig. 5.7, where we show the regression line and the probability distribution of Y, for these different values of X. (More correctly, we have graphed three examples of the conditional probability density function of Y, given different values of X.)

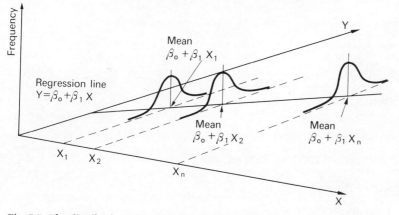

Fig. 5.7 The distribution of possible Y values for given X

The second assumption stated that if we selected two families at random and calculated the corresponding errors made by predicting, from the regression line, the holidays they would take, knowledge of the first error made would tell us nothing about the error made in predicting the second family's holiday habits. Even if we know the error made by our previous prediction we can still do no better than to use just the regression line and the probability distribution of the error term. Since we never have an infinite sample size from which to observe the regression line and the error variance we are forced to estimate the three parameters β_0, β_1 and σ^2 from the limited observations available. Using these observations the best regression equation can be calculated using the normal equations. The values we obtain for the parameters $\hat{\beta}_0$ and $\hat{\beta}_1$ are then used as estimates of the two parameters β_0 and β_1 in the linear model.

† Mean of $Y_i = E(Y_i) = E(\beta_0 + \beta_1 X_i + e_i)$
$$= \beta_0 + \beta_1 X_i + E(e_i)$$

since β_0, β_1 and X_i are constant. But we have assumed the errors all have mean zero, i.e. $E(e_i) = 0$, and therefore $E(Y_i) = \beta_0 + \beta_1 X_i$.

In the same way we use the sample data to calculate $\hat{\sigma}^2$ as an estimate† of σ^2, the true variance of the error variable. The formula for this‡ is

$$\hat{\sigma}^2 = \frac{1}{n-2} \sum_{i=1}^{n} (Y_i - \hat{Y}_i)^2.$$

The estimate of the error variance is just an average of the observed squared errors.

5.2.5 *Calculating the parameters*

With the formulae so far derived, we can go on to estimate the three parameters of the regression model, β_0, β_1 and σ^2. The necessary calculations for the holiday data introduced in Table 5.1 are shown on the following page in Table 5.2.

Substituting the calculated values into the normal equations gives,

$$\hat{\beta}_1 = \frac{\sum_{i=1}^{n} (X_i - \overline{X})(Y_i - \overline{Y})}{\sum_{i=1}^{n} (X_i - \overline{X})^2}$$

$$= 4244.56/5084020 = 0.00083488,$$

and

$$\hat{\beta}_0 = \overline{Y} - \hat{\beta}_1 \overline{X}$$

$$= 1.26 - 0.00083488 * 1780.7 = -0.22667082$$

we find the estimated regression line is:

$$\hat{Y}_i = -0.226671 + 0.00083488 * X_i.$$

By calculating $\hat{Y}_i$ for each observation of X_i we obtain predicted holiday lengths, and by subtracting these predicted levels from the actual levels $(Y_i - \hat{Y}_i)$ we obtain the error associated with each observation. For example, for the first observation, $X_1 = 482$, and therefore substituting this value into the estimated regression line gives a predicted value of:

$$\hat{Y}_1 = -0.226671 + 0.00083488 * X_1$$

$$= -0.226671 + 0.00083488 * 482$$

$$= 0.175741$$

and therefore

$$Y_1 - \hat{Y}_1 = 0.024259.$$

---

† Technically $\hat{\sigma}^2$ is an estimator; that is, a rule for calculating a numerical estimate from the observations. The estimated standard deviation $\hat{\sigma}$ is often called the standard error of estimate.
‡ Proof of this result is given, e.g. in: Wonnacott and Wonnacott, 1970, Ch. 2. It requires the use of calculus.

Table 5.2
Calculating the parameters

X_i	Y_i	$X_i - \bar{X}$	$Y_i - \bar{Y}$	$(X_i - \bar{X})(Y_i - \bar{Y})$	$(X_i - \bar{X})^2$	$\hat{Y}_i$	$Y_i - \hat{Y}_i$	$(Y_i - \hat{Y}_i)^2$	$(Y_i - \bar{Y})^2$
482	0.2	−1,298.7	−1.06	1,376.62	1,686,622	0.175741	0.024259	0.000588	1.1236
1,300	0.8	−480.7	−0.46	221.12	231,072	0.858673	−0.058673	0.003443	0.2116
2,400	2.1	619.3	0.84	520.21	383,532	1.777041	0.322959	0.104303	0.7056
1,400	1.2	−380.7	−0.06	22.84	144,932	0.942161	0.257839	0.066481	0.0036
3,100	2.2	1,319.3	0.94	1,240.14	1,740,552	2.361457	−0.161457	0.026068	0.8836
2,150	1.4	369.3	0.14	51.70	136,382	1.568321	−0.168321	0.028332	0.0196
1,500	0.8	−280.7	0.46	129.12	78,792	1.025649	−0.225649	0.050917	0.2116
1,925	1.6	144.3	0.34	49.06	20,822	1.380473	0.219527	0.048192	0.1156
1,200	0.6	−580.7	−0.66	383.26	377,212	0.775185	−0.175185	0.030690	0.4356
2,350	1.7	569.3	0.44	250.49	324,102	1.735297	−0.035297	0.001246	0.1956
17,807	12.6	0	0	4,244.56	5,084,020	12.599998	−0.000002	0.360260	3.9040

$\bar{X} = 1,780.7$ $\sum\limits_{i=1}^{n} (X_i - \bar{X})(Y_i - \bar{Y}) = 4,244.56$ $\sum\limits_{i=1}^{n} (X_i - \bar{X})^2 = 5,084,020$

$\bar{Y} = 1.26$ $\sum\limits_{i=1}^{n} (Y_i - \hat{Y}_i)^2 = 0.360260$ $\sum\limits_{i=1}^{n} (Y_i - \bar{Y})^2 = 3.9040$

Squaring and summing these error terms provides us with an estimate of the error variance:

$$\hat{\sigma}^2 = \frac{1}{n-2} \sum_{i=1}^{n} (Y_i - \hat{Y}_i)^2$$

$$= 0.360260/8 = 0.0450325$$

and an estimate of the standard deviation of the distribution:

$$\hat{\sigma} = \sqrt{0.0450325}$$

$$= 0.21221 \quad \text{to five significant figures.}$$

Note that because of the disparity between the sizes of the X and Y measurements, we are forced to carry a large number of decimal places throughout the calculations in order to be confident that the result is of a specified accuracy: here given to five significant figures.

With the three parameters estimated we have to consider the more fundamental question of model construction. From the observations collected we have been able to build a simple linear model linking input (in this case family income) with output (weeks holiday). As we pointed out in an earlier section alternative models could be developed to describe the same data. Is the linear model adequate or would another model prove better?

§5.3 Testing the adequacy of a model

The problem associated with the linear regression model can now be summarized. The analyst collects n pairs of observations $(X_1, Y_1), (X_2, Y_2) \ldots (X_n, Y_n)$ and proceeds to calculate:

1. Estimates of the parameters of the linear relationship, $\hat{\beta}_0$ and $\hat{\beta}_1$.
2. The error variance estimate $\hat{\sigma}^2$.

However, there is now a third stage he must go through:

3. Testing the adequacy of his model.

This third requirement is less easily met than the first two, simply because there are no simple formulae that classify an equation as good or bad. Instead we have to make a judgement. The criteria on which it would be made include such factors as:

3(*a*)   The strength of the relationship between X and Y.
3(*b*)   The adequacy of the linear model to represent any such relationship.
3(*c*)   The validity and reliability of the assumptions made in setting up the forecasting model.

5.3.1 The correlation and multiple correlation coefficients

The correlation coefficient. In everyday speech we will regularly suggest that two variables are correlated, by which we generally mean not only that they co-vary, but that the observed association did not occur by accident. This observation is the basis for the *correlation coefficient* which is a measure of the strength of the *linear* relationship (or association) between two variables, X and Y.

Suppose that by using least squares we estimated the slope parameter in the linear model: $Y = \beta_0 + \beta_1 X + (\text{error})$ by $\hat{\beta}_1$. We might think that $\hat{\beta}_1$ was a suitable measure of the relationship between X and Y. Unfortunately, we can change the value of $\hat{\beta}_1$ just by changing the scale of measurement of either X or Y,† and this in no sense changes the strength of the relationship between X and Y. In order that our measure be independent of the measurement scales of the variables we therefore standardize the units of measurement‡ to obtain the correlation coefficient, which is usually denoted by r:

$$r = \hat{\beta}_1 \frac{\hat{\sigma}_X}{\hat{\sigma}_Y}$$

and making the jump of substituting for the different estimators we get the usual formula:

$$r = \frac{\sum\limits_{i=1}^{n} (X_i - \overline{X})(Y_i - \overline{Y})}{\sqrt{\sum\limits_{i=1}^{n} (X_i - \overline{X})^2 \sum\limits_{i=1}^{n} (Y_i - \overline{Y})^2}} .$$

Using the calculations already made in Table 5.2 for the holiday survey we find

$$r = 4244.56 / \sqrt{5084020 * 3.9040} = 0.9523.$$

As we have shown, r is a measure of the linear relationship between X and Y. Figure 5.8 shows how it varies with different spatial configurations. In the first diagram X and Y are independent and the observations are randomly scattered about the joint mean. The second shows all the observations on a line and in this case r has a value of 1 indicating a perfect association. In the third all observations are close to the line, while in the fourth they are more scattered; and because high values of one variable are associated with low values of the other r is therefore negative and in fact smaller than in the previous illustration. In the last case r is again zero; however, there is clearly a relationship between X and Y; r only measures the strength of a linear association between X and Y while the true relationship is non-linear.

The multiple correlation coefficient. In forecasting we are concerned with explaining (and predicting) the movements of the dependent variable using a model based on the

---

† For example, if we change the units of Y from weeks' holiday to days' holiday this multiplies each Y measurement by 7 and by referring back to the formula for $\hat{\beta}_1$, we see that this is therefore multiplied by a factor of 7. Similarly, by changing the income variable X from pounds to dollars (at an exchange rate of $2.40 = £1$), we will decrease $\hat{\beta}_1$ by $(1/2.40)$.
‡ Recall from Ch. 4 that a standardized measurement Z is given by $Z = (X - \overline{X})/\hat{\sigma}_X$, $\hat{\sigma}_X$ being the estimated standard deviation of X. From the above footnote standardizing X has the effect of multiplying $\hat{\beta}_1$ by $\hat{\sigma}_X$, while standardizing Y, divides $\hat{\beta}_1$ by $\hat{\sigma}_Y$.

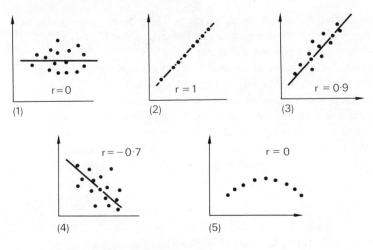

Fig. 5.8 *The correlation coefficient*

independent variable. A basic source of information on the model's ability to explain the variation in Y is provided by the n residual errors, $Y_1 - \hat{Y}_1, Y_2 - \hat{Y}_2, \ldots Y_n - \hat{Y}_n$. These may be used to decompose the variation in Y, $\sum_{i=1}^{n} (Y_i - \overline{Y})^2$ into two components, the variation explained by the model and the residual variation. (In the remainder of this chapter we will omit the upper and lower limits in the summation $\sum_{i=1}^{n}$ unless there is a possibility of confusion.)

It can be shown that:

$$\sum (Y_i - \overline{Y})^2 = \sum (\hat{Y}_i - \overline{Y})^2 + \sum (Y_i - \hat{Y}_i)^2$$

In words:

'Sum of Squares Total adjusted for mean' = 'Sum of Squares explained by regression' + 'Sum of Squares for error'

($\sum Y_i^2$ is often called 'Sum of Squares Total'; we use the 'Sum of Squares Total adjusted for mean' for $\sum (Y_i - \overline{Y})^2$ to discriminate between the two. The 'Sum of Squares for error' is often called 'Residual Sum of Squares'.)

The left-hand side, $\sum (Y_i - \overline{Y})^2$ we may think of as the variation of Y about its mean value $\overline{Y}$; and in trying to predict Y by $\hat{Y}$ we would expect that the total variation in $\hat{Y}$ would be approximately equal to the variation in Y.

We see from the equation that if the model exactly fits the data, i.e. $Y_i = \hat{Y}_i$, then the sum of squares for error is zero and the model explains all the variation in Y. If, on the other hand, there is no relationship between Y and X the model explains no part of the variation in Y and the best prediction of Y is just the mean of the probability distribution of Y, i.e. $\hat{Y}_i = \overline{Y}$ for all values of i. In this latter case therefore, the variation in Y explained by the model is zero.

By dividing through the above equation by 'the variation in Y', $\Sigma(Y_i - \overline{Y})^2$, we derive the following equation:

$$1 = R^2 + \frac{\Sigma(Y_i - \hat{Y}_i)^2}{\Sigma(Y_i - \overline{Y})^2}$$

where

$$R^2 = \frac{\Sigma(\hat{Y}_i - \overline{Y})^2}{\Sigma(Y_i - \overline{Y})^2}.$$

R is called the *multiple correlation coefficient* while its square, R^2, is called the coefficient of determination. By referring to the above equation it is clear that R^2 is always positive and less than 1. From the discussion in the preceding paragraph R^2 may be interpreted as:

$$R^2 = \frac{\text{variation in Y explained by the model}}{\text{variation in Y}}.$$

It therefore measures the proportion of the variation in Y explained by the model; it is a measure of the strength of the relationship between X and Y.

Returning to the holiday example we may calculate the multiple correlation coefficient from the calculations already made in Table 5.2.

Now $R^2 = \dfrac{\Sigma(\hat{Y}_i - \overline{Y})^2}{\Sigma(Y_i - \overline{Y})^2}$, but from the above formula

$$= 1 - \frac{\Sigma(Y_i - \hat{Y}_i)^2}{\Sigma(Y_i - \overline{Y})^2}$$

$$= 1 - \frac{0.360260}{3.9040}$$

$$= 0.9077.$$

Family income explains 91 per cent of the variation in the length of family holidays. Because R^2 measures the proportion of Y's variation explained by the model it can be thought of as a measure of the explanatory power of the forecasting model. The above exposition is valid for *any* model of the form:

Y = f(X) + (error).

On the other hand, while we introduced the correlation coefficient as a measure of the strength of the *linear* association (we use 'association' as opposed to 'relation' when there is no causal mechanism implied) between X and Y, its square, r^2 also may be interpreted as the linear equivalent of R^2. It measures the proportion of variation explained by the linear model,[†]

$Y = \beta_0 + \beta_1 X + $ (error).

---

† It follows from this argument that if we calculate R^2 using a linear forecasting model, it will equal r^2.

From the holiday–income survey we computed $R^2 = 0.9070$ for the linear model, as well as $r = 0.9523$ and of course $0.9070 = (0.9523)^2$.

To summarize, R^2 is a useful summary measure of the explanatory strength of any forecasting model, while r only measures the strength of the linear relationship (or association) between X and Y. They both are given in a standard computer print-out.

5.3.2 A hypothesis test of $\beta_1 = 0$

Even when R^2 appears high, suggesting a strong relationship between the dependent variable Y and the independent variable X, we still need to consider the statistical possibility that the observed relationship is purely random. Now if $\beta_1 = 0$, there is no linear relationship between X and Y; any observed relationship must have occurred by chance. But the observed relationship is measured by our estimate of β_1, $\hat{\beta}_1$ and our problem now becomes one of considering if our estimate $\hat{\beta}_1$ is compatible with β_1 being zero.

If we repeated the estimation of β_1 with a different set of data, we would derive a new estimate of β_1 because the calculation depends on the new observations we have just collected. Our slope estimate, $\hat{\beta}_1$, is therefore a random quantity with a probability distribution. To examine if the observed relation could have occurred by chance, we therefore analyse whether the probability distribution of the $\hat{\beta}_1$'s could have a mean value of zero. More formally, we test the *null hypothesis* $\beta_1 = 0$ against the alternative hypothesis $\beta_1 \neq 0$. To be convinced of the existence of a linear relationship between X and Y we would wish there to be little possibility that the observed relationship (as measured by $\hat{\beta}_1$) occurred by chance. It is the classical *hypothesis testing* situation discussed in all elementary statistical texts (see, e.g. Mendenhall and Reinmuth, 1974, Chs 8 and 9).

Before going any further we need to make one additional assumption which concerns the shape of the probability distribution of the error term. If we can assume that it is normal it can be shown that the distribution of $\hat{\beta}_1$ is also normal. Now we may make use of the theory of hypothesis testing with the normal distribution to examine whether our observed value of $\hat{\beta}_1$ is compatible with the hypothesis that $\beta_1 = 0$.

There are four components in testing such an hypothesis; we will illustrate them by reference to the income–holiday data.

1. We specify the null hypothesis; here $\beta_1 = 0$.
2. We specify an alternative hypothesis. Typically the alternative hypothesis is $\beta_1 \neq 0$ although in the holiday example we are interested only in testing the hypothesis that higher income is associated with longer holidays, since it is implausible to suggest that long holidays are associated with lower incomes. If our estimate of β_1 was negative we would generally regard it as support for the null hypothesis. Such a test is called *one-tailed* (i.e. $\beta_1 < 0$ or $\beta_1 > 0$) in contrast with the *two-tailed* test mentioned earlier ($\beta_1 \neq 0$).
3. We specify the *significance level* of the hypothesis test. This is just the probability that the null hypothesis ($\beta_1 = 0$) is rejected in favour of the alternative, when the null hypothesis is in fact correct. In setting this probability we have to take into

account a second type of error, the obverse of the first. It is the error made in mistakenly rejecting the alternative hypothesis when it is in fact true. These two types of error:

(*a*) rejecting the null hypothesis when it is true;
(*b*) accepting the null hypothesis when it is false;

should be balanced, exactly in the same way as in a criminal trial the court tries to compromise between two errors of judgement it can make, that of convicting an innocent man or releasing one who is guilty. These two possibilities are weighed against each other in every judicial system. Likewise in a forecasting situation there are dangers if a variable is included in a forecasting model when it is not related to the dependent variable Y, and there are dangers if an important variable is omitted from the model. The solution, somewhat arbitrary by nature, is to set the significance level for rejecting the null hypothesis at a fairly conservative 5 or 10 per cent. The probability of accepting a false null hypothesis is then kept low by using an adequate sample size.

4. We compute the t test statistic:

$$t = \hat{\beta}_1/(\text{estimated standard deviation of } \hat{\beta}_1), \text{ i.e. } t = \frac{\hat{\beta}_1}{\hat{\sigma}} \sqrt{\Sigma(X_i - \overline{X})^2}.$$

Under the null hypothesis $\beta_1 = 0$, by repeatedly collecting new observations, computing fresh parameter estimates of $\hat{\beta}_1$, and then calculating the above t statistic we would find that t had (unsurprisingly, considering its name) a Student t-distribution, with $(n - 2)$ degrees of freedom (Mendenhall and Reinmuth, 1974, pp. 213–20) as shown in Fig. 5.9. The shape of this distribution depends on the available degrees of freedom. The origin of this term lies in the idea that the degrees of freedom of the t statistic depend on both the number of observations n and also how many have been 'used up' in estimating the regression parameters. In the holiday example we have 'used up' two degrees of freedom in estimating the parameters of the line β_0 and β_1. The t-distribution in this case, with ten observations has $(n - 2)$, or eight degrees of freedom.

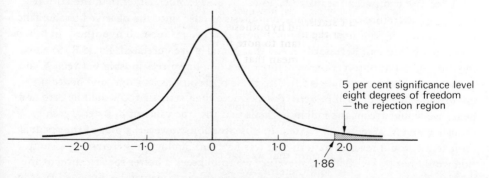

Fig. 5.9 The Student t-distribution and rejection region for a one-tail test

With these four steps completed we can show how the testing is done. The choice of a significance level determines a region in the tails of the t-distribution which is called the *rejection region*. If we fix the significance level at 5 per cent then under the null hypothesis there is a 5 per cent chance of observing a t value within the rejection region. Consequently, if the computed t value falls within that region, either:

(*a*) an unlikely event has occurred; or

(*b*) the null hypothesis is false.

We accept the second explanation. A high t value is regarded as substantial evidence that the hypothesis $\beta_1 = 0$ is false.

We will now use the holiday survey to illustrate the four step procedure:

1. Specifying the null hypothesis: $\beta_1 = 0$.
2. And the alternative hypothesis: $\beta_1 > 0$.
3. Fixing the significance level: 5 per cent.
4. Computing the t statistic:

$$t = \frac{\hat{\beta}_1}{\hat{\sigma}} \sqrt{\Sigma (X_i - \overline{X})^2}$$
$$= (0.00083488/0.212209) * \sqrt{5084020}$$
$$= 8.871.$$

From the first three steps, the rejection region therefore lies in the right tail of the t-distribution, a large positive value of t giving support for the alternative hypothesis, $\beta_1 > 0$. With ten observations and two of these used up in estimating the regression line there are eight $= n - 2$ degrees of freedom left in the data. Referring to a set of statistical tables (see, e.g. Mendenhall and Reinmuth, 1974, p. 529) we see that the critical value corresponding to a significance level of 5 per cent in the right tail and eight degrees of freedom is 1.86. That is:

Probability (observing t > 1.86: given the null hypothesis is true) = 0.05.

There is a 5 per cent probability of observing a t-value > 1.86, so consequently the critical region, in which the null hypothesis is rejected, is just the observed values of t > 1.86. The computed t statistic is, however, 8.871, much larger than the critical t-value. We therefore reject the null hypothesis as false since the observed t-value falls in that critical region. It is important to note that even if the null hypothesis of $\beta_1 = 0$ is rejected it does not necessarily mean that X and Y are unrelated. Fig. 5.8 (5) above showed a series of observations generated by a non-linear relationship between X and Y. However, if a straight line is fitted to these observations its slope, and hence the calculated value of $\hat{\beta}_1$, will be zero. Furthermore the t statistic too would be zero and hence we would accept the null hypothesis that the true value of β_1 is zero, even though Y and X were in fact related. In this situation, however, a plot of the residual error terms would reveal a pattern that was far from random; our regression assumption would not be satisfied and therefore we would seek a better specification of the relationship between X and Y. How such an analysis is made will be discussed later in this chapter.

A more dangerous error occurs when $\hat{\beta}_1$ is significantly different from zero, because the analyst is inclined to argue that a change in X will cause a concomitant change in Y. If X were the only variable affecting Y then the statement might well be true, but a more typical situation is where both X and Y are moving in sympathy with a third variable Z which affects them both. A justly celebrated example of this type of mistake is provided by the reported relationship between church attendance and number of illegitimate children in the US, said to be observed in the years 1750–1910. While you might expect the number of illegitimate children to decrease with increasing church attendance exactly the opposite occurred. Propriety is restored by the realization that both variables increase with population and it is this third variable that explains the apparent relationship between piety and illegitimacy. We will return to this subject of causality in Chapter 8, when it forms a basis for a discussion of causal models of cost and demand.

5.3.3 Analysis of variance – the 'F' test

In §5.3.1 the total sum of squares of the dependent variable Y, adjusted for mean, was decomposed into the sum of squares explained by the regression and the sum of squares due to residual variation, i.e.:

$$\Sigma(Y_i - \overline{Y})^2 = \Sigma(\hat{Y}_i - \overline{Y})^2 + \Sigma(Y_i - \hat{Y}_i)^2.$$

This division forms the basis of the Analysis of Variance (ANOVA) approach to testing whether the model explains a significant part of the variation in Y.

To perform the test we need to tabulate each component sum of squares, together with its associated degrees of freedom. This procedure is set out in Table 5.3. Note that in column (3) the degrees of freedom of the sum of squares due to the regression has only one degree of freedom with which to explain the variation in Y since it is already known that the regression line runs through the joint means $(\overline{X}, \overline{Y})$, and thus out of the two degrees of freedom available in the choice of parameters, one has already been used. By dividing each sum of squares (column 2) by the associated degrees of freedom (column 3) we obtain the mean square variation (column 4). Note that the mean square residual variation is in fact the estimated error variance $\hat{\sigma}^2$.

Table 5.3
The analysis of variance table

Source of variation (1)	Sum of squares (2)	D.F. (3)	Mean square (4)	F (5)
Due to regression	$\Sigma(\hat{Y}_i - \overline{Y})^2$	1	$\Sigma(\hat{Y}_i - \overline{Y})^2$	$\Sigma(Y_i - \overline{Y})^2/\hat{\sigma}^2$
Residual variation	$\Sigma(Y_i - \hat{Y}_i)^2$	$n - 2$	$\Sigma(Y_i - \hat{Y}_i)^2/(n - 2) = \hat{\sigma}^2$	
Adjusted total	$\Sigma(Y_i - \overline{Y})^2$	$n - 1$	$\Sigma(Y_i - \overline{Y})^2/(n - 1)$	

Finally, in column 5, we calculate the F statistic as the ratio between the mean square variation due to the regression and the residual mean square variation.

$$F = \frac{\text{mean square variation due to regression}}{\text{mean square variation due to residuals}}.$$

When X and Y are unrelated, the best forecast of Y is just $\overline{Y}$ and therefore the mean square regression is zero; it follows that F is zero. If the model is a perfect predictor, the residual variation is zero and F is infinite. The larger the value of F the more variation in Y is explained by the model. This leads us to a hypothesis test of whether the model explains a significant part of the variation in Y. The F statistic, like the t statistic is a random variable with its own distribution, and in a similar way the shape of its distribution depends on the degrees of freedom in both the numerator and denominator of the above ratio (i.e. 1 and n − 2). As with the t statistic we follow four steps in testing the model's explanatory ability:

1. Set up the null hypothesis: no part of Y's variation is explained by the model. In the single variable linear model this is equivalent to $\beta_1 = 0$.
2. Specify an alternative hypothesis: Y's variation is partially explained by the model. In the single variable linear model this translates as $\beta_1 \neq 0$.
3. Calculate the test statistic: F.
4. Set a significance level: of 1 per cent (say).

These four components define a critical region, found by using a set of tables of the F distribution. (Mendenhall and Reinmuth, 1974, pp. 532–5. For a discussion of the F test, see pp. 229–38.)

We will illustrate the procedure with reference to the holiday–income data. By referring back to the calculations shown in Table 5.2 we may substitute these actual values into Table 5.3, giving the results shown in Table 5.4:

Table 5.4
Analysis of variance and the holiday–income data

Source of variation	Sum of squares	D.F.	Mean square	F
Due to regression	3.543740	1	3.543740	78.694
Residual variation	0.360260	8	0.045032	
Adjusted total	3.904000	9		

The critical F value for a 1 per cent significance level with one degree of freedom in the numerator and eight in the denominator is 11.26.

i.e. Prob. (observed F value > 11.26: given null hypothesis is true) = 0.01.

But we observed an F value of 78.694. We therefore accept the alternative hypothesis that the linear model explains a part of the variation in Y. Another way of putting the same thing is to say that we accept that X and Y are linearly related, and that $\beta_1 \neq 0$.

Both the F and t statistics test the same hypothesis in the special case considered. They are related through the formula $F = t^2$, and we can confirm this by calculating t^2: $t^2 = (8.871)^2 = 78.694$, the same as the calculated F value. If we accept a hypothesis using one test, we will accept it using the other and vice versa. The more complicated models of Chapter 6 include a larger number of independent variables and this increases the degrees of freedom in the numerator of the F ratio. Such situations as these can only be analysed using the F distribution. Computerized regression programs may well use both methods, as appropriate.

5.3.4 The validity of the model assumptions

The third question, raised in the introduction to §5.3 has yet to be fully answered. 'Are the assumptions of the model met?' These assumptions can be broken down into two components:

(a) The assumption that the linear model, $Y = \beta_0 + \beta_1 X + e$, is correct; and
(b) That if the linear model is correct, e is distributed normally with a mean of zero and constant variance, and any two errors e_i, e_j, are independent of each other (and therefore any two observations Y_i, Y_j are also independent, depending as they do on the error term).

The first component could be called structural and the second technical.

By testing the hypothesis $\beta_1 = 0$, and examining the strength of the relationship between X and Y we have given a partial answer to the structural question. If we say β_1 is non-zero and R^2 explains sufficient variation of Y, then this is equivalent to accepting the linear model as at least partially correct. However, this does not rule out the possibility that an alternative model would be better.

When we turn to the technical assumptions, not only will the behaviour of the error term need to be scrutinized, but in doing this we would expect to obtain additional information about the way in which the current model could or should be improved. Here we will discuss some simple visual methods for checking on a number of the technical assumptions.

Visual inspection of the residuals. The normality assumption is the most easily dismissed. It is not used directly in deriving the parameter estimates β_0 and β_1 but in testing their significance. So long as the number of observations remains large (n > 30 is regarded as sufficiently large), then the t and F tests are adequate, whether or not the assumption holds (one renowned exception is in forecasting stock market prices). Consequently it is unusual for this to be tested and collating the observations into a frequency histogram, a method illustrated in §4.5, is a sufficient check that nothing very peculiar is going on. The other error assumptions are more important, for they lead the analyst back to the model, perhaps to change the estimates or to consider an alternative model. The simplest method of examination of the residuals is visual, and we will leave alternative analytical methods to Chapter 6.

Let us suppose that the observations on two variables X and Y are taken over a

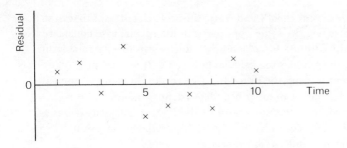

Fig. 5.10 Time plot of residuals

period of time. Assuming some theoretical underpinning, we can hypothesize a linear relationship from which we can calculate the residuals, as is shown in Fig. 5.10. If the assumptions about the error hold, then the observations will appear to be nothing more than a random sample from an unknown probability distribution, a phenomenon discussed in §4.5. The probability distribution will have a sample mean of zero; because as we showed when discussing least squares the sum of the residuals is always zero. However, it is quite common for the errors to be correlated over time or their variance to change. How would such a plot of the residuals help in deciding whether this is happening?

Figure 5.11(*a*) shows a situation where there appears to be a cyclical fluctuation in both the sign and the size of error. For example, knowledge that at time period 6 the error was small and negative, at period 7 larger and still negative suggests that at period 8 the error will again be negative and quite large. If the errors were really independent then instead of having a sequence of signs +++++ −−−−+ you would expect the plusses and minuses to be scattered at random. In the above sequence there is first a run of five +'s, then four −'s and finally one +, three runs in all. The sequence may be written (+++++) (−−−−) (+), making it easier to count the runs. In fact a statistical test has been developed based on the number of runs observed in the residuals (Draper and Smith, 1966, pp. 95−9). In the above example three seems low and this impression is confirmed if we choose to go through the formal testing procedure of the runs test, described in the reference below. We will not give the details here as we describe an alternative testing procedure in Chapter 6.

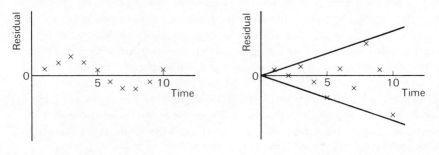

Fig. 5.11(a) Errors are correlated   *Fig. 5.11(b) Variance is changing*

While there is no pattern in the signs of the residuals in Fig. 5.11(*b*) the magnitude of the errors appears to be growing. Again the analyst is trying to recognize order in the data and use the information to build a more accurate model. Here the growth of the residuals over time suggests that the error variance is also increasing with time, a contradiction of the assumption that the errors have constant variance. A possible way round the failure of the constant variance assumption is to use the model:

$$\frac{Y}{t} = \beta_0 + \beta_1 X + e,$$

instead of

$$Y = \beta_0 + \beta_1 X + e.$$

(Wonnacott and Wonnacott, 1970, pp. 132–5; Draper and Smith, 1966). The idea behind using the new model is to transform the Y observations to a new variable (Y/t) which *does* satisfy all the assumptions of the regression model.

There is often a good reason for the error variance to increase. For example in predicting long-term sales two possible models are:

$$S_t \text{ (Sales at t)} = f(t) + (error); \text{ or}$$
$$S_t = f(t) * (error).$$

In one model the error is additive, and in the other multiplicative. But if sales are increasing rapidly it is reasonable to expect the fluctuations about the regression curve to increase in amplitude, as occurs in the multiplicative model. Another common pattern shown by the residuals is illustrated in Fig. 5.12. Here the errors are increasing over time and this systematic compounding of error can be removed by using a model which includes a time trend. This visual impression of systematic error would again be supported by the runs test which would have suggested that something peculiar was going on, there being only two runs of residuals in this data. To spot a failure in the error assumption it is useful to plot the residuals $(Y_i - \hat{Y}_i)$ against the corresponding estimated values of Y_i, $\hat{Y}_i$ as well as the independent variable X_i. In normal circumstances the residuals should always appear as a horizontal band round the origin (Fig. 5.10)

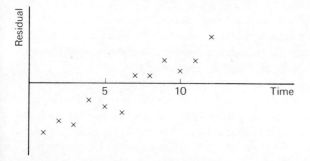

Fig. 5.12 *Trend in residuals*

and there should not be an extreme number of runs, either too few or too many. If there appears to be evidence that some systematic distortion is occurring in the residuals, then the model has to be changed to take into account the failure of the basic regression assumptions. To take this failure into account a number of suitable approaches are discussed in Chapter 6.

§5.4 The sensitivity of the forecast

5.4.1 Confidence intervals

In a forecasting situation the decision maker is rarely interested in just a single forecast. It is important for him to know the accuracy of a forecast as well. One way of making a forecast more useful is to attach probabilities to each of the possible forecast outcomes, so that the forecast appears as a range of possible outcomes rather than just a point estimate. Thus a forecaster, asked to predict the course of sales over the next year might use a linear regression equation that predicted a sales increase of 14 per cent. However, it would be misleading to act as if this forecast were true when there was a good chance that the possible sales increase could be as high as 20 per cent or as low as 8 per cent. We therefore need to know how accurate we expect the forecast to be.

Fortunately, the assumptions of the regression model lead directly to a means of specifying the accuracy of a forecast. Suppose that $\hat{\theta}$ (theta capped) is to be used to estimate an unknown parameter, where $\hat{\theta}$ might for example be a coefficient in a regression equation, and θ (theta) the true parameter in the regression model. Such an estimate would be based on a random sample of observations and like the estimates we have already talked about, the sample mean, the regression coefficients $\hat{\beta}_0$ and $\hat{\beta}_1$ etc., $\hat{\theta}$ has a probability distribution with a mean and variance. We will suppose that $\hat{\theta}$ is what is called an *unbiased* estimate of θ; that is, the mean (average) value of $\hat{\theta}$ is θ (using expectations, $\hat{\theta}$ is an unbiased estimate of θ if $E\hat{\theta} = \theta$). Calling the standard deviation of $\hat{\theta}$, $\sigma_{\hat{\theta}}$ it can be shown that in general the quantity (it is of course random because $\hat{\theta}$ is based on a set of random observations):

$$Z = \frac{\hat{\theta} - \theta}{\sigma_{\hat{\theta}}}$$

has a probability distribution which is approximately normal with mean zero, and variance of 1 when $\hat{\theta}$ is based on a large number of observations. This theorem holds true for $\overline{X}$ as an estimate of the population mean, as well as the regression coefficients $\hat{\beta}_0$ and $\hat{\beta}_1$ which are unbiased estimates of β_0 and β_1, respectively.

Because the distribution of Z is known, for any given constant a — measured in terms of standard deviation — we are able to calculate Prob. [|Z| < a], and this is just the shaded area in Fig. 5.13. Looked at the other way round, we can also calculate the value of a, which corresponds to any given probability. This concept is easily illustrated by referring to Fig. 5.13. The fixing of the Prob. [Z| < a], represented by the shaded area, has the effect of also fixing a. For example, if we wish to be 95 per cent certain that Z falls within the interval (−a, +a) we choose a so that the shaded area under the

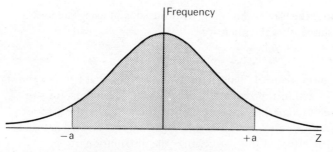

Fig. 5.13 Confidence limits

curve is 0.95. By referring to tables for the normal probability distribution, a is therefore 1.96 standard deviations:

Prob. $[-1.96 < Z < +1.96] = 0.95$.

Since $Z = (\hat{\theta} - \theta)/\sigma_{\hat{\theta}}$, this may be re-written in the form:†

$P[\hat{\theta} - 1.96\ \sigma_{\hat{\theta}} < \theta < \hat{\theta} + 1.96\ \sigma_{\hat{\theta}}] = 0.95$.

The estimate $\hat{\theta}$ lies within 1.96 standard deviations (of size $\sigma_{\hat{\theta}}$) of the parameter θ, with probability 0.95. The lower end point of the interval, $\hat{\theta} - 1.96\ \sigma_{\hat{\theta}}$ is called the lower confidence limit, while $\hat{\theta} + 1.96\ \sigma_{\hat{\theta}}$ is the upper confidence limit, of this 95 per cent *confidence interval*.

In general, we may construct a $(1 - \alpha)$ per cent confidence interval in exactly the same way. Let $z_{\alpha/2}$ be the value from the tables corresponding to a probability level in each tail of $\alpha/2$ then the Prob. $[|Z| < z_{\alpha/2}] = 1 - \alpha$ and therefore the $(1 - \alpha)$ per cent confidence interval is given by:

A lower confidence limit $= \hat{\theta} - z_{\alpha/2}\ \sigma_{\hat{\theta}}$;
An upper confidence limit $= \hat{\theta} + z_{\alpha/2}\ \sigma_{\hat{\theta}}$.

5.4.2 A confidence interval for the forecast
(In some texts this is called a prediction interval, the term confidence interval being reserved for the estimation of EY_p, *the mean of* Y_p, *rather than* Y_p *itself, with which we are concerned.)*

In the previous section we discussed confidence intervals very generally. Here we specialize the argument to the situation of linear regression. In order to predict the value of Y corresponding to an input value X_p we will first estimate the regression line $Y = \beta_0 + \beta_1 X + (\text{error})$, the predicted value of Y_p being just $\hat{Y}_p = \hat{\beta}_0 + \hat{\beta}_1 X_p$. It is now possible to use arguments similar to those in the last section to find a confidence interval for Y_p.

† $0.95 = \text{Prob.}\ [-1.96\ \sigma_{\hat{\theta}} < \hat{\theta} - \theta < 1.96\ \sigma_{\hat{\theta}}]$
    $= \text{Prob.}\ [1.96\ \sigma_{\hat{\theta}} > \theta - \hat{\theta} > -1.96\ \sigma_{\hat{\theta}}]$
and the result follows by adding $\hat{\theta}$ to both sides of the inequality.

Using the assumption that the error is normally distributed, and using the ideas of the last section, it can be shown that the quantity:

$$(\hat{Y}_p - Y_p)\big/\sqrt{\mathrm{var}(\hat{Y}_p - Y_p)}$$

is normal with mean zero and variance 1. This means, for example, that 95 per cent of the time the forecast $\hat{Y}_p$ lies within approximately two standard deviations (of size $\sqrt{\mathrm{var}(\hat{Y}_p - Y_p)}$) of the true outcome Y_p. Unfortunately while we know the forecast $\hat{Y}_p$ from the regression equation, $\mathrm{var}(\hat{Y}_p - Y_p)$ is unknown, and it therefore has to be estimated from the data. The effect of this is to change the distribution of $(\hat{Y}_p - Y_p)\big/\sqrt{\hat{\mathrm{var}}(\hat{Y}_p - Y_p)}$ from the normal to the t with $(n - 2)$ degrees of freedom. (We use $\hat{\mathrm{var}}(\hat{Y}_p - Y_p)$ to mean the estimate of the variance of $[\hat{Y}_p - Y_p]$).

The 95 per cent confidence interval then becomes:

$$\hat{Y}_p \pm t_{0.025}\sqrt{\hat{\mathrm{var}}(\hat{Y}_p - Y_p)}\dagger.$$

The t value is that taken from a t distribution with $(n - 2)$ degrees of freedom such that $P[|t| < t_{0.025}] = 0.95$ as described on page 91.

Before the interval can be computed we require an estimate of $\hat{\mathrm{var}}(\hat{Y}_p - Y_p)$. It is given by the formula:

$$\hat{\mathrm{var}}(\hat{Y}_p - Y_p) = \hat{\sigma}^2\left(1 + \frac{1}{n} + \frac{(X_p - \overline{X})^2}{\Sigma(X_i - \overline{X})^2}\right),$$

where $\hat{\sigma}^2$ is the usual estimate of the error variance, discussed in §5.2.4.

As usual we will use the holiday–income data to show how a confidence interval is constructed. Suppose we wish to calculate the 90 per cent confidence interval for the holidays taken when family income, $X_p = £3,000$. In the general formula of footnote($\dagger$) below, $\alpha = 0.1$. With ten observations the appropriate t distribution has $10 - 2 = 8$ degrees of freedom, and consequently $t_{\alpha/2} = t_{0.05} = 1.860$. $\hat{\sigma}^2$ has already been estimated in §5.2.5 and is equal to 0.0450325. The point forecast of the length of holiday taken by a family with an income of £3,000 is given by substituting X_p in the estimated regression line:

$$Y = -0.22667 + 0.00083488\,X,$$

which gives a value of

$$\hat{Y}_p = -0.22667 + 0.00083488 * 3{,}000 = 2.27797 \quad \text{to five significant figures.}$$

The estimated variance of $\hat{Y}_p - Y_p$ is taken from the above formula:

$$\hat{\mathrm{var}}(\hat{Y}_p - Y_p) = 0.0450325 * \left(1 + \frac{1}{10} + \frac{(3{,}000 - 1780.7)^2}{5084020}\right)$$

$$= 0.06270440,$$

therefore the standard deviation is 0.25041 to five significant figures.

$\dagger$ The $(1 - \alpha)$ per cent confidence interval for Y_p is:
$$\hat{Y}_p \pm t_{\alpha/2}\sqrt{\hat{\mathrm{var}}(\hat{Y}_p - Y_p)}$$

Thus, the 90 per cent confidence limits for Y_p are:

2.27797 ± 1.860 * 0.25041; or

1.8 and 2.7,   accurate to one decimal place.

Thus we would expect 90 per cent of families with an income of £3,000 to take a holiday of between 1.8 and 2.7 weeks.

To show the importance of the approach developed here, consider the following simple example. Suppose a forecast for electricity demand by 1985 implied the building of three new power stations while the standard deviation of the forecast was sufficiently large that the upper confidence limit meant as many as four stations needed to be built, while the lower required only two. Before any decision could reasonably be made more information would have to be gathered. However, if the forecast was such that we were 99 per cent certain that exactly three stations needed to be built, then the decision becomes self apparent. The added precision of the second forecast is sufficient to limit the range of possible courses of action to one only. By attaching a confidence interval to each forecast the sensitivity of each course of action may be tested against the extremes of the forecast.

The usefulness of a forecast can therefore be measured by the width of the appropriate confidence interval; the most helpful forecast is that we are 100 per cent confident that $\hat{Y}_p$ will occur. We are rarely so fortunate, but a narrow confidence interval will still decrease the riskiness of the corresponding decision, of which the forecast is just one of the information inputs. Referring to the general formula for the confidence interval we can see the width of the interval depends on the components of the estimated standard deviation of $\hat{Y}_p$, $\sqrt{\hat{var}(\hat{Y}_p - Y_p)}$ where

$$\sqrt{\hat{var}(\hat{Y}_p - Y_p)} = \hat{\sigma} \sqrt{1 + \frac{1}{n} + \frac{(X_p - \overline{X})^2}{\Sigma(X_i - \overline{X})^2}}$$

As X_p moves away from $\overline{X}$ the interval grows wider, and as either n or $\Sigma(X_i - \overline{X})^2$ increases the interval narrows. More important, the width depends quite critically on the standard error. Figure 5.14 shows how the interval depends on X_p.

In summary, we are now able to see how important it is to calculate the distribution of possible forecast outcomes as well as to find a single best estimate. In applications where decisions are sensitive to forecast accuracy it is apparent that we want a forecasting model that not only introduces no systematic bias into a forecast, but also has an estimated standard deviation which is small enough to ensure a narrow prediction interval. The effect will be to minimize the risk of decision making.

§5.5 Sensitivity testing and forecasting — an example

The problem. In 1973, a traffic control system company decided that because of the substantial changes caused by the oil crisis, existing plans to increase production capacity to meet an expected sales increase over the next 5 years, would have to be re-examined.

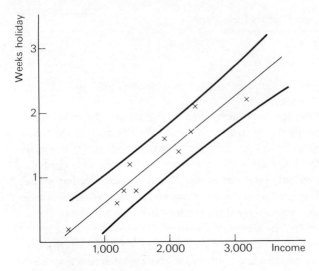

Fig. 5.14 A confidence interval for forecasting

While in the short term, company sales could be forecast quite accurately from data on new construction plans and proposed traffic schemes issued by public authorities, such plans tend to be implemented within a short period and therefore current figures could not provide much information on possible sales 5 years ahead. Instead it was decided to examine the relationships between sales and the Gross Domestic Product (GDP) because it was thought that:

1. The rate of investment in roads appeared to be a function of the level of GDP.
2. Long-term forecasts of GDP are available from semi-official sources (we discuss these in Ch. 9) and these would reflect the expected changes in the economy due to the oil crisis.

The data. Fortunately production capacity had not been limited over the 12 years from 1961 to 1972 and therefore the sales figures for these years could reasonably be used to represent demand for the company's traffic control system. The raw data used in building the sales forecasting model is shown below in Table 5.5.

The next decision to be made in building the forecasting model concerned the choice of measurement units for both sales and GDP. While it was preferable to relate the growth in investment in roads through GDP with the number of control systems sold, because each system was to a certain extent individually designed, it was only feasible to measure demand in terms of an 'average' unit. Initially, actual GDP was used as the independent variable producing an equation with an R^2 of 0.89 though with a large standard error of sixteen (compared with $\overline{Y} = 91.4$), but a visual examination of the residuals made it apparent that the errors were not independent. This was supported by there being only three runs in the twelve observations.

Table 5.5
Sales and GDP data, 1961–72 (indexed in 1970 at 100)

Year	Sales of 'average' units in thousands	GDP £ thousand millions	GDP at 1970 prices	Year	Sales of 'average' units in thousands	GDP £ thousand millions	GDP at 1970 prices
1961	21.3	24.20	78.4	1967	95.5	38.84	93.1
1962	26.0	25.28	79.3	1968	120.6	37.26	97.2
1963	40.2	26.88	82.7	1969	130.6	39.17	98.7
1964	69.1	29.19	87.2	1970	138.4	42.79	100.0
1965	76.8	31.16	90.1	1971	140.2	48.16	100.6
1966	84.7	33.06	91.4	1972	153.1	53.48	102.8

Source: National Income and Expenditure 1973, Government Statistical Service, HMSO, London.

One possible reason for the failure of the independence assumption was the careless use of actual GDP rather than GDP, measured at constant prices. Using actual figures confused two quite separate components, real growth in national income which has a consequent effect on investments in roads and traffic systems, and inflation, which is unlikely to affect the number of 'average' units sold.

The forecasting model. With the variables suitably defined a linear regression model, $Y = \beta_0 + \beta_1 X + (\text{error})$ was estimated, Y being the number of 'average' units sold in thousands while X was GDP in constant (1970) prices, indexed at 100 in 1970. The results of a computerized regression calculation are shown below:

Variable	Mean	Sum of squares	Standard deviation
Y	91.375000	23371.4	46.09414
X	91.797667	786.9692	8.458284

Regression equation: $Y = -407.83 + 5.4384 X$
Degrees of freedom = 10
Standard error: $\hat{\beta}_0 = 10.159$; $\hat{\beta}_1 = 0.11025$
t statistic: $\hat{\beta}_0 = -40.144$; $\hat{\beta}_1 = 49.328$
$R^2 = 0.996$
Standard error of estimate = 3.09278.

Notes:
1. The 'Sum of squares' figure for variable X (say) is merely $\Sigma (X_i - \overline{X})^2$.
2. The estimated standard deviation of a parameter is often called the standard error of that parameter.
3. The t statistic for $\hat{\beta}_1$ (say) is given by the formula $t = \hat{\beta}_1/(\text{standard error of } \hat{\beta}_1)$; i.e. t = 5.4384/ 0.11025 = 49.328. The cap above the standard error of $\hat{\beta}_1$, has the same meaning as usual and shows the standard error has been estimated from the data. Like $\hat{\beta}_1$ the estimate of the constant term, $\hat{\beta}_0$ is random and therefore has an associated mean and standard deviation. Its t value is calculated as above using the formula: $t = \hat{\beta}_0/(\text{standard error of } \hat{\beta}_0)$.

Examination of the residuals and the t statistics suggested that the basic regression assumptions held. The equation was therefore thought to be a plausible explanation of the systematic movements of sales. However, the forecast of sales 5 years ahead was a critical information input into the decision on plant investment. The forecasting accuracy had to be considered before the company went ahead with its investment.

Forecasting and sensitivity testing. The forecasts for the years 1973 through 1977 were derived by first using forecasts of the real growth in GDP. The GDP forecasts are given in Table 5.6 with the corresponding sales forecast calculated using the regression equation:

$Y = -407.83 + 5.4384 X$

Table 5.6
Sales forecasts and 90 per cent confidence limits, 1973–77

Year	GDP (forecast)	Sales ('000s units)	90% confidence limits
1973	108.0	179.5	6.7
1974	107.0	174.1	6.6
1975	109.5	187.7	6.8
1976	113.3	208.3	7.2
1977	119.3	241.0	8.0

For example, the sales forecast for 1977 was:

$Y = -407.83 + 5.4384 * 119.3 = 241.0,$
    : sales of 241,000 units.

The calculation of confidence limits was made using the formula given in §5.4.2, and repeated below for convenience.

$$\hat{Y}_p \pm t_{\alpha/2}\ \hat{\sigma} \sqrt{1 + \frac{1}{n} + \frac{(X_p - \overline{X})^2}{\Sigma (X_i - \overline{X})^2}}\ .$$

The entry in the column headed 'confidence limits' is just the latter term in this expression. The necessary calculations for the 1977 entry are shown below. It uses the following values taken from the results of the previous page:

$n = 12 : \alpha = 0.1$: Degrees of freedom $= 12 - 2 = 10$
    $\hat{\sigma} = 3.09278 \quad \Sigma (X_i - \overline{X})^2 = 786.9692.$

Therefore, the appropriate critical t value has ten degrees of freedom and is

$t_{0.05} = 1.812.$

Substitution in the above formula gives:

$$1.812 * 3.093 * \sqrt{1 + \frac{1}{12} + \frac{(119.3 - 91.791667)^2}{786.9692}}$$
$$= 8.0 \quad \text{to one decimal place.}$$

Using the point forecast of the volume of demand for 1977 it was possible for the company to calculate the expected return for the different size plants under consideration and to decide between the various investment options. In this particular case the policy of adding a medium-sized plant to production capacity looked the most attractive. Before finally accepting this option it was thought necessary to test whether the decision remained unaltered if forecast demand reached either its upper or lower confidence limits. If the addition of a medium-sized plant still seemed the most appropriate policy the company could be more confident as to the decision's correctness.

One further test of sensitivity was considered. The confidence interval for demand was constructed, contingent on the forecasts of GDP being correct. This will rarely be the case; in fact the failure to predict the oil crisis occasioned the re-assessment of the investment plans. The simplest way of incorporating errors in the independent variable is to recalculate the forecast confidence intervals under various assumptions about GDP. For example, the per cent growth rates of real GDP on which the initial set of forecasts were made were 5.1, −1, 2.4, 3.4 and 5.3 per cent. The events of early 1974 quickly made these forecasts look optimistic. The forecast of an increase in GDP in 1976/77 was due to the belief that commodity prices would ease and North Sea oil would come on-stream. While the former still seemed likely, the latter event had already been delayed until 1978/79. Using a set of new and pessimistic forecasts of GDP it was again possible to check the sensitivity of the decision to invest in a medium-sized plant.

Comment. The method of sensitivity testing proposed here is quite crude, although it fits well with the decision theory framework proposed in § 3.2 for assessing projects. It is particularly useful in identifying variables which critically affect the decisions to be made. If, as is quite likely, a change in the basic assumptions about the growth of GDP produces a substantial shift from what had been the optimal decision then it is probable that more time and money could profitably be spent in forecasting the behaviour of the economy in order to decrease the riskiness of the decision. A second source of error is the possible omission from the forecasting equation of further independent variables which, like GDP, have a systematic effect on demand. We will discuss the type of variables to be included in a model for forecasting demand and also suitable methods of doing this in Chapter 8.

References

Draper, N. R. and **Smith, H.** (1966) *Applied Regression Analysis*, Wiley, New York.

Frank, Charles, R. (1971) *Statistics and Econometrics*, Holt, Rinehart and Winston, New York.

Mendenhall, W. and **Reinmuth, J. F.** (1974) *Statistics for Management and Economics*, 2nd edn, Duxbury, Calif.

Wonnacott, Ronald J. and **Wonnacott, Thomas H.** (1970) *Econometrics*, Wiley, New York.

6

Multiple regression

§6.1 Introduction

In the previous chapter we described the simplest of regression models, a linear model in which only one input variable is used to describe the behaviour of the variable which we wish to forecast. Usually there are several factors which have a systematic effect on the dependent variable. Multiple regression provides a suitable method for including this added complexity in a forecasting model. Figure 6.1 illustrates how three independent variables, likely to affect Q, the annual retail sales of washing machines (the example is discussed in detail in Chapter 8) may be included in a multiple regression forecasting model.

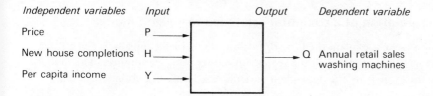

Fig. 6.1 Variables used to forecast the retail sales of washing machines

Here P is the average installed price of the washer, H is the number of new housing units completed in that year and Y is the per capita income. The principle that is used to construct a model using these variables is to describe Q as a function of the input variables. This may be written:

Q = f(P, H, Y) + (error),

and read, Q is a function of P, H and Y plus random error. For each set of values of P, H, and Y there is one corresponding value of f(P, H, Y). The above model suggests that we can find a function of the variables which will approximate the dependent variable, except for some small amount of error.

The easiest function to try is linear in the independent variables. If there are p input variables with which to describe the behaviour of the dependent variable Q, the linear multiple regression model is:

$$Q = \beta_0 + \beta_1 X_1 + \beta_2 X_2 + \cdots + \beta_p X_p + \text{(error)}.$$

For example, we might try to forecast the sales of washing machines Q by postulating a linear relationship between Q and the three independent variables, price, the number of new houses built and income, i.e.:

$$Q = \beta_0 + \beta_1 P + \beta_2 H + \beta_3 Y + \text{(error)}.$$

The problem the analyst faces in using such a model are similar to those raised in the previous chapter; how to estimate the parameters, how to find confidence limits for the forecast, and how to test the validity of the model. While the techniques used are very similar, the increase in data makes the calculations by hand (or desk calculator) much more time-consuming and difficult. As in the case of only one variable, the principle of least squares is used to estimate the parameters in the model. Using the methods of matrix algebra it is possible to find formulae for all the quantities which are of interest to us in interpreting the estimated model. We will not give them here. Draper and Smith (1966) in *Applied Regression Analysis* do this job well. Instead we will assume the reader has access to a computer. Not only does this eliminate much of the possible error in calculation, but the analyst is then able to concentrate on the design of the most suitable forecasting model and the interpretation of the results.

§ 6.2 Interpretation of a computer-estimated regression model

In this section we will explain the type of information which typically is given to an analyst who has estimated a multiple regression model using a computer. The model we propose for estimating the dependent variable Y is linear in two independent variables X_1 and X_2, i.e.:

$$Y = \beta_0 + \beta_1 X_1 + \beta_2 X_2 + \text{(error)},$$

where we will suppose, β_1 and β_2 are expected to be positive.

The above assumptions on the form of the model and the sign of the coefficients are made after referring to any relevant previous studies, and any other available information. In the holiday—income problem used throughout the previous chapter, for example, we postulated that income is earned to satisfy family needs, among which we include taking holidays. With increased income the opportunity to take longer holidays is also increased and therefore the relationship between income and length of holiday is expected to be positive. In the same way we will suppose that in our current example an analysis of earlier work leads us to expect the variables X_1 and X_2 to have a positive influence on Y. The data used for estimating the proposed regression model is shown in Table 6.1.

Table 6.1

Data for computer example

Observation No.	Y	X_1	X_2
1	0.50	1.47	3.01
2	0.83	1.51	5.20
3	0.77	1.53	2.39
4	1.25	2.31	6.83
5	0.91	2.50	4.10
6	1.10	2.46	4.88
7	0.45	1.51	1.20
8	0.89	2.71	3.87
9	1.17	2.70	4.25
10	1.50	2.74	7.12

In estimating the equation we have used a typical computer multiple regression package, and the remaining presentation will be concerned with the interpretation of the output from this package. The first part of the printout is presented in Table 6.2(*a*).

Table 6.2(*a*)

Multiple regression printout: Part 1

```
MULREG
   REGRESSION NUMBER (1)¹          DEPENDENT VARIABLE IS (1)²
   INDEX ³        MEANS ⁴          STANDARD DEVIATIONS ⁵
     2            2.144                .565097
     3            4.285               1.84532
     1             .937                .327653

   CORRELATION COEFFICIENTS ⁶

    .999998 ⁷      .783729              .879174
    .783729       1.0                   .573098
    .879174        .573098             1.0
```

Notes to Table 6.2(a)

1. Most regression programs can be instructed to estimate a number of alternative models from one set of data. Where this is done successive models will be numbered sequentially. In this case we are looking at the first regression run.

2. The dependent variable in the particular model run is indicated by an index number which shows the position in which that variable appears in the data block of input variables.

3. In a similar way each independent variable included in the model is indicated by its index number in the block of input data.

    Normally programs give the option of entering data on the complete set of values observed for each variable in turn; alternatively data can be entered observation by observation. Here the data were entered through a time-share terminal, observation by observation, in the form of data statements, for example:

    9901 DATA 0.50, 1.47, 3.01
    9902 DATA 0.83, 1.51, 5.20
    9903 DATA 0.77, 1.53, 2.39

4; 5. The program first calculates the *means* and *standard deviations* of each variable, and prints the result next to the appropriate index.

6. The next item printed is the *correlation coefficient* for each pair of variables, a measure already discussed in §5.3.2. The table is slightly difficult to read. The position of an entry defines the two variables used in calculating the correlation; for example, 0.783729 is in the first row and the second column and is therefore the correlation between variable index 1 and variable index 2, that is Y and X_1. Similarly, 0.573098 is the correlation between X_1 and X_2.

7. The correlation between a variable and itself is of course, 1. Sometimes a value like 0.999998 is printed instead, an error due to machine rounding error, which is unimportant in subsequent calculations.

This exhausts Part 1 of the printout. Table 6.2(*b*) shows the remainder.

Table 6.2(*b*)
Multiple regression printout: Part 2

INDEX	B [2]	STANDARD ERROR [3]	T—RATIO [4]
0	−6.82727E−02 [5]	.161103	.423782
2	.241644	8.88602E−02	2.71937
3	.113696	2.72119E−02	4.17818

VARIANCE−COVARIANCE MATRIX OMITTED [1]

R—SQUARED [6] = .889588   R = .94318

STANDARD ERROR OF EST [7] = .123451   D.F. [8] = 7 [9]

PROBLEM COMPLETED

Notes to Table 6.2(b)

1. A matrix is a rectangular array of numbers arranged into columns and rows. *The variance—covariance matrix* is usually an optional part of the printout, used only rarely in interpreting a regression model, although many calculations are based on

it, in particular, the calculation of the confidence interval of §5.4. In this case we have chosen to omit it.

2. The model $Y = \beta_0 + \beta_1 X_1 + \beta_2 X_2 + e$ is estimated by

$$\hat{Y} = \hat{\beta}_0 + \hat{\beta}_1 X_1 + \hat{\beta}_2 X_2,$$

with $\hat{\beta}_0$ etc. being the least squares estimate of β_0 etc. These estimates $\hat{\beta}_0$, $\hat{\beta}_1$ and $\hat{\beta}_2$ depend on the observed values of Y, X_1 and X_2 and are random quantities because the Y's are random. The estimates of the coefficients $\hat{\beta}_0$, $\hat{\beta}_1$ and $\hat{\beta}_2$ are listed under the heading 'B' or '*B coefficients*'. The estimated model in the example is:

$$Y = -0.0682727 + 0.241644\ X_1 + 0.113696\ X_2.$$

3. Because the Y's are random the coefficient estimates are random and consequently have variances which can be estimated from the observations. The entries under the heading '*standard error*' are the square roots of the estimated parameter variances. They are used in the calculation of confidence intervals for the B coefficients, and in computing the *t-ratio* shown in the last column.

4. The t-ratio (or alternatively the F-ratio) is the statistic used for testing whether any of the regression coefficients are significantly different from zero. But as we noted in §5.3.2 this is equivalent to analysing if the addition of a variable, let us say, X_2, significantly improves the model's ability to explain the variation in Y as compared with the situation where X_2 is omitted. The t-ratio thus tests the hypothesis 'the regression coefficient of X_2 is zero when X_1 is included in the model', against a one- or two-sided alternative.

The procedure for computing the t statistic is to divide the B coefficient by its corresponding standard error. In a test of $\beta_2 = 0$ against the alternative, $\beta_2 \neq 0$, a large t value implies the rejection of the null hypothesis. A value of $|t|$ of larger than 2 (the coefficient estimate is more than twice its standard error) is close to being significant.

Exact critical t values for a given significance level and the appropriate number of degrees of freedom may be found by referring to any set of standard tables. When the multiple regression printout gives a t value for $\hat{\beta}_2$ that is not significant (at a given significant level) the alternative and simpler model:

$$Y = \beta_0 + \beta_1 X_1 + (\text{error})$$

needs to be considered. Accepting the null hypothesis that $\beta_2 = 0$ tells us that the addition of X_2 to the model adds nothing to its ability to explain the variation in Y. However, before X_2 is excluded because its coefficient is not significant there are other factors to consider and these we will discuss more fully in §6.7.

5. *6.82727E−02* is a common and convenient way of printing the number 0.0682727. It is derived from the fact that $0.0682727 = (6.82727) * 10^{-2} = 6.82727E{-}02$. '−02' is the index of 10 and has the effect of shifting the decimal point two places to the left. Similarly, with the number 8.35E + 01, 'E + 01' shifts the decimal point one place to the right, and therefore this is an alternative way of writing 83.5.

6. *R-Squared* is the square of the multiple correlation coefficient and has already been

discussed in §5.3.1. It measures the proportion of the variation of Y that is explained by the model.

7. *The standard error of estimate* (**Stand. Error of Est.**) was also discussed earlier in §5.2.4. In developing a multiple regression model, as in the simple linear model discussed in Chapter 5, a number of assumptions are made. One of them is that the errors are normally distributed (allowing the analyst to use the t test), independent of each other, with constant variance σ^2. The standard error is the estimate of σ. It is a major determinant of the width of the forecast confidence interval and should therefore be comparatively small in relation to the Y values for the forecast to be useful.

8. *The degrees of freedom* (**D.F.**) are connected to the number of observations and the number of parameters in the model. In the example discussed here there are n = 10 observations, and parameters β_0, β_1 and β_2, a total of three parameters. If there had been p independent variables included in the linear model, in general there would be (p + 1) corresponding parameters. In this example p = 2. The degrees of freedom here are $10 - 3 = 7$. With p independent variables the degrees of freedom are $(n - p - 1)$. This concept is used to find the critical value for the t test which has $(n - p - 1)$ degrees of freedom.

Interpretation. The R^2 value is quite high at 0.89 although the number of degrees of freedom (7) is barely adequate, there being ten observations and three parameters to be estimated. An R^2 value of 1 is always possible if the number of parameters is equal to the number of observations, and therefore there are no residual degrees of freedom left in the data. R^2 alone is not a sufficient measure of the model's accuracy, and it has to be combined with both the degrees of freedom and the standard error.

With so few observations it is impossible to be confident that the errors are distributed normally, and as that assumption forms the basis for the t and F tests their validity is open to question. However, it is known that even if the normality assumptions are incorrect, the hypothesis tests of the parameters are usually accurate enough. *A priori* we hypothesized that β_1 and β_2 were both positive. For a one-tailed test, at a significance level of 5 per cent, with seven (= n − p − 1) degrees of freedom the critical t value is 1.895. Both the observed t values are significant and therefore we accept the hypothesis that both X_1 and X_2 separately contribute to explaining the variation in Y.

It is worth noting here that the t value for $\hat{\beta}_0$, the constant term, is not significantly different from zero; however, the decision on whether to include it or not should be made on *a priori* grounds rather than statistical. The linear model is an approximation to the true functional relationship between Y and the independent variables X_1 and X_2, an approximation only valid for certain sets of values, which in general do not include values close to the origin. The constant term therefore may be interpreted as the average effect on Y of variables which have not been included in the equation; *not* the value of Y when X_1 and X_2 are both zero. Unless the theoretical model is valid close to the origin and it also suggests that β_0 is zero, this constant term is retained in the equation. With these reservations borne in mind, what conclusions can be drawn?

The first and most obvious is that increases in either X_1 or X_2 will produce a corresponding increase in Y. By substituting actual (or predicted) values for X_1 and X_2 we can also forecast the future values of the dependent variable from the regression equation, although the standard error of estimate is 0.12345, 13.2 per cent of the mean value of Y. Such a value indicates that the confidence interval is wide as a proportion of Y and therefore forecasts based on the model may well not be useful.

In summary, by using the relationship between Y and X_1 and X_2 we have been able to explain a significant part of the variation in Y. Whether in fact the forecasting equation is useful depends on the cost of inaccuracy. However, by using a computer to do the calculations the analyst has not made a major investment in any particular model. He can therefore devote much more of his time to exploring alternative models until his needs for accuracy are met.

§ 6.3 Non-linear models

In §5.3 we remarked that it was quite possible for Y to be related to X and yet the correlation coefficient between them could still be zero. The example we considered there was where all the observations lay on a quadratic. Obviously Y and X are related and yet their correlation is zero. There is no *linear* relation between the two. Multiple regression can quite easily be extended to include situations such as this where the relationship between dependent and independent variables is *non-linear*. Instead of the relation of Y to X being a straight line, Y may be related to X in a variety of ways, two often encountered examples being:

$Y = \beta_0 + \beta_1 X^2$; or

$Y = \beta_0 + \beta_1 \log X$.

However, both non-linear relationships are very similar to the simple linear regression model, for they can be re-written as:

$Y = \beta_0 + \beta_1 Z$.

In the first case, by substituting $Z = X^2$ we return to the original equation and in the second the transformation, $Z = \log X$ has the same effect. In the next two sections we develop these ideas to allow the methods of Chapters 5 and 6 to be used extensively in the analysis of non-linear models such as these.

But why use a non-linear model? The first answer is that it may well describe the data better. Sales of many products — for example, chlorine and polythene — have been increasing at a rate faster than would be implied by a linear model, for as we will show in Chapter 7 the linear model implies a declining rate of growth in the market. In markets such as these, new end-uses of the product have continually been discovered, keeping the rate of growth high. A second reason is that quite often there are natural restrictions on the dependent variable which need to be incorporated in the forecasting model. It would be peculiar if in predicting market penetration the forecast was of a penetration greater than 100 per cent. Thirdly, the basis of all empirical forecasting models is founded on the theoretical relationships between independent and dependent variables, and this may sometimes imply using a non-linear model.

6.3.1 *Transformations to the standard linear model*

The usual method of analysing non-linear models is to search for a transformation which takes the non-linear model into the standard linear regression model, which can then be estimated using the methods of the last section.

Polynomial models. The simplest example of a non-linear model is the polynomial:

$$Y = \beta_0 + \beta_1 X + \beta_2 X^2 + \cdots + \beta_p X^p + e$$

where e obeys the usual error assumptions. This is very similar to the standard multiple regression model:

$$Y = \beta_0 + \beta_1 Z_1 + \beta_2 Z_2 + \cdots + \beta_p Z_p + e$$

$Z_1, Z_2, \ldots Z_p$ being the independent variables. To turn one into the other we make the transformation $Z_1 = X$, $Z_2 = X^2$ through to $Z_p = X^p$ and the two models are then identical; the parameters $\beta_0, \beta_1 \ldots \beta_p$ can now be estimated using the methods described in §6.2. The values of $Z_1, Z_2 \ldots$ to Z_p can of course be calculated from the given observations on X. Consequently, the analyst is able to transform the raw data (this is often done automatically by the computer) into a form which is suitable for use as the input into the standard multiple regression computer program. Although there is originally only one input variable, because of the transformation there are p variables $Z_1, Z_2, \ldots Z_p$ used in the regression calculations.

A situation where polynomial regression is useful is in inventory control. Figure 6.2 shows a graph of the total cost of an inventory system, as it varies with the amount re-ordered. The costs are made up of two basic components: the cost of placing an order and the cost of storing the goods. We will suppose that because of the assumptions on which it is based, the usual inventory model (as discussed in §1.8) is hard to justify. Instead, over a short period of time different re-order policies have been tried and their corresponding costs calculated. The observations are seen to fall close to the sketched quadratic. Certainly a straight line would not represent the data accurately. More important, in the search for an optimum re-order quantity a line (with a negative slope) suggests that the larger the amount ordered at any one time, the lower your costs, which is unlikely since the total costs are partly made up of inventory costs.

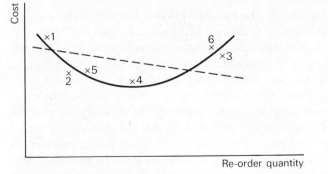

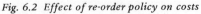

Fig. 6.2 Effect of re-order policy on costs

The general non-linear model. Most of the time there is an obvious transformation which turns a non-linear model into the standard multiple regression model. However, any model which by a transformation of the variables may be re-written in the form of the standard regression equation is called *intrinsically linear* to distinguish it from other models where no such simplifying transformation exists.

One particularly useful model which is intrinsically linear is the exponential growth model. It has been used to describe the growth in world population, growth in industrial capital or pollution and a variation of the model is often used to describe the relation between demand, price and income.

In contrast to the standard model $Y_t = \beta_0 + \beta_1 t$, which has a declining growth rate, the growth rate of the exponential model is constant. Table 6.3 and Fig. 6.3 show the exponential function:

$Y = a \exp(b * t)$:†

for values of b of 0.5, 1 and 2, where a is a constant independent of time.

Table 6.3
The exponential: $y = \exp(t)$

t	0	0.25	0.50	0.75	1.00	1.25	1.50	1.75	2.00
y	1.00	1.28	1.65	2.12	2.72	3.49	4.48	5.75	7.39
t	2.25	2.50	2.75	3.00	3.25	3.50	3.75	4.00	5.00
y	9.49	12.2	15.6	20.1	25.8	33.1	42.5	54.6	148.00

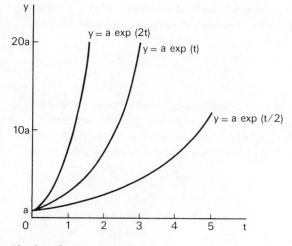

Fig. 6.3 The exponential

† 'exp(b * t)' is an alternative way of writing 'e^{bt}' where e = 2.718 . . . We use 'exp' rather than 'e' to distinguish it from the error term.

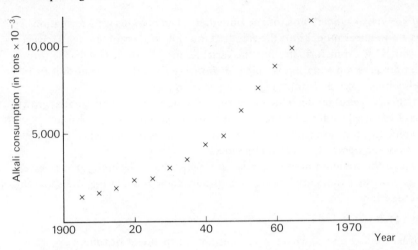

Fig. 6.4 Alkali consumption per 5 years: 1901—70 (Source: Industrial Marketing Management, 1972, p. 168)

The graph's most obvious feature is its growth rate given by the formula:

$$= y_t/y_{t-1} = a \exp(b * t)/a \exp(b * [t-1])$$
$$= \exp(b).$$

Figure 6.4 illustrates the use of the exponential growth model. It shows the consumption of alkali in the UK and Eire, and we see immediately that no straight line will fit the data so as to ensure that the error assumption of independence is valid. Consumption is growing too fast. If we compare the data with the exponential models of Fig. 6.3 we can see the similarity between the two.

We will therefore fit the exponential model:

$$Q_t = \alpha \exp(\beta t) * (\text{error}),$$

where Q_t represents consumption; the time trend t takes on initial value 1 for the interval 1901—05; α and β are parameters to be estimated and the error random variable is assumed to have multiplicative effect on consumption. Superficially, this is not similar to the linear model, but if logarithms† are taken of both sides the model appears in the more familiar form:

$$\log Q_t = \log \alpha + \beta t + (\text{error}).$$

Let $\log Q_t = Y_t$, $\log \alpha = \beta_0$, and $\beta = \beta_1$, and the model can be written in the standard form:

$$Y_t = \beta_0 + \beta_1 t + (\text{error}).$$

† Recall that all logarithms are to the base 'e', therefore, $\log_e (\alpha \exp \beta t) = \log_e \alpha + \log_e (\exp \beta t)$, but $\log_e (\exp \beta t) = \beta t$, using the definition of a logarithm.

Table 6.4
Raw and transformed data on alkali consumption

t	Q_t	log Q_t	t	Q_t	log Q_t
1	1,375	7.226	8	4,316	8.370
2	1,589	7.371	9	4,891	8.495
3	1,870	7.534	10	6,390	8.762
4	2,316	7.748	11	7,578	8.933
5	2,360	7.766	12	8,734	9.075
6	2,964	7.994	13	9,755	9.186
7	3,412	8.135	14	11,237	9.327

Making the usual assumptions about the structure of the error term we may estimate β_0 and β_1 using the observations graphed above in Fig. 6.4 and given in Table 6.4. The estimated parameters of the transformed variables are $\hat{\beta}_0 = 7.0248$, $\hat{\beta}_1 = 0.16738$ and $\hat{\sigma} = 0.05148$ and the transformed model is: $Y_t = 7.0248 + 0.16738\ t$. Using the estimates of β_0 and β_1 we may now estimate the parameters in the original model. Because $\log_e \alpha = \beta_0$, it follows that $\hat{\alpha} = \exp(\hat{\beta}_0) = 1124.4$ and $\hat{\beta} = \hat{\beta}_1 = 0.16738$.

Confidence intervals can be constructed in the usual way, by transforming a confidence interval for Y back to a confidence interval for the original Q. For example, suppose we wish to construct 90 per cent confidence limits for Q_{15}, the consumption for the years 1971–75, then we first construct a 90 per cent confidence interval for Y_{15}. Using the method of §5.4 the 90 per cent confidence interval with 12 ($= n - 2$) degrees of freedom is:

Prob. $[9.430 \leqslant Y_{15} \leqslant 9.641] = 0.90$

with a point estimate, $\hat{Y}_{15} = 7.0248 + 0.16738 * 15 = 9.5355$.

Transforming back now in the raw sales data where $Y_{15} = \log Q_{15}$

Prob. $[9.430 \leqslant \log Q_{15} \leqslant 9.641] = 0.90$

and simplifying:

Prob. $[\exp(9.430) \leqslant Q_{15} \leqslant \exp(9.641)] = 0.90$

and it follows therefore that the 90 per cent confidence interval for Q_{15} is: $12,400 \leqslant Q_{15} \leqslant 15,380$, with a corresponding point estimate of $\hat{Q}_{15} = \exp(\hat{Y}_{15}) = 13,840$.

A second important example of the use of the logarithmic transformation in an exponential model is that of a Cobb–Douglas production function which relates output Q to labour L and capital K, arguing that the output of a firm depends on the capital and the labour it employs. The model proposed is:

$$Q = \alpha v L^{\beta} K^{1-\beta}$$

where v is an error random variable. By taking logarithms the equation becomes:

$\log Q = \log \alpha + \beta \log L + (1 - \beta) \log K + \log v.$

Using the transformations:

$Y = (\log Q - \log K): \beta_0 = \log \alpha: \beta_1 = \beta: X = (\log L - \log K): e = \log v$

we arrive at the following equation:

$Y = \beta_0 + \beta_1 X + e,$

which may now be estimated using the usual methods.

We have discussed the exponential model to show how a non-linear model — which is however, intrinsically linear — is estimated. The method is always the same. A transformation is found which takes the non-linear model into the standard multiple regression model. The transformed data are used to estimate the parameters in the standard model which then allows the analyst to calculate the parameter estimates in the original model. It is a method which works most of the time but as we shall see in Chapter 7 there are situations where a model which is intrinsically non-linear should be employed. Thus a non-linear model is considered appropriate when:

1. There are *a priori* grounds for the choice of functional form. This evidence may be gathered from earlier studies, both empirical and theoretical, or from the analyst's subjective feelings about the form of the relationship.
2. Examination of the data suggests that a linear model would be inadequate. This is discussed further in §6.6.

As we showed with the simple sales example of Chapter 5, the specification of the appropriate model is critical and it should not be dictated by the arithmetic convenience of the standard multiple regression model.

§6.4 Dummy variables

Suppose we wish to forecast the demand for international air travel. In specifying a model we might isolate two components of the growth of civil aviation. One factor increasing its popularity has been the trend in technical performance in the industry as it moved from an uncomfortable and hazardous form of transport to its present state of development. A second factor increasing demand has been the spread of affluence and the general increase in service in advanced economies.

Reflecting these factors we might specify a model:

$A_t = \beta_0 + \beta_1 t + \beta_2 Y_t + (\text{error})$

where Y_t is *per capita* income; A_t is miles travelled *per capita* on scheduled flights; and technological improvements are measured through the time trend.

In fitting such a model to time series data gathered from different countries, however, we would not expect it to predict equally well for all countries for a variety of reasons. Demand might be affected by geographical and behavioural differences between cultures, data collection and definition would be subtly different and so on. One solution to this is to run the model separately for each country, although this would drastically reduce the number of observations available to estimate each forecasting equation. A better procedure is to create a variable which allows us to separate out 'country' effects while still using all the observations to estimate a single equation.

Thus let us define a variable P which is assigned a value on the basis of the nationality of an observation. Thus in a two-country situation we may take:

P = 1   if the observation is French;

 = 0   if the observation is American.

P is called a *dummy variable.*

We can then pool the French and American observation and use them in estimating the model:

$$A_t = \beta_0 + \beta_1 t + \beta_2 Y_t + \beta_3 P + e_t.$$

When we consider the demand in US we are in effect using the model:

$$A_t = \beta_0 + \beta_1 t + \beta_2 Y_t + e_t,$$

while in France the model is:

$$A_t = (\beta_0 + \beta_3) + \beta_1 t + \beta_2 Y_t + e_t,$$

and β_3 therefore represents the difference in *per capita* travel between the two countries if income and time were the same. Normal regression techniques can be used to estimate the four parameters $\beta_0, \beta_1, \beta_2, \beta_3$, the only modification is that in entering the data we create a new variable, P, to represent the origin of the observation. The prepared data is shown in Fig. 6.5. Using dummy variables significantly extends the possible uses of regression analysis, since the method allows the analyst to incorporate the effect of a non-numerical input variable into the model. In the previous example, the country of origin of the observation was postulated as affecting demand for air travel. Similarly the social class of an individual may well affect his drinking habits and the management style operating in a factory could affect its output. In all these cases it is hard if not impossible to assign a numerical measure to the variable. They are

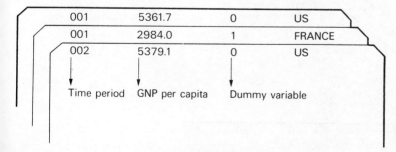

Fig. 6.5 Data input when dummy variable is present

categorical variables which assign the observations to different classes depending on the value of that variable. In the air travel example the two classes are French and American.

A second illustration of the same point is provided by the following hypothetical example showing the consumption of beer against time. The data are shown in Table 6.5 and plotted in Fig. 6.6. Looking at the grouped data it appears that consumption during the war is somewhat at variance with consumption both pre- and post-war. In particular there are shifts in consumption associated with the beginning and end of the war, and when the function of beer is considered it is clear why there should be such a change in behaviour. Two of the data points, 1939 and 1946 are difficult to classify either as war years or non-war years, so they have been dropped from the analysis in both the following models.

Table 6.5
Beer consumption in millions of gallons, 1935—49

Year	Consumption of beer	Year	Consumption of beer	Year	Consumption of beer
1935	23	1940	29	1945	33
1936	23	1941	30	1946	32
1937	25	1942	31	1947	33
1938	25	1943	32	1948	34
1939	27	1944	32	1949	34

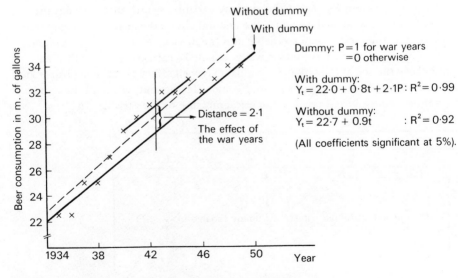

Dummy: $P = 1$ for war years
$\qquad = 0$ otherwise

With dummy:
$Y_t = 22 \cdot 0 + 0 \cdot 8t + 2 \cdot 1P : R^2 = 0 \cdot 99$

Without dummy:
$Y_t = 22 \cdot 7 + 0.9t \qquad : R^2 = 0 \cdot 92$

(All coefficients significant at 5%).

Fig. 6.6 Beer consumption in millions of gallons, 1935—49

The broken line in Fig. 6.6 is the regression line if the data is analysed without dummy variables, while using a dummy variable gives the considerably more accurate solid lines as estimates. Examination of the calculated residuals where no dummy was included shows that they are initially negative, then positive and then again negative. This is caused by the omission of one of the independent variables — 'the war years' variable. In general, correlation of this form in the residuals is a sign a variable has been omitted. The problem will be discussed in greater detail in §6.6. It is sufficient to say here that the estimated regression line without the dummy variable is inaccurate, with a larger error variance due to omitting an important explanatory variable. (The estimates are also biased. When a variable which should be in the regression equation is omitted the estimated coefficients in the incorrect equation, besides having high variances, also estimate the 'wrong' thing. The average (expected) value of the estimates $\hat{\beta}_0$, $\hat{\beta}_1$ etc. differ from the parameters they estimate, β_0, β_1 etc., an undesirable quality for an estimator to possess. This is called *bias*. Recall from Chapter 5 that an estimator $\hat{\beta}$ of β is biased if $E\hat{\beta} \neq \beta$.)

Another important use of dummy variables is to capture seasonal fluctuations in data. If beer sales had been considered on a quarterly instead of annual basis we would have noticed that the pattern of consumption is seasonal, being particularly high in the summer. These seasonal effects can be measured by including three dummy variables, Q_{1t}, Q_{2t} and Q_{3t} in the equation:

$$C_t = \beta_0 + \text{(other causal factors)} + \beta_p Q_{1t} + \beta_q Q_{2t} + \beta_r Q_{3t} + e_t$$

and setting the values for these variables in line with seasonal changes:

	Q_1	Q_2	Q_3
spring observation	0	0	0
summer observation	1	0	0
autumn observation	0	1	0
winter observation	0	0	1

Thus, in the first quarter we are using in effect the model:

$$C_t = \beta_0 + \cdots + e_t,$$

while in the second:

$$C_t = (\beta_0 + \beta_p) + \cdots + e_t.$$

Similar equations hold for the third and fourth quarters. β_p in the equation above represents the average amount of goods sold in the second quarter each year above (or below) the level sold in the first quarter, other factors remaining unchanged and similarly for the remaining dummy parameters β_q and β_r. We can use exactly the same approach to pool data from various sources. A study of savings patterns using data from ten countries could net out 'country effects' by using nine dummy variables. In general with n qualitative classes there are $(n - 1)$ inter-class differences and therefore we use only $(n - 1)$ dummy variable to describe these differences, i.e. in the seasonality example β_p, β_q, and β_r measure the differences between goods sold in summer, autumn and winter respectively compared with the goods sold in spring.

To summarize the discussion, we have argued that by including dummy variables in a regression equation the analyst is able to take into account qualitative variables which may systematically affect the behaviour of the dependent variable, thereby considerably extending the flexibility of basic regression analysis.

§ 6.5 Lagged variables

If we wished to forecast the amount of money lent by a building society, one obviously important independent variable is the amount of money deposited in the society. But money is not lent out immediately. There is a time lag (which may be quite short).

If L_t = money lent in time period t,

and D_t = money deposited in time period t,

then a possible model to forecast loans might be

$$L_t = f(D_{t-\gamma}) + e_t$$

when γ is the time lag between the money being deposited and it being lent out. The simplest regression model describing the relationship is:

$$L_t = \beta_0 + \beta_1 D_{t-\gamma} + e_t.$$

Unfortunately we do not know the length of the lag and we therefore have to find some method for estimating it. If we are lucky we can use information gathered from previous studies. Usually though we have to experiment for ourselves. An *ad hoc* method which is helpful is to calculate the correlation coefficient between L_t and $D_{t-\gamma}$ for different values of the lag γ, selecting that value of γ which maximizes R^2. This method is equally appropriate when there are other independent variables in the equation, say X_t and Z_t. Suppose the forecasting equation is:

$$L_t = f(X_t, Z_t, D_{t-\gamma}) + e_t.$$

After we have decided on the functional form of the equation we may estimate its parameters and R^2, the coefficient of determination. Different values of γ give us different values of R^2. We again select the value of γ which maximizes R^2.

More generally the effect of a change in the dependent variable is not confined to one time period. Rather it will be spread out over a number of periods. For example, consumers do not instantaneously adjust their habits to a new price level. The previous price level also has an effect. We may reflect this characteristic in a model where the effect of a variable is distributed over a number of time periods, i.e.:

$$Y_t = \beta_0 + \beta_1 X_t + \beta_2 X_{t-1} \ldots \beta_r X_{t-r+1} + \cdots + e_t.$$

(We use the linear model here for convenience. The arguments hold for all of the models we have discussed.) The immediate difficulty with such a model is that unless the number of non-zero parameters is small or the number of observations is large, there are too many parameters to be estimated. We therefore have to make some simplifying assumptions about the parameters. Let us consider the problem of measuring the effect of advertising on the demand for a consumer good. It is fairly clear that advertising has a cumulative effect on demand. People are made aware of the product well before they may buy it. It therefore seems appropriate to include the level of advertising from many previous time periods as a determinant of demand; but as remarked above, before we can estimate the parameters we need to make some simplifying assumptions.

Referring back to the previous equation with Y demand and X advertising, the first thing to note is that an outlay of one unit of advertising at time t has an effect on current demand of β_1. However, the same expenditure will effect sales at t + 1 by an amount β_2 and sales at t + 2 by an amount β_3 and so on. The cumulative effect of that expenditure is therefore $(\beta_1 + \beta_2 + \beta_3 + \ldots)$. Also we would expect that the amount spent on advertising in a particular time period will have a decreasing effect on time. The period in which it is spent will produce the greatest effect on sales, the next period somewhat less, etc. Consequently,

$$\beta_1 > \beta_2 > \beta_3 > \cdots \beta_r > \cdots.$$

Let us now simplify further by supposing the coefficients are related by the equation:

$$\beta_{i+1} = \lambda\beta_i, \quad \text{for i = 1, 2, \ldots,}$$

where λ (lambda) lies between 0 and 1. Because

$$\beta_{i+1} = \lambda\beta_i = \lambda^2\beta_{i-1} = \lambda^i\beta_1$$

this forces the coefficients to decrease as the time lag between sales and advertising grows longer. With this simplification the equation becomes:

$$Y_t = \beta_0 + \beta_1X_t + \beta_1\lambda X_{t-1} + \beta_1\lambda^2 X_{t-2} + \cdots e_t.$$

Similarly:

$$Y_{t-1} = \beta_0 + \beta_1X_{t-1} + \beta_1\lambda X_{t-2} + \beta_1\lambda^2 X_{t-3} + \cdots + e_{t-1}.$$

If the last equation is multiplied by λ and subtracted from the first, the equations simplify considerably to:

$$Y_t - \lambda Y_{t-1} = \beta_0(1 - \lambda) + \beta_1X_t + v_t,$$
$$\text{where } v_t = e_t - \lambda e_{t-1},$$

and this may be written: $Y_t = \beta_0(1 - \lambda) + \beta_1X_t + \lambda Y_{t-1} + v_t.$

The above equation is a little different than the previous lagged models that we discussed, for it includes a lagged *dependent* variable Y_{t-1}. However, if the usual assumptions hold, the parameters may be estimated using least squares. (Some estimation problems do arise from the dependent variables also being used as if it were an independent variable. They are discussed in §8.3.) Let us suppose that using the above model we derived the equation:

$$Y_t = 0.7 + 1.4X_t + 0.3Y_{t-1}.$$

In this equation it is possible to test the hypothesis $\lambda = 0$ using the t test, and we will suppose the λ is significant (at the 5 per cent level). From the above estimates we may find $\hat{\beta}_0$ and $\hat{\lambda}$, estimates of the parameters in the original model by solving:

$$\hat{\beta}_0(1 - \hat{\lambda}) = 0.7 \text{ and } \hat{\lambda} = 0.3,$$

implying that:

$$\hat{\beta}_0 = 1,$$

which we may combine with our knowledge that:

$$\hat{\beta}_1 = 1.4;$$

and so in this way use the coefficients in the estimated equation to calculate the structural parameters that reflect the assumed causality. From our estimate that the effect of advertising expenditure decays at a rate of 70 per cent we can calculate the effect of a unit increase in advertising expenditure on demand. The total effect of the unit increase is the sum of its effect in the current period β_1, its effect in the next period, $\lambda\beta_1$, its effect two periods ahead $\lambda^2\beta_1$, etc.,

$$= \beta_1 + \lambda\beta_1 + \lambda^2\beta_1 + \cdots\dagger$$
$$= \beta_1/(1 - \lambda)$$
$$= 1.4/(1 - 0.3)$$
$$= 2,$$

a long-term cumulative effect of 2 compared with its short-term effect of 1.4. Using the so-called Koyck model we have been able to estimate the model's parameters as well as the long- and short-term effect of changes in advertising expenditure.

The Koyck model is one of a number of ways of simplifying the general distributed lag model. We have shown its use with regard to the cumulative effect of advertising, an example we will discuss in much more detail in Chapter 8. As we did in the last two sections, we have developed a further generalization of the standard multiple regression model which significantly enhances our ability to model such situations as advertising effectiveness realistically.

§6.6 Validity of the multiple regression model

In §5.3.4 we showed that a visual examination of the regression residuals was a useful diagnostic tool in assessing whether or not the basic assumptions of regression hold. The same methods work equally well in the case of multiple regression. In the first part of this section we will extend our discussion of dependence in the error term to describe a numerical test of this crucial regression assumption:

(*a*) The errors are independent of each other.

In the second part we discuss an assumption peculiar to multiple regression:

† Recall that the sum of the geometric progression: $a + ar + ar^2 + \cdots = a/(1 - r)$.

(b) The explanatory independent variables are not linearly related to each other.

In other words this second assumption states that it should not be possible for any one of the independent variables to be 'explained' by a linear combination of some or all of the other independent variables.

6.6.1 Correlation in the error term (autocorrelation)

Autocorrelation (or serial correlation) in the error term is a term used to describe a situation in which the error made at one point in time gives information about the error made at a subsequent point in time. Autocorrelation is important in forecasting because of its frequent occurrence, and it has two significant effects. In a situation of autocorrelation:

1. The variance of the estimated parameters increases. This implies the estimated regression line is likely to differ considerably from the true line.
2. The variance of the error term is seriously underestimated when least squares is used to estimate the parameters in the model.

These two statements taken together suggest that not only is the estimated line less accurate than is indicated by the standard error estimates of the parameters calculated in the usual way, but also that the error variance is also underestimated, giving a spurious impression of the accuracy of the parameter estimates, and the fit of the model.

Testing autocorrelation. How does one recognize autocorrelation? How to deal with it? Both questions are easier asked than answered and the research literature is extensive and still increasing. To understand the suggested test and the changes necessary to the basic linear model let us consider the two variable model:

$$Y_t = \beta_0 + \beta_1 X_t + e_t,$$

where it is assumed that e_t is related to e_{t-1} (the error at time $t - 1$) by the equation:

$$e_t = \rho e_{t-1} + v_t, |\rho| < 1.$$

If we assume that v_t is well behaved, in particular it is not autocorrelated, we have above a simple example of autocorrelation. We call ρ (rho) the first-order autocorrelation coefficient. When $\rho = 0$ the errors are independent of each other and consequently we may identify autocorrelation through a test of the hypothesis $\rho = 0$. The test we describe is named after its originators Durbin and Watson. It is based on the test statistic:

$$d = \frac{\sum_{t=2}^{n} (\hat{e}_t - \hat{e}_{t-1})^2}{\sum_{t=1}^{n} \hat{e}_t^2},$$

where $\hat{e}_t = Y_t - \hat{Y}_t$. It can be shown that $0 < d < 4$, and when $\rho = 0$, d is close to 2. If

125

the errors are positively correlated d will tend to be small, and if negative, d is large (and greater than 2). The testing procedure has the usual four components:

1. We specify the null hypothesis, $\rho = 0$;
2. We specify an alternative, $\rho \neq 0$ (though it could equally well be a one-sided alternative);
3. The significance level is fixed; and
4. The test statistic d is computed.

From these four steps a critical region is defined.

Unlike previous tests of hypothesis that we have discussed, the critical region in which the null hypothesis is rejected and the acceptance region, in which it is accepted do not include all possible values of d. There are two regions of indeterminancy, as is illustrated in Table 6.6. For a given significance level (and given n, and p, p being the number of parameters in the model) two critical values are obtained from tables given in, for example, Kane, 1969; Johnston, 1972 (Kane discusses this in more depth than this book but remains as readable as possible in pp. 357–73). The lower value we designate as d_L, and d_U is the higher.

Table 6.6

The Durbin–Watson test

Value of d	0		d_L	d_U	2	$(4-d_U)$	$(4-d_L)$	4
D e c i s i o n	Reject the null hypothesis in favour of the alternative of positive autocorrelation ie accept $\rho > 0$		Neither accept nor reject the null hypothesis	Accept the null hypothesis ie accept $\rho = 0$		Neither accept nor reject the null hypothesis	Reject the null hypothesis in favour of the alternative of negative autocorrelation ie accept $\rho < 0$	

If $d < d_L$, as the above table shows, the null hypothesis is rejected in favour of the alternative of positive autocorrelation ($\rho > 0$) while if $d_L < d < d_U$ the test is indeterminate. A similar procedure exists for $d > 2$ except that the alternative hypothesis is of negative autocorrelation ($\rho < 0$). Typically, the Durbin–Watson statistic is automatically printed in most computer programs and from the test just described we are able to decide whether or not there is autocorrelation in the error term.

With luck we will be able to go on to the interpretation of our regression results, confident that there is no autocorrelation in the error term. However, if we accept the hypothesis of autocorrelation, because of its important effects on the parameter estimates, we have to develop methods for repairing the least squares assumptions.

Repairing an autocorrelated model. (Of the remainder of this section, 6.6.1, only the summary should be read the first time through.) Suppose there is evidence of autocorrelation in the error term; what approaches may be tried to alleviate the problem? As we pointed out earlier the assumption is important in the interpretation of the forecasting model. However, evidence that the errors are autocorrelated does not necessarily mean that the model is well specified and the error structure is time dependent. As we showed in our discussion of beer sales in relation to the use of dummy variable, autocorrelation is as often evidence of the omission of an important independent variable from the model. Only when the analyst believes that every relevant measurable variable has been included should he accept the need to investigate the error structure of the model.

The simplest procedure adopted in the event of positive autocorrelation is to work with first differences, the corresponding model being:

$$Y_t - Y_{t-1} = \beta_0 + \beta_1(X_t - X_{t-1}) + v_t$$

where v_t is the random error variable obeying the usual assumptions of independence, constant variance etc. More generally, if ρ is the first order autocorrelation coefficient the analyst works with the model:†

$$Y_t - \rho Y_{t-1} = \beta_0(1 - \rho) + \beta_1(X_t - \rho X_{t-1}) + v_t,$$

v_t obeying the usual error assumptions.† If ρ were known the parameters β_0 and β_1 (as well as the standard error of v_t) could be calculated. Unfortunately ρ is unknown and has to be estimated from the data. The simplest method of estimation which we use later in an example is to approximate ρ using the formula:

$$\hat{\rho} = 1 - d/2,$$

where d is the Durbin–Watson statistic readily available from the printout of most multiple regression computer packages. With this estimated value of $\hat{\rho}$ we may now transform the basic variables X and Y to $X_t^* = X_t - \hat{\rho}X_{t-1}$ and $Y_t^* = Y_t - \hat{\rho}Y_{t-1}$.

The last stage of the analysis is to estimate the parameters in the model:

$$Y_t^* = \alpha_0 + \alpha_1 X_t^* + v_t.$$

We see in comparison with the previous regression equation that:

$$\hat{\alpha}_0 = \hat{\beta}_0(1 - \hat{\rho}) \text{ and } \hat{\alpha}_1 = \hat{\beta}_1.$$

† The basic model on which this is based is:
$$Y_t = \beta_0 + \beta_1 X_t + e_t$$
with
$$e_t = \rho e_{t-1} + v_t.$$
Multiplying the corresponding formula for Y_{t-1} by ρ and subtracting this new equation from Y_t we get:
$$Y_t - \rho Y_{t-1} = \beta_0 + \beta_1 X_t + e_t - \rho(\beta_0 + \beta_1 X_{t-1} + e_{t-1})$$
$$= \beta_0(1 - \rho) + \beta_1(X_t - \rho X_{t-1}) + (e_t - \rho e_{t-1})$$
but $e_t - \rho e_{t-1} = v_t$, and we have derived a model suitable for estimation.

We have therefore succeeded in calculating the parameter estimates, $\hat{\beta}_0$, $\hat{\beta}_1$, and $\hat{\rho}$ in the original regression model:

$$Y_t = \beta_0 + \beta_1 X_t + e_t$$

and

$$e_t = \rho e_{t-1} + v_t.$$

A forecast. (Omit on first reading.) To obtain a forecast from this autoregressive model at time (t + 1) we substitute the predicted value of X, X_{t+1} to obtain:

$$\hat{Y}_{t+1} = \hat{\beta}_0 + \hat{\beta}_1 X_{t+1} + \hat{e}_{t+1}$$

where $\hat{e}_{t+1}$ is a forecast of the error at time (t + 1). Normally of course − because the mean of the error is zero and it is independent of earlier errors − the error at (t + 1) is expected to be zero. Here though, because of the autocorrelation we may utilize our knowledge of the error at t to obtain a forecast of the error at (t + 1):

$$\hat{e}_{t+1} = \hat{\rho} e_t.$$

Combining the two equations we obtain the final forecast:

$$\hat{Y}_{t+1} = \hat{\beta}_0 + \hat{\beta}_1 X_{t+1} + \hat{\rho} e_t.$$

Durbin's method. (Omit on first reading.) A better method of estimating the parameters in the basic autocorrelated regression model:

$$Y_t = \beta_0 + \beta_1 X_t + e_t$$

and

$$e_t = \rho e_{t-1} + v_t$$

is to first use least squares to estimate the parameters in the model:

$$Y_t = \alpha + \rho Y_{t-1} + \alpha_1 X_t + \alpha_2 X_{t-1} + v_t,$$

from which we derive an estimate $\hat{\rho}$ of ρ. We may then compute the new variables $Y_t^* = Y_t - \hat{\rho} Y_{t-1}$, $X_t^* = X_t - \hat{\rho} X_{t-1}$, and again use least squares to estimate:

$$Y_t^* = \beta_0(1 - \hat{\rho}) + \beta_1 X_t^* + v_t.$$

From this latter equation we obtain estimates of β_0 and β_1, and from the first stage of the procedure, an estimate of ρ.

To find a forecast we again use the formula:

$$\hat{Y}_{t+1} = \hat{\beta}_0 + \hat{\beta}_1 X_{t+1} + \hat{\rho} e_t.$$

If the error variance of v_t is σ^2, the variance of e_t is $\sigma^2/(1 - \rho^2)$.

Summary. Autocorrelation is important and unfortunately the subject is also technically difficult. Generally an unsatisfactory Durbin−Watson statistic is a sign that a significant independent variable is missing from the regression model. If the analyst is unable to find that variable he is forced to make some attempt to remove the autocorrelation. We discussed two appropriate methods and showed how the parameter estimates may be used to produce a forecast. Like any powerful technique however, basic regression methods cannot be applied automatically without running substantial risks of mis-application and autocorrelation is a subject which demands that the analyst is careful and creative in his use of the standard regression models. In this section we have discussed some of the many ideas that have been proposed to deal with this difficult problem.

6.6.2 Multicollinearity

Multicollinearity is a problem both as important and as widespread as autocorrelation. It arises when the independent variables are linearly related among themselves. To explain this definition, let us first consider a simplified example where the dependent variable Y is related to two independent variables X_1 and X_2 through the equation:

$$Y = X_1 + X_2 + (error).$$

For the moment we will neglect the error term. Suppose that by chance the analyst had collected his observations in such a way that $X_1 = 2X_2$. Using these observations he could well have estimated the above relationship as $Y = 3X_1/2$ or $Y = 3X_2$: all these models are equally good at explaining Y's variation. So long as the analyst only intended to predict Y for further observations in which the relationship between the two independent variables, $X_1 = 2X_2$ still held, his predictions would be correct which-ever of the three models he selected. Nevertheless, with multicollinearity present in the data the coefficients in the estimated model cannot be interpreted. Because of the relationship between X_1 and X_2, the analyst is unable to identify the correct forecasting model. Moreover, as soon as the relationship between X_1 and X_2 fails, a prediction based on either of the latter two models is wrong.

Another way of thinking about the problem is to visualize the observations. With two independent variables they generally lie in a plane. However, when X_1 is linearly related to X_2 all values of X_1 and X_2 fall on a line; and therefore lie in one dimension rather than two. This loss of a dimension in the observed values of the independent variable means that we cannot properly identify the relationship between Y and the independent variables for we only know how Y varies along the line $X_1 = 2X_2$ and not in the remainder of the plane. It is almost as bad if the two variables X_1 and X_2 are only highly correlated as distinct from being perfectly collinear. The problem described above still remains. It is difficult if not impossible to estimate the parameters of the model or even to decide which of the independent variables should be included in the regression model.

Let us now generalize our discussion of multicollinearity to the case where there are p independent variables. If any one of them can be written as a linear sum of the others then the variables are said to be collinear and the estimation of a unique regres-sion model is impossible. When the independent variables are only close to collinear the estimates of the parameters in the multiple regression equation become very imprecise. That is, specific estimates are likely to be extremely inaccurate. Because the significance of a coefficient depends on its variance, a large variance may well lead to a variable being omitted while in fact it is extremely important in explaining the variation of Y, but the particular (collinear) observations used in the analysis have disguised this.

The problem of multicollinearity in time series studies is particularly acute since many of the explanatory variables will tend to increase with time, so that it becomes impossible to determine whether, for example, income growth or a time trend is causing an increase in the demand for air travel, discussed earlier. In forecasting, if an important variable is omitted because it varies linearly with other explanatory variables in the model, but later, during the period of time for which the forecast is being made, changes its behaviour and moves independently of those variables, the forecast is likely to be highly inaccurate. Air travel again offers an example, for if income were omitted from the model it would then forecast an increase in air traffic whether or not the economy continued to grow; not a desirable characteristic of a demand model in this particular market.

A further consequence of multicollinearity is that the estimates of the coefficients become very unstable, and the addition of extra observations may well alter them considerably. Therefore if the relationship was estimated using two different sets of data the analyst might well obtain two substantially different sets of parameter estimates, and as we argued earlier, it is therefore impossible to interpret the coefficients or decide on their relative importance.

As with autocorrelation there are two questions to be asked. How to recognize multicollinearity when it exists, and secondly, what to do about it? Multicollinearity in the data can be checked by two quite simple procedures. Quite often the computer printout contains the entry 'determinant value'. If this is close to zero then it is likely that the input variables are collinear. The second method is discussed later in §6.7.2. More sensitive tests for multicollinearity are developed further by Johnston (1972), while Hamilton (1972) gives an illustration of how one procedure for checking multicollinearity is performed. Although with multicollinearity present in the data it is common practice to drop one of the input variables, we have already illustrated the dangers inherent in this approach in the air traffic example. Two possible methods may be more helpful. The first is obvious and more easily said than done.

1. Collect more data. It is sometimes possible to change the level of aggregation of the analysis. Instead of using average data, for income (say), the income parameter can be estimated using information gathered from individuals in the population. As a second example, if the aim of the forecaster is to predict air travel in Europe, it may be possible to use data from individual countries, hopefully destroying any multicollinearity that may exist between income and the time trend.
2. Base the model on variables which behave independently of each other. This might well mean a search for new explanatory variables, which may be based on transformations of the original variables. The simplest approach is to work with first differences as shown on p. 127. This will also often minimize the autocorrelation in the error term. It is of course important that the transformed equation conforms to the usual assumptions. A more difficult alternative (see a discussion on Factor

Analysis in Johnston (1972)) is to argue that there is an underlying structure of separate, 'basic factors' in the independent variable which explains the interrelationships (and therefore the multicollinearity). The model should therefore be constructed using these non-collinear factors.

6.6.3 Summary

In developing the multiple regression model a number of assumptions are made. Often they will be violated, and the forecaster needs to decide whether or not this matters, and if so how to alter the model to take this into account.

Both multicollinearity and autocorrelation are dangerous to the forecaster because they make the interpretation of the regression model difficult if not impossible. More important, it is likely that the forecasts produced by models in which either of these two assumptions fail will be grossly inaccurate.

In discussing the basic regression assumptions we pointed out that they could be classified into the structural and the technical. While multicollinearity and autocorrelation are technical in nature, producing for example parameter estimates with higher variances than if the standard regression model were valid, their presence is symptomatic of a structural failure at the level of model construction. Without a satisfactory solution to both problems we are even unsure of our basic model as well as the parameter estimates.

§ 6.7 The best regression equation

6.7.1 General principles

In the last few sections we have developed methods for modelling quite complicated situations. To deal with the failure of some of the basic regression assumptions it was necessary to transform the variables, perhaps by taking first differences rather than using the raw data. Sometimes the model contained lagged and dummy variables. It is easy to see that in an exploratory study where there is little guide as to the variables which we might on *a priori* grounds expect to influence Y, the number of original independent variables in the equation is likely to be large. Ten is not an exceptional number and yet if the analyst considered all the possible linear regression equations based on those variables he would have to examine 1,023 equations. Since each of the variables can be transformed and combined with any of the others there is an infinity of equations to be considered.

It is important to recognize why an examination of the many plausible alternative models is desirable. The analyst has only a limited number of observations from which to decide (and estimate) the forecasting model he wishes to use. While previous theoretical and empirical work will help him in ruling out many possibilities there are still as many left to consider, each one of which could well be the 'best' forecasting model. His only approach to selection can be to find a parsimonious method for examining as many of these models as cost allows. The results of the analyst's examination will not be definitive. Instead, he will be left with a number of models, some of which contain a lot of explanatory variables, some only a few. They will fit the data equally well and be equally well-specified in their ability to comply with the regression assumptions. Some considerations argue for accepting a model which includes many of the independent variables while some argue against such a complicated model.

The following criteria are suggested as reasons for selecting as simple a model as is consistent with earlier accepted theory as well as the new observations.

1. Ease of interpretation. The forecast user usually demands a plausible and comprehensible model. (We should perhaps add that in our experience plausibility occasionally works in the opposite direction in that a variable statistically and theoretically non-significant may have to be included in the model to satisfy the user of the model's validity.) A model which includes a large number of explanatory variables bearing a complicated functional relationship to Y is hard to interpret. Similarly the parameter estimates should also have an interpretation in the system being modelled. Because multicollinearity (a condition which is more likely as more explanatory variables are included in the model) makes the estimates unreliable and very sensitive to changes in the data base, the model and its parameters are difficult to interpret. Consequently the model should be built with as few explanatory variables as possible, each of which measures a separate phenomenon (subject of course to the model complying with the regression assumptions).

2. Significance of the coefficients. The coefficient estimates in the chosen model should be statistically significant. However, because each variable is included in the model only if there are *a priori* grounds for believing it to be important. (We use 'important variable' to mean that it forms part of the causal linkages between the independent and dependent variables) this rule should not be rigidly applied. On the other hand because a variable is known to be important does *not* mean it should necessarily be included in the regression equation. It may well be that an important variable is not significant in the model because of its high correlation with other variables in the equation which together do a slightly better job of explaining Y's variation. (We should be confident, if possible, that the observed correlation between the 'important' variable and the other independent variables in the model is not spurious.)

3. Cost of data collection and model maintenance. It is costly on staff and computing time to constantly monitor the performance of a forecasting model to make sure it remains valid, and to update and store the necessary data from which the model is constructed. This cost increases as a function of model complexity.

4. Degrees of freedom. With the addition of more variables (and parameters) to the model the degrees of freedom available within a given set of data are reduced, thereby making the usual tests of the model's validity less reliable, e.g. the t- and F-tests. Forecasting accuracy as measured by the standard error of estimate is also dependent on the degrees of freedom being large.

On the other hand there is an important argument in favour of including all *a priori* relevant variables in the model.

5. *Danger of omitting an important variable.* If an important variable is dropped from a regression model the remaining coefficient estimates are biased and have a high variance. The variable may be dropped either because the theoretical model was ill thought-out or because the estimate of the variable's coefficient was not significant. (Usually a low significance level (say 10 per cent) is chosen and this takes partial account of this possibility.) Consequently omitting an important variable leads to the possibility of omitting further important variables from the equation. There is also, of course, a drop in forecasting accuracy.

Dropping an important variable from the equation because of the non-significance of its coefficient can easily happen just because it stayed comparatively constant in the data used for the model's construction. A recent example of this is the price of fuel oil. Prior to the oil crisis of 1973/74, price was believed to be unimportant as a short-term determinant of demand and would not have been included in a forecasting model. With the large increase in prices in late 1973 we saw that demand responded immediately. *A priori* a variable may be thought to be important in explaining the variation in Y. From the data collected, however (as in the above example prior to 1973) it may happen that its coefficient is non-significant. Before that variable can reasonably be dropped from the model the analyst has to assure himself that the variable in question is unlikely to be important in the time period in which the model is expected to be valid.

In summary there are arguments both in favour and against the inclusion of a large number of theoretically relevant variables in a regression model. Econometricians would generally agree that data and degrees of freedom permitting, one should err on the side of including variables in the model rather than excluding them.

6.7.2 Examination of all possible models

To understand the problem of selecting a regression model further, it is helpful to consider an example. Let us suppose that we need only consider four variables in the construction of a particular regression model, and to further simplify the problem, suppose we restrict ourselves to linear models in these variables. The possible models to be examined are of the form:

$$Y = \beta_0 + \beta_1 Z_1 + \beta_2 Z_2 + \beta_3 Z_3 + \beta_4 Z_4 + e,$$

with some of the coefficients perhaps zero.

We will use four particular variables X_1, X_5, X_7, and X_8 to correspond to the variables Z_1, Z_2. Z_3 and Z_4 in the above equation. They are taken from the example given in the next section, and their observed values are listed in Appendix 3 (p. 268) together with the corresponding values of the dependent variable Y.

Using the basic summary statistics. In this section we will concentrate on developing some *ad hoc* procedures for selecting a regression model from the $2^4 - 1 = 15$ possible linear models. Let us assume, on theoretical grounds, that each of the four explanatory variables is related to the dependent variable and we also have no reason to believe that any one of them should *not* be omitted. To decide between the various plausible models the analyst is often confronted with a vast number of equations to compare. Fortunately with only fifteen alternatives, comparison of each forecasting equation with every alternative is easily practicable. The following procedure is suggested:

1. Classify all fifteen equations into four categories defined as follows:
   (*a*) includes all equations using just one independent variable;
   (*b*) includes all equations with two independent variables;
   (*c*) includes all equations with three variables;
   (*d*) contains the equation using all four variables.

2. Rank the equations within each set by their respective values of R^2. Alternative criteria are sometimes used in computer packages. Because R^2 is always increased by the addition of a new variable, it may be worthwhile to correct its value to take into account the one degree of freedom that has been lost by including this extra term. If there are p variables in the equation the corrected R^2 is defined as $\bar{R}^2 = R^2 - p(1 - R^2)/(n - p - 1)$.

3. Select those equations in each set with high values of R^2.

4. Compare the selected equations. Using the variables shown above we obtain Table 6.7.

Table 6.7
Various regression equations: summary statistics. The number of observations, n = 20.

Set	Selected variables	R^2	Standard error	Durbin– Watson
a	X_1	0.518	2.42	1.71
	X_7	0.507	2.45	1.21
b	X_1, X_7	0.679	2.03	1.98
	X_5, X_7	0.697	1.97	2.03
	X_7, X_8	0.687	2.01	0.94
c	X_1, X_7, X_8	0.811	1.60	1.42
	X_5, X_7, X_8	0.942	0.887	1.69
d	X_1, X_5, X_7, X_8	0.945	0.891	1.69

Note that although X_1 forms the 'best' single variable equation, with X_7 a close alternative, the equation with highest R^2 in category *b* does not include X_1. This phenomenon re-occurs when we consider category *c* with the equation $\hat{Y} = f(X_5, X_7, X_8)$ explaining some 13 per cent more of the variation in Y than either of the alternatives including X_1. The intuitive explanation is that when X_7 and X_8 together are included in the equation, X_5 explains much more of the residual variation in Y than X_1 does. X_1 and 'X_7, X_8' overlap in explaining the same part of the variation in Y.

The addition of X_1 to the above forecasting equation increases R^2 only slightly (and

$\bar{R}^2$ would show a decrease). This is because X_1 is close to being collinear with X_5, X_7 and X_8, although the determinant value (of 0.44) suggests that multicollinearity is not a substantial problem here. This is further supported by an examination of the parameter estimates and their estimated errors calculated both with X_1 and without X_1 in the equation. The standard errors increase (showing some degree of multicollinearity) but not substantially enough to affect either the parameter estimates or their 'significance' as we can see from the two sets of parameter estimates given below and in the printout in Appendix 3. Finally if we now turn to examine the standard error of estimate we find that the equation including only X_5, X_7 and X_8 has the lowest standard error.

However, before a conclusion can be reached, it is necessary to examine the proposed equation in the light of the points listed in §6.7.1 to check the internal validity of the equation. The assumptions made about the error term have to be verified and the Durbin–Watson test applied to investigate serial correlation. The calculated Durbin–Watson statistic for each regression is shown in Table 6.7. With three explanatory variables in the equation and a significance level of 10 per cent (a two-tail test) the critical d values are: $d_L = 1.00$ and $d_U = 1.68$ while with four variables in the equation $d_L = 0.90$ and $d_U = 1.83$. Consequently with the three-variable model we can reject the hypothesis of autocorrelation while the Durbin–Watson statistic falls in the indeterminate region for the four-variable case. Thus we cannot discriminate between the two models from the evidence of the Durbin–Watson statistic.

We see that the final decision on the inclusion of X_1 has therefore to be based on theoretical grounds. We hypothesized in the introduction to the example that no single variable was thought to be essential to the theoretical structure of the model. The addition of X_1 brings about only a small increase in R^2 and produces an increase in the standard error. We may drop it from the equation with one last proviso; the stability of the estimated regression coefficients is important and if the discarding of a variable substantially alters these coefficients then the variable cannot be superfluous for it is having a significant effect on the dependent variable which has now to be explained by only those variables left in the equation (Rao and Miller, 1971, pp. 29–43 usefully expand these ideas). Therefore with X_1 excluded:

$$\hat{\beta}_1 = 0; \quad \hat{\beta}_2 = 3.424; \quad \hat{\beta}_3 = 0.050; \quad \hat{\beta}_4 = 0.810;$$

but with it included:

$$\hat{\beta}_1 = 0.047; \quad \hat{\beta}_2 = 3.135; \quad \hat{\beta}_3 = 0.047; \quad \hat{\beta}_4 = 0.781.$$

The parameters are seen to change only slightly and therefore on the basis of the measures so far considered we will use the equation:

$$Y = -77.218 + 3.424X_5 + 0.050X_7 + 0.810X_8$$

for forecasting.

The F test. The F test introduced in Chapter 5 may be extended to test whether the addition of one or more variables to the model significantly improves the model's explanatory power. This is done by decomposing the variation of Y into three components:

1. That explained by the 'basic' multiple regression model using the variables $X_1, \ldots X_k$.
2. That due to the addition of variables $X_{k+1} \ldots X_p$.
3. The residual variation that is left unexplained.

Thus:

$$\left\{ \text{Variation in Y} \right\} = \left\{ \begin{array}{l} \text{Variation due} \\ \text{to } X_1, \ldots X_k \end{array} \right\} + \left\{ \begin{array}{l} \text{Additional variation} \\ \text{due to } X_{k+1}, \ldots X_p \\ \text{given } X_1 \ldots X_k \text{ are} \\ \text{in model.} \end{array} \right\} + \left\{ \begin{array}{l} \text{Residual} \\ \text{variation} \end{array} \right\}$$

From this decomposition we generalize our earlier definition of the F statistic to:

$$F = \frac{\text{mean additional variation explained by adding } X_{k+1} \ldots X_p}{\text{Residual variation}}$$

where there are $(p - k)$ degrees of freedom in the numerator and $(n - p - 1)$ in the denominator.

We may therefore test the effect of adding a group of variables to our basic forecasting model.† Two special cases are particularly important for analysing the regression equation:

1. When $k = p - 1$, this is equivalent to testing the addition of the pth variable to the model with null hypothesis that $\beta_p = 0$. We have already discussed this test in §6.2 when we used the t-statistic in the same situation. As before F and t are related through the formula $F = t^2$ and both are formally equivalent. The F test described here is often called 'partial' or 'sequential' to distinguish it from the test's other uses.
2. When $k = 0$, we are testing whether the model explains any more of Y's variation than would be explained by the chance fluctuations of the X's and Y's with no linear relationship between them. It is an overall test of the model's explanatory power. This is formally equivalent to testing the null hypothesis $\beta_1 = \beta_2 = \cdots = \beta_p = 0$ against the alternative that at least one of the parameters is non-zero. If all the parameters are accepted as zero we reject the model as having no explanatory power at all.

The overall F statistic may also be used as a summary of how well the total model fits the data, and as we shall see in the next section the partial F test is used repeatedly in testing whether a variable should be included in an existing model.

Turning points. A turning point in a time series is a time when the series changes direction, from increasing to decreasing or vice versa. Figure 6.7 shows precisely what

† In fact the same basic idea may be used to test complex hypotheses, e.g. in the model $Y = \beta_0 + \beta_1 X_1 + \beta_2 X_2$ we may test $\beta_1 = \beta_2$.

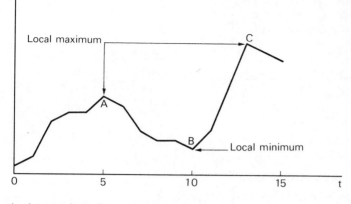

Fig. 6.7 Turning points

is meant by the definition. Points A and C are called local maxima and point B is a local minimum; 'Local' because it is only in a short time period about the point that the point is a maximum or minimum. In the diagram, C is *the* maximum while *the* minimum value of Y_t is at time 0. Note that if the dependent variable were a percentage change or a first difference a turning point in the *level* variable Y_t is identified by a change of sign in the change variable. (If the change variable C changes sign at t, C_t is positive (say) while C_{t-1} is negative. That is, $Y_t - Y_{t-1} > 0$ while $Y_{t-1} - Y_{t-2} < 0$ and consequently Y_{t-1} is a minimum.)

Turning points are important because they often require substantial changes of plan to protect the individual or organization from their effects. A company geared to meet the needs of an expanding market is not well equipped to shield itself in a recession. Of equal seriousness, is the prediction of a turning point, when in fact, the predicted event does not occur. Forecasting models therefore can be compared on their ability to predict turning points as well as the common criteria of the last sections.

Summary. In summary, when all possible regression equations are analysed simple rules of thumb, like 'use the equation with maximum R^2', are inadequate for selecting the most suitable forecasting equation. Error specification, significance, standard error, and turning point forecasts have to be considered as well as the implication for the underlying theory that acceptance of a particular model might have. We have suggested a simple procedure for analysing the many possible alternative models. As we pointed out earlier such a procedure is impractical for large data sets, wasteful as it is of both the analyst's and the computer's time. In the next section, 6.7.3, we describe a practical alternative, step-wise regression.

6.7.3 Step-wise regression
The aim of the step-wise regression computing procedure is to select a suitably specified regression equation as economically as possible. We may illustrate the procedure through the following flow chart (Fig. 6.8) showing the basic steps, which we will

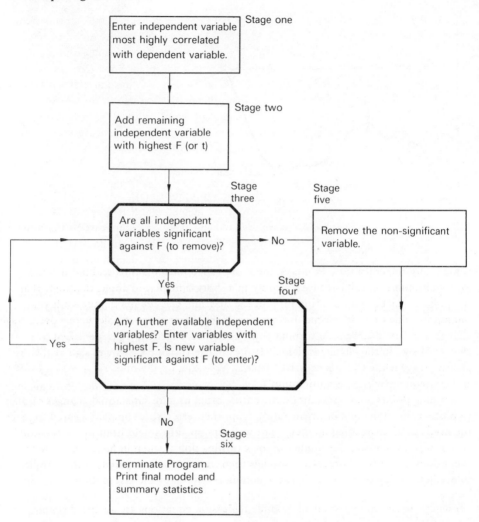

Fig. 6.8 Step-wise regression flow chart

discuss in relation to the example printed out in full in Appendix 3 (p. 268) and discussed later in §6.8.

At the first stage the independent variable most highly correlated with the dependent variable is selected as the 'best' one-variable model and the summary statistics printed.† In the example this is X_1. Next, all remaining variables are examined for inclusion in the 'best' two-variable model that *includes* X_1. The variable with highest F (or t) value is then included in the step-wise model,‡ and this

† The variable most highly correlated with Y also has the largest F (or t) statistic.
‡ An equivalent criterion is to select the variable with highest *partial correlation* coefficient. The partial correlation between X and Y, when a further set of factors Z may affect the relationship, is a measure of how X and Y covary when Z is held constant.

is seen from Appendix 3 to be X_7. The procedure next tests the variables in the model for significance.† Both X_1 and X_7 remain significant and we therefore go on to stage 4.

At the fourth stage the remaining independent variables are examined and again the one with highest F is chosen for inclusion. Before it is accepted, however, its F value is examined for significance.‡ X_5 is chosen in our example and it has a significant F. The program next returns to stage 3 and examines all variables for significance. With X_5 joining X_1, X_7 and X_8 in the four-variable model the significance of X_1 falls and it is removed at step 5, the results of course being printed. The process is completed when there are no independent variables remaining to be considered which have an F value (to enter) that is significant. In the example X_4 joins X_5, X_7 and X_8 in the final model, $Y = f(X_4, X_5, X_7, X_8)$.

The procedure is not guaranteed to find the optimum equation containing a given number of variables, even if by optimum we only mean 'highest R^2', because all possible equations have not been considered. Accordingly, in complicated situations the early selections made by the procedure can possibly mislead the analyst. This danger is easily avoided by going through the procedure twice using two different sets of F levels. The effect of a high F (to enter) is to scan the variables stringently before they are included in the regression equation. A high F (to remove) likewise will easily eliminate a variable as other variables are brought into the equation which explain that same part of Y's variation. High F values therefore will produce an equation including only a small number of variables. Low values obviously have the reverse effect and with both levels set at zero an equation including all the variables will necessarily result (we are assuming multicollinearity is not a problem).

To ensure finding a usable forecasting equation the analyst should therefore make two computer runs, one with high F values (equivalent to a significance level of 5 or 10 per cent) and the second, with low F values. By comparing the two results on such dimensions as the stability of the coefficients, R^2, and the standard error, the analyst will gain some considerable understanding of the variables to include in the final equation. Finally, most step-wise regression programs allow the user the option of specifying whether certain variables should be included (or excluded) from the final equation. The reason for such a facility is as we have stressed before, that significance is not the same as importance. The selection of those variables to appear in the final model remains an art which cannot be compressed into any automatic procedure.

§ 6.8 The best regression equation — an example

Typically, many forecasting studies using econometric models consider a large number of variables in the attempt to produce a workable forecasting equation. In this section we consider the step-by-step development of such a model which we hope is flexible enough to act as a guide in many different situations.

---

† When the calculations are computerized instead of fixing a significance level the analyst fixes an F *value* which we call F (to remove); we take it to be 4 in our example. If F(observed) < F(to remove), that particular variable is dropped from the equation.
‡ This value is called F (to enter). As with the F (to remove) value set at the previous step, it is usually fixed by the analyst. Here again we take it to be 4.

The problem

Let us consider the following hypothetical example of an attempt to forecast the *per capita* sales of a durable consumer product. On *a priori* grounds a large number of variables qualify for possible inclusion in a sales forecasting model and in Chapter 8 we go on to consider these variables in more detail. Here, for the sake of a manageable exposition we will use only a limited number of variables, all of which may plausibly be said to influence industry sales.

One difficulty in establishing a causal structure in sales forecasting models is that while there may be general agreement about the variables to be included this does not extend to agreement about the form in which they are to be measured. An *ad hoc* procedure for choosing between two alternative measures of the same influence is to calculate the correlations between Y and each alternative measure and to include the one with the higher correlation. A better procedure when the degrees of freedom are sufficiently large is to include all the different measures in the preliminary model, allowing weak significance tests to discriminate between them. Those variables remaining after this weak screening test are then included in the final stage of the analysis which consists of a careful consideration of a variety of linear and non-linear equations.

Suppose that in our hypothetical example the following much shortened list of variables are accepted as suitable for inclusion in the last part of the analysis:

X—1: Index of time in years, 1955 = 1.0.

X—2: An index of real *per capita* consumer expenditure on all durables, starting with a value of 100 in 1955. The price deflator used is the consumer price index. (For some remarks on UK price indices see, e.g., Morrell, 1973, pp. 168—74. For some general discussions, see Mendenhall and Reinmuth, 1974, and Fox, 1968.)

X—3: X_2, lagged one period.

X—4: Average unit price/(Price index of consumer durables).

X—5: Proportionate change† in real disposable *per capita* income, measured by $(Y_t - Y_{t-1})/\frac{1}{2}(Y_t + Y_{t-1})$, Y_t being *per capita* income.

X—6: Availability of credit, measured as the percentage of the purchase price required to be paid back in the first year.

X—7: Three-period moving average of advertising expenditure, measured in pence *per capita* * 100, the amount being deflated by an advertising price index.

X—8: Index of new household formations, 1956 = 100.0.

X—9: Sales of the durable goods, measured in units sold *per capita* * 100. (In the models given below the dependent variable X—9 is designated Q to distinguish it from the independent variables.)

The product under consideration might be a household consumer durable in the same category as beds, kitchen equipment and so on. On *a priori* grounds we would expect sales for this class of goods to arise from two sources — new sales, which will broadly be a function of new household formations, and replacement sales where an existing item of equipment is discarded as old or obsolete. We expect both classes of

† It is more usual to measure proportionate change by: $(Y_t - Y_{t-1})/Y_{t-1}$.

sales to be influenced by changes in the real price of the product, i.e. relative to similar products (X—4) as well as the ability of consumers to make the purchase (X—2), (X—3), (X—5), reflected in income changes and the availability of credit (X—6). The increased likelihood that, all other factors being equal, a new household would tend to generate a higher level of purchase on this type of durable is represented by including new household formations (X—8) as a variable. Finally, advertising (X—7) is included since it may either increase the overall rate of purchase or else shift the purchases that are made from one period to another.

The independent variables (excluding time) formed a causal model linking the potential market for the consumer durable and the total money available for spending on durables to the *per capita* industry sales. An examination of the observations on these variables, however, shows that many of them contain a trend component. To avoid the type of spuriously high correlation that may occur when both dependent and independent variables move with time, time was included explicitly and therefore each coefficient in the model

$$Q_t = \beta_0 + \sum_{i=1}^{8} \beta_i X_{it} + e_t$$

represents the responsiveness of demand to a change in the corresponding variable, all other variables, including time being kept constant. (*Notes:* 1. To make a difficult equation a little easier to read, the subscripts X_{it} are used rather than the more easily printed computer notation $(X-1)_t$; 2. Reasons for including time in the forecasting model are given in §8.3.1. Rao and Miller, 1971, pp. 99—104 discuss the implications for the interpretation of the regression coefficients.)

Before proceeding to combine the variables into a forecasting model we should re-emphasize that the methods outlined here allow us to judge the statistical plausibility of the equation. However, whether or not it is a best equation in any but a statistical sense can only be resolved by considering the need for accuracy as dictated by the sensitivity of the corresponding decision process. Indeed, a simple model based only on the history of the time series may well be adequate for this purpose. In the following discussion we will assume that the equation should provide as accurate forecasts as are reasonably possible. Given these introductory words, let us return to the technical problem of selecting the 'best' equation. Suppose that the analyst has available twenty yearly observations on both the eight independent variables and the dependent variable of *per capita* sales. These values are given in Appendix 3.† We wish to use these observations to select a forecasting equation and make a forecast for the next 5 years which includes some idea of the accuracy of the predictions. In the next section we describe a method of analysis.

† The accuracy of the raw data changes from variable to variable. While we know the precision of the computations in the computer program is very high this tells us little about the overall accuracy of the results which of course depend on the raw data. Often variables such as GDP are published to many significant figures which because of errors in compilation and data collection gives a spurious accuracy to them. This is true in the data used here, for example the income data is to six significant figures, much higher than the accuracy of the observation. The procedure for dealing with the problem is to use the data as given and to round the final results (conservatively).

The analysis — the regression runs

Runs 1 and 2. The first regression run was made using the basic linear model

$$Q_t = \beta_0 + \sum_{i=1}^{8} \beta_i X_{it} + e_t, \, t = 1 \ldots 20,$$

where the parameters are estimated from the twenty observations (shown in Appendix 3), and the dependent variable Q is designated X—9 in the data matrix. In the step-wise procedure low F values were used in this initial run so that the analyst was able to see the estimated equation with all variables included. A complete version of the printout is given in Appendix 3 for the second run which was made with high F values.

In Table 6.8 we repeat the summary statistics for each step of this first run. Because low F values were used no variables were displaced by the inclusion of additional variables.

Table 6.8
The summary statistics, the linear model: Run 1

Step	Variable entering	R^2	$\overline{R}^2$	Standard error	Overall F	Degrees of freedom	Variables with 'significant' F coefficient (F > 4)[1]
1	X—1	0.518	0.491	2.42	19.3	18	X—1
2	X—7	0.679	0.641	2.03	18.0	17	X—1, X—7
3	X—8	0.811	0.778	1.61	22.8	16	X—1, X—7, X—8
4	X—5	0.945	0.930	0.891	65.0	15	X—7, X—8, X—5
5	X—4	0.964	0.951	0.751	74.5	14	X—7, X—8, X—5, X—4
6	X—6	0.965	0.947	0.764	60.1	13	No change
7	X—3	0.967	0.948	0.769	51.0	12	No change
8	X—2	0.968	0.945	0.803	41.0	11	No change

The summary statistics immediately suggested that the approximate number of variables to include in the equation was five. Standard error was minimized and the overall F statistic, used as a measure of the model's fit was maximum. Introducing X—6, X—3 and X—2 only produced a small increase in R^2 while $\overline{R}^2$ decreased. However, by checking the regression coefficients for significance it was noted that at step 8, only X—4, X—5, X—7 and X—8 were 'significant' and this had been true from step 5. The addition of X—5 to the equation at step 4 had made the partial F associated with X—1 drop below 4 (to a value of 0.924) as can be seen on p. 268 (Appendix 3).

In run 2, the same model was used as in the first run except that the F values were increased to 4. The output is printed in Appendix 3. The first four steps were identical to run 1. At step 5 the high F (to remove) forced X—1 to be dropped, giving a final equation containing X—4, X—5, X—7 and X—8. The corresponding summary statistics were:

$R^2 = 0.962$; standard error = 0.741; overall F = 95.55; $\overline{R}^2 = 0.952$; degrees of freedom = 15; Durbin—Watson = 2.43.

The two critical values of the Durbin—Watson statistics were: $d_U = 1.83$; $d_L = 0.90$ at the 10 per cent significance level, and the test statistic was $4 - d = 4 - 2.43 = 1.57$. The test was therefore inconclusive (see §6.6.1) and the suspicion of autocorrelation in the error term was not eradicated. A brief examination of the residuals did not support the hypothesis that they were related to either Q or any of the independent variables.

Run 3. The third run was made to see if the suggested autocorrelation could be easily removed. The general model to be used in run 3 in the attempt to eliminate autocorrelation was:

$$Q_t - \rho Q_{t-1} = \beta_0 + \beta_1(1 - \rho)X_{1t} + \sum_{i=2}^{8} \beta_i(X_{it} - \rho X_{it-1}) + e_t$$

where ρ is the assumed (or estimated) value of the autocorrelation. In run 3 a simple estimating procedure was used to calculate ρ.

First, though, a check to see if an important variable had been omitted was made. The initial analysis had included all the variables thought relevant by both the forecaster and the forecast user so that this possibility was rejected. Consequently, the method (explained in §6.6.1) for repairing the autocorrelated error term of estimating ρ by $1 - d/2$ was used. With d at 2.43 the estimate of ρ was thus -0.215. Although the specification of the model was improved (not in itself too surprising as we have chosen ρ to eliminate the first-order serial correlation) the estimated coefficients and their standard errors were similar to those in the simple model of run 2. Usually the summary statistics, e.g. R^2 and the standard error, are suitable for comparing different models.[†] The standard error of estimate in particular was seen to be important as a measure of forecasting accuracy when compared with the mean and standard deviation of the dependent variable. Unfortunately, by transforming the dependent variable its distribution is also changed. With runs 1 and 2 we made the standard assumptions about Q_t (independent, normal, etc.) while in the model of run 3 we have to make the standard assumptions about $Q_t - \rho Q_{t-1}$. It follows that standard error comparisons between runs 1 and 2 and run 3 cannot be made.

Ideally, since our concern was to forecast Q, up to k periods ahead we would have compared the estimated accuracy[‡] of the forecasts of Q_{t+k} using alternative models. There are no simple ways of estimating the variance of Q_{t+k} for the difference model shown above. We had to search out other alternatives. We therefore compared models

---

[†] Rao and Miller, 1971, pp. 13—20, gives further explanation. It is possible to extend the available theory to compare the summary coefficients for certain transformations of the dependent variable: pp. 107—11 e.g. a log transformation.

[‡] We have used the word 'accuracy' here to convey what is technically called 'mean square error'. The 'accuracy' of an estimator (forecast) is made up of two components, the variance of the estimator and the average bias. For example, if the analyst makes a forecast, say, for example, that GNP will rise at the constant rate of 4 per cent for the next 5 years, then the variance of that forecast is zero. It may be, however, a bad forecast because it is highly biased. Throughout the last two chapters we have aimed at forecasting models which are correctly specified and therefore unbiased. The forecasting variance is then the only important measure of forecasting 'accuracy'.

2 and 3 on their ability to predict turning points. In §6.7.2 it was argued that possession of this characteristic in a forecasting model was particularly important in many business decisions. First, however, we had to derive a forecast of the level variable, Q_t for run 3, for the dependent variable used in that run is $Q_t - \hat{\rho}Q_{t-1}$. The first prediction is lost through the lagging procedure and therefore we assumed that $\hat{Q}_1 = Q_1$. With Q_1 pre-determined and $Q_2 - \hat{\rho}Q_1$ estimated from the forecasting equation, $\hat{Q}_2$ was easily found from our knowledge of $\hat{\rho}$ and Q_1. The remaining estimates were found by repeating this process. Unfortunately, use of the lag model of run 3 offered no improvement in predicting the turning points of the series and was therefore discarded.

Summary of runs 1–3. The analysis so far has concentrated on statistical criteria of selection. By comparison with run 1 (when low F values were used) model 2 seemed to provide the best statistical fit using the various criteria of R^2, standard error, etc. The variables finally included in model 2 were relative price, proportionate change in disposable *per capita* income, advertising expenditure and an index of new household formations. The next step in the analysis of the various alternative models was to examine this estimated forecasting equation (given below) to check the plausibility of its economic implications.

$$Q_t = -64.986 - 5.372X_{4t} + 3.537X_{5t} + 0.03761X_{7t} + 0.7630X_{8t}.$$

In referring to run 2 (output given in Appendix 3) it was noted that the signs of the estimated regression coefficients were as expected with the relative price variable having a negative sign. Since most households possess the product, new household formations, $X-8$, was significant in the final forecasting model. It was surprising that the income level variables, $X-2$ and $X-3$, were non-significant while the proportionate change variable $X-5$ was included in the final model. It may perhaps be explained by the durable nature of the product and the heavy household usage. A substantial jump in income was seen as encouraging the product's early replacement while the level of a consumer's income did not appear to affect his frequency of purchase; consequently it was the proportionate change variable, which appeared important. A further explanation of the findings was that the *amount* spent in the purchase of each unit depended on income. Because the dependent variable was '*number* of units sold *per capita*' income was unimportant in the models of demand developed here.

Before concluding the economic analysis of the forecasting equation it was thought desirable to check the relative importance of the independent variable in explaining fluctuations in the dependent variable. This cannot be done directly from the regression coefficients because these depend on the scales chosen in measuring the dependent and independent variables. To get round this we need to standardize the regression coefficient linking Q and X_i by their relative standard deviations, using the following formula:

$$\hat{\beta}_i^* = \hat{\beta}_i \frac{\hat{\sigma}_i}{\hat{\sigma}_Q}$$

where $\hat{\sigma}_Q$ is the sample standard deviation of the dependent variable Q, and $\hat{\sigma}_i$ the standard deviation of X_i. $\hat{\beta}_i^*$ is the so-called *beta coefficient* of X_i.

The beta coefficients† from run 2 were calculated by hand with the following results:

$$\hat{\beta}_4^* = -0.213; \hat{\beta}_5^* = 0.534; \hat{\beta}_7^* = 0.492; \hat{\beta}_8^* = 0.472.$$

As would be expected with a household necessity, price was not as important as percentage change in income, advertising or new household formations. Usually advertising is thought of as unimportant in determining the total market sales but rather, it is used as a strategic weapon for increasing market share. Its importance here gave support to the hypothesis that the market could be usefully separated in two parts: new purchases, represented by X—8 and replacement, the frequency of which depended on a change in income; the product's price and the associated advertising expenditure.

From the above considerations it was concluded that the model

$$\hat{Q} = \hat{\beta}_0 + \hat{\beta}_4 X_4 + \hat{\beta}_5 X_5 + \hat{\beta}_7 X_7 + \hat{\beta}_8 X_8$$

was suitable for use in general-purpose forecasting, although in specific application it would be necessary to confirm that the accuracy of the model was sufficient to be an aid in decision making. Nevertheless, before the investigation was thought complete certain transformations of the new data were considered as a basis for an alternative forecasting model.

Transformations — the final runs
The first four runs were made using a model in which the effects of the different independent variables were assumed additive. However, there was no *a priori* reasoning behind the choice; rather, it was thought to be a reasonable approximation to perhaps some more complicated functional alternatives. It was equally plausible to consider the multiplicative model:

$$Q = \beta_0 \left[\prod_{i=1}^{8} X_i \beta_i \right] * (\text{error}); \text{ or taking logs; } \log Q = \beta_0 + \sum_{i=1}^{8} \beta_i \log X_i + (\text{error}).$$

The usual assumptions were made about the error and the parameters were then estimated. Two runs were made, the first with low F values, the second with high. The runs showed much the same pattern as with the additive models although when low F values were used, the model including the transforms of the four variables of run 2, price, proportionate income change, etc.; however, the transforms of time and also the credit variable X—6 had t values larger than 1.5. The credit variable had the

---

† The beta coefficients are identical to the estimated parameters in a regression model using only standardized variables. A change in the units of measurement only produces proportionate changes in the size of the corresponding regression coefficient and the standard error. Consequently the variables included in that model remain the same as in the old model while its parameters reflect the relative importance of the different independent variables.

expected negative sign. Even then, it was still impossible to differentiate between the various models by the usual criteria.

A number of further attempts were made to improve on the forecasting equations developed in the earlier runs. Because the market could only grow slowly a log transform of time was included in the additive model. It produced no noticeable improvement. Finally, the possibility that the effects of price and advertising could not be approximated by the additive model was tested by including a further independent variable in the additive model (**Price**) * (**Advertising**). However, it was found to be non-significant and it was decided that both the linear model and the multiplicative model were adequate explanations of the variability of sales.

Conclusions
Of the models considered three had seemed particularly plausible:

Model 2: Additive with independent variables
        X−4, X−5, X−7, X−8.

Model 5: Multiplicative with independent variables
        X−4, X−5, X−7, X−8.

Model 6: Multiplicative with independent variables
        X−1, X−4, X−5, X−6, X−7, X−8.

The final forecasts were made by considering the performance of all three models over the next 5 years.

In order to produce the forecasts the values of the independent variables had to be specified for that period. These are reproduced in Appendix 3 together with the printout of the corresponding forecasts for model 2. The values of the independent variables were premised on a 3-year period of government restraint on spending and income to deal with the aftermath of the oil crisis in 1973; with the coming on-line of North Sea oil it was thought likely that there would be substantial increases in the income variables, a relaxation of credit restrictions and with the beginnings of a boom in sight there would be a concomitant increase in advertising expenditure. Throughout that period relative price was expected to fall. New housing formations were also thought likely to respond to the fluctuations of the national economy.

The forecasts produced using the above three models (the confidence intervals for the multiplicative models were calculated as shown in §6.3.1. Formulae for the calculation are given in Draper and Smith, 1966, pp.121−2) were broadly similar and the results for run 2 are shown below in Table 6.9. All three models are particularly sensitive to the forecast changes in the income variable X−5 and the index of new household formations X−8. For example, referring back to the estimated model of run 2:

$$Q_t = -64.986 - 5.372X_{4t} + 3.537X_{5t} + 0.03761X_{7t} + 0.7630X_{8t}$$

and the extrapolation data, we see that X_5 varies from a minimum value of 0.5 in forecast year 2 (1976) to 4.0 in year 5 (1979), causing an increase of 13 in the dependent sales variable Q, some 40 per cent of the total increase from year 2 to year 5. A second point about all three models is that they perform worst in the 'bad' years when the market environment is unusually hostile. The models have all been constructed from a data base which did not include similar conditions. It is at just these times that we would wish for the most accurate forecasts.

Table 6.9
The forecasts derived from the additive model

	Model 2		
Year	*Forecast*	*Upper limit*	*Lower limit*
1	15.5	17.1	14.9
2	6.0	8.45	3.55
3	10.8	12.9	8.83
4	20.6	22.0	19.3
5	34.7	36.7	32.7

To complete the forecast it is necessary to embed the three alternative models into the decision-making system of which the forecast information forms a part. Simple sensitivity testing would be carried out (as illustrated in §5.5) testing in year 1, for example, a likely range of 15.5 to 16.6 sales units, against the extremes of 14.6 and 18.3 the values derived from combining the results of all three models. Supported by the comparative sizes of the β coefficients it was clear that the macro-economic forecasts of change in income and new household formations were critical in defining the minimum level of sales in any forthcoming slump. Again the stability of the decision would be tested against a more pessimistic economic scenario, formulated perhaps on the assumption of a delay in the coming on-line of North Sea oil.

As is usual in any realistic application of forecasting we are confronted with a choice of models which 'statistically' fit the data. If a final point forecast is a necessary input to the decision, it can only be constructed by reference to the forecast users who will add their subjective knowledge of market behaviour, in particular its response to a slump, to arrive at a conclusion.

The final forecast and its associated confidence limits may well bear little relationship to those shown above in Table 6.9. However, the payoff to the organization comes from the synthesis of formalized experience as encapsulated in a number of plausible statistical models, and managerial experience. It follows from this view that the management information system should monitor the performance not just of the models themselves but of the alteration in decision making that they produce. In this way the true nature of forecasts as an instrumental step in improved decision making is recognized.

References

Draper, N. R. and Smith, H. (1966) *Applied Regression Analysis*, Wiley, New York.
Fox, Karl (1968) *Intermediate Economic Statistics*, Wiley, New York.

Hamilton, James L. (1972) 'The demand for cigarettes: advertising, the health scare and cigarette advertising ban', *Review of Economics and Statistics*, vol. 54.

Johnston, J. (1972) *Econometric Methods*, 2nd edn, McGraw-Hill, New York.

Kane, Edward J. (1969) *Economic Statistics and Econometrics: an Introduction to Quantitative Economics*, Harper and Row, New York.

Morrell, J. (ed.) (1973) *Management Decision and the Role of Forecasting*, Penguin, Harmondsworth.

Rao, P. and Miller, R. L. (1971) *Applied Econometrics*, Wadsworth, Calif.

Progression — Part 2

These three chapters have considered the methodology of forecasting. Our aim has been to 'popularize', if such a term does not seem too inappropriate, the structures and methods of time-series modelling which are successfully applied in forecasting as we show in the next part of the book. However, we did not intend just another overview of forecasting methods. This has been done often — see for example an excellent article:

Adams, G. F. and de Janosi, P. E., 'Statistics and econometrics of forecasting', in Butler, W. F. and Kavish, R. A. (eds) (1966) *How Business Economists Forecast*, Prentice-Hall, Englewood Cliffs, New Jersey.

On the contrary, we have aimed to describe the ideas and methods behind elementary time series, linear regression and multiple regression so that the reader will be able to use these building blocks in applications within his organization. We have omitted most formulae and their proofs.

Yeomans, K. A. (1968) *Applied Statistics*, Allen Lane, Harmondsworth, Middlesex

gives the formulae and shows how to make the calculations, while **Draper** and **Smith** (1966) (*see Ch. 6 References*) is perhaps the standard text and is both well written and thorough. It does, however, require the use of matrix algebra. It is also primarily concerned with production problems, so topics such as multicollinearity and autocorrelation are given only passing mention.

Our omission of formulae is of course, not accidental. Regression, time-series decomposition, and exponential smoothing are all part of a typical computer package available cheaply to almost all organizations whatever the size. It is difficult enough interpreting the output of such package without worrying unnecessarily about how it was obtained.

Robinson, C. (1971) *Business Forecasting*, Nelson, London

takes a similar view to us of the mathematical level necessary to the understanding of forecasting methodology. However, our approach may well require supplementing by reference to the basic statistical ideas we use throughout. For the reader who has forgotten his elementary statistics, we have recommended **Mendenhall** and **Reinmuth** (1974) (*see Ch. 6 References*) while at a slightly more formal level **Frank** (1971) Ch. 1 through 8 (*see Ch. 5 References*) will take the reader slowly through the basic ideas of statistics with a view to its econometric applications later.

Two books at an intermediate mathematical level are: **Fox** (1968) Ch. 1 through 7 (*see Ch. 6 References*) and:

Clelland, **R. C.** *et al.* (1973) *Basic Statistics with Business Applications*, 2nd edn, Wiley, New York;

while **Wonnacott** and **Wonnacott** (1970) (*see Ch. 5 References*) is particularly clear. Part 1 describes much of the material we cover in greater depth without using matrix algebra (but with calculus needed).

For an advanced mathematical treatment **Johnston** (1972) (*see Ch. 6 References*) and:

Christ, Carl (1966) *Econometric Models and Methods*, Wiley, New York

for example, are both standard works.

Part 3
Applications

At this stage we turn to consider the way in which the forecasting methodologies developed in earlier sections can be applied to specific forecasting problems. For purposes of exposition, applications of non-causal models (Chapter 7) and causal models (Chapter 8) have been discussed separately, but this is not an indication that there is any clear-cut difference in the situations in which these two types of model can be used. For many applications causal and non-causal approaches are very real alternatives, and the choice between them depends on cost effectiveness rather than statistical criteria. In fact, the simple, cheap naive models may be used both in the long or short term as benchmarks with which to evaluate the more expensive causal models,

Of course, there is an important philosophical difference between a naive model which produces forecasts over which the decision maker has no control and a causal model which includes decision variables which may then be used to influence the forecast outcome. Consequently, in the longer term, more and more stress is placed on the selection of desirable futures from those that are socially and technically feasible. To emphasize this, Chapter 9 'National economic forecasting' and Chapter 10 'Long-range forecasting and technological change' suggest a mixture of both causal and non-causal models to meet the decision maker's forecasting needs.

7
Benchmark forecasting

§7.1 Introduction

The forecasting methods discussed in this chapter are described as benchmark forecast because they serve as a standard against which forecasts of alternative models can be compared. Because benchmark forecasting models have little or no structural content they are normally cheap enough to construct and operate for them to be used automatically, both to signal a need for a more sophisticated forecasting effort and to evaluate the outcome of such effort where it is made.

§7.2 Short-term forecasting

Naive short-term forecasting is generally required where many detailed but continuing control decisions have to be made to maintain operations in a normal state. Sales forecasting (Harrison, 1967, describes the forecasting method then used in ICI) is a typical application; because while reasonably stable production and purchasing policies are advantageous the susceptibility of short-run sales to fluctuations make such policies difficult to operate. In this situation the task is not to generate exact forecasts of randomly varying sales, (since such random variation is better handled using inventories), so much as to provide an early warning that a permanent change has occurred in the level round which the sales series fluctuates. The priority for the forecasting technique is then to separate out the 'true' and 'random' elements in a series of observations and to provide reliable signals for a management by exception approach.

Of course while it is easy to make a theoretical distinction between true and random components, in practice the two are inextricably mixed. All we can hope to do is to adopt a forecasting model where the costs of responding to the transmission of random information are roughly in balance with the costs incurred where true information is not transmitted and no action is taken. In choosing any particular short-term model we are implicitly making assumptions about the form of the 'true' generator of the data series we are trying to forecast and in the next sections the implications of this choice in terms of some widely used naive forecasting models are considered.

§7.3 Short-term forecasting: methodology

In §4.7.2 the use of the moving average technique was illustrated. In selecting this technique we are making an implicit assumption that the time series is generated by four components: trend, cycle, seasonal and random. It follows that once trend, cyclical and seasonal fluctuations are removed, all residual variation is random and that the best forecast is given by using the trend, cyclical and seasonal components alone. For example, using the moving average approach on quarterly data, we calculate the centred four-period moving average through which the original sales data can be deseasonalized, and a linear trend is then fitted by using least squares to estimate the parameters of the equation. To transform this forecast to actual rather than seasonally adjusted sales we need to multiply by the appropriate seasonal index.

In interpreting the forecast it is important to recognize the limitations of this method. Smoothing the observations through using moving averages makes only partial use of the recent observations. Moreover, while the separate use of four seasonal factors is intuitively appealing it does mean that the least squares criterion is applied only to seasonally adjusted data and not to the whole model. A further limitation is imposed by the initial assumption that all residual error after adjustment for seasonality and trend is random and contains no 'true' component. Usually, however, the error contains a systematic component which indicates a true change in the circumstances affecting the series we are forecasting and in discarding this information we weaken the model's ability to reflect changes in the behaviour of the underlying time series.

In the late 1950s an alternative to the moving average approach was developed. Holt (1957) and Brown (1959) suggested that because most time series are subject to systematic changes it is reasonable to give more weight in forecasting to recent observations than to early ones, simply because current observations provide a more accurate guide to the current 'true' generator of the series. To put this into effect Brown derived the basic exponential smoothing equation introduced in §4.8. To predict the value of Y, T periods ahead, we use:

$$\hat{Y}_{t+T} = S_t = pY_t + (1 - p)S_{t-1}, \quad \text{for } 0 \leqslant p \leqslant 1$$

where p is the smoothing parameter, S the smoothed value of the series, Y the observed value, and $\hat{Y}$ the forecast. The absence of trend and seasonal components means that S_t, the current value of the smoothed series is the estimate of Y_{t+T}. An inspection of the equation shows that the higher the value of p, the closer S_t is to Y_t until when p takes on the value 1, the smoothed series is identical to the original series. The significance of the choice of p is that in setting its value we are making an implicit judgement about the distribution of true and false information in the current observation Y_t.

7.3.1 Choice of the smoothing parameter
The significance of the value selected for the smoothing parameter p in governing the responsiveness of a forecasting system to systematic changes in the observations has

already been discussed in §4.8. The general effect on the responsiveness of the system for different values of p is illustrated in Fig. 7.1 (Brown, 1963). For example, if a step change occurs the new observations recorded will, of course, now fluctuate around this new level. The smoothed series S_t responds to the change, based as it is on both the new and the old observations and as more of the new observations are included, S_t will more and more reflect the new level of the series. Figure 7.1 shows how the speed of response depends on the value of the smoothing parameter p. Here the values of p, the smoothing parameter are plotted against the number of additional observations required after a step change has occurred in the underlying series before 90 per cent of the step change is reflected in the smoothed estimates of the series.

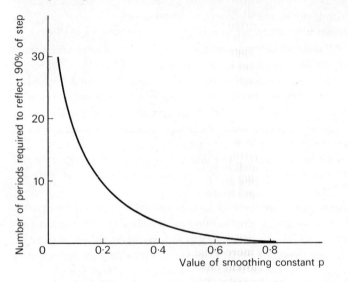

Fig. 7.1 Responsive to a step change with p, *the smoothing constant varying*

The diagram shows for example that with the smoothing parameter set at p = 0.2 ten new observations are needed before S_t reflects 90 per cent of the step increase. With p = 0.6, however, only two observations are needed. Inspection of the diagram suggests that with a smoothing constant between 0.2 and 0.4 the smoothed series S_t responds quite quickly to step changes. Ideally of course the choice of a smoothing constant would be made by carefully balancing the costs associated with over-responsiveness and under-responsiveness in any dependent decisions. Fortunately however, the forecasting errors are not sensitive to even quite large changes in the smoothing constant and in practice a value of p between 0.1 and 0.3 can be chosen by trial and error. However, if the series is unstable a higher value for p may be used and it is in these situations that some of the more complicated methods we describe later become useful.

More formal criteria can be used to select an appropriate value for p. (These criteria, like least squares, are also used to assess the forecasting model's accuracy. A further criterion, Theil's U is often used but we are sceptical as to its merits. See for example; Bliemel, 1973, pp. 444–6.) Two common criteria are to choose p to:

1. Minimize the error variance

$$\frac{\Sigma (Y_i - \hat{Y}_i)^2}{n - 1}$$

which is equivalent, of course, to minimizing

$$\Sigma (Y_i - \hat{Y}_i)^2; \text{ or,}$$

2. Minimize the mean absolute deviation

$$\frac{1}{n} \Sigma |Y_i - \hat{Y}_i|,$$

often designated by MAD.

The difference between the two is that MAD gives comparatively less weight to extreme errors. Because both these measures tend to be insensitive to small changes in p, an initial value is chosen arbitrarily, say p = 0.1, and the error variance or MAD calculated. The results are then compared with those obtained by setting new values for p, say of 0.2 then 0.3 until by iteration, preferably using a computer, the best smoothing constant is selected. It is worth repeating, however, that although it is possible to select p to satisfy some criterion of fit using historic data, that does not mean it will be optimal in the future.

7.3.2 Trends and seasonal components in exponential weighted moving averages
So far the exponential moving average model we have considered has not included the seasonal and trend components of a typical time series. These are taken into account by developing a further smoothing equation for each component. The general model at time t for forecasting T periods ahead is:

$$\hat{Y}_{t+T} = (S_t + T * R_t) * F_{t+T-L}$$

where S_t is the estimate of the constant factor (this term is the smoothed level of the series after removal of the seasonal component) at time t, R_t the trend at time t and F_t the seasonal component at time t, where the seasonal component has a periodicity of L. By setting the values of three smoothing parameters p, q and r, the three components of the series are calculated using the following equations:

(1) the *constant factor* at time t,

$$S_t = p \frac{Y_t}{F_{t-L}} + (1 - p)(S_{t-1} + R_{t-1});$$

(2) the *seasonal factor* at time t,

$$F_t = q \frac{Y_t}{S_t} + (1 - q)F_{t-L};$$

(3) the *trend factor* at time t,

$$R_t = r(S_t - S_{t-1}) + (1 - r)R_{t-1}.$$

The equations are calculated recursively. Suppose we know S_{t-1}, R_{t-1} and the values for F between F_{t-1} and F_{t-L}. A new observation of Y_t allows us to use the first equation to calculate S_t. S_t is then substituted into equations (2) and (3) to calculate F_t and R_t.

Once these calculations are complete the three components can be used in the forecasting model:

$$\hat{Y}_{t+T} = (S_t + T * R_t) * F_{t+T-L}$$

to predict Y_{t+T} for values of T from 1 to L. That is, we can use this equation without modification to forecast ahead up to a full cycle of the seasonal component (usually a year). If we wish to extend the forecast further we just re-use the last estimate of the appropriate seasonal factor (e.g., F_t is the appropriate seasonal index for forecasting Y in periods t + L, t + 2L, etc.). An inspection of the equations used to isolate each component reveals a similar structure. The equation for each factor consists of the most recent observation together with the previous smoothed value of that same factor. For example, in determining the trend factor, S_t is the deseasonalized level of the series at time t, and, therefore, $S_t - S_{t-1}$, the increase in level at time t, is then the latest value of the trend. The equation then weights the most recent observation of trend $(S_t - S_{t-1})$ by r and the previous estimate, R_{t-1} by $(1 - r)$, in exactly the same way as in the basic equation of exponential smoothing.

Before a forecast can be made, initial values of the three factors, constant, trend and seasonal have to be made. Because the periodicity of the seasonal factor is L there are L initial values F_1 to F_L required. If there are a large number of historical data points available, the fact that the forecasting model is not sensitive to the starting values means that it is unimportant how they are selected. Usually, though, at least two complete seasons are required to initialize the data, before either an average or an exponentially smoothed average can be calculated. To illustrate the use of this technique and to compare it with the results obtained using the basic equation for exponential smoothing discussed earlier in the chapter we have fitted the two models to the data in Table 7.1. The data for the years 1969 and 1970 have been used to calculate the initial values but the two measures of forecasting accuracy — the mean absolute deviation, and the standard error of the forecast — are only calculated on the remaining 3 years of data.

The forecasts in columns (3), (4) and (5) of Table 7.1 are based on three different forecasting models. The first includes S_t, the constant factor, R_t, the trend and F_t the quarterly seasonal. As we noted above, using all three components the forecast T periods ahead is given by $\hat{Y}_{t+T} = (S_t + T * R_t) * F_{t+T-4}$. The seasonal factor that is used is the latest smoothed seasonal index calculated for the season in which t + T falls. The results of using this model are shown in column (3). Column (4) contains the forecasts when the trend factor R_t is discarded, the forecast being:

$$\hat{Y}_{t+T} = S_t * F_{t+T-4}.$$

156

Table 7.1

Exponentially smoothed sales of consumer product 1971—73 adapted to include seasonal and trend factors

Data used to calculate initial values

Year/Quarter	Sales	Year/Quarter	Sales
1969/1	34.9	1970/1	35.6
2	33.6	2	34.0
3	33.0	3	33.1
4	39.7	4	41.4

Year/Quarter (1)	Sales (2)	*Exponential smoothing with trend and seasonals* (3)	*Exponential smoothing with seasonals* (4)	*Exponential smoothing* (5)
1971/1	35.5	35.867	35.680	36.069
2	34.5	34.286	34.118	35.955
3	33.8	33.558	33.417	35.664
4	42	41.484	41.065	35.291
1972/1	35.9	36.201	35.881	36.633
2	34.8	34.923	34.617	36.486
3	34	34.143	33.87	36.149
4	43.1	42.206	41.781	35.719
1973/1	36	36.538	36.187	37.195
2	35.7	35.281	34.952	36.956
3	35.1	34.611	34.284	36.705
4	44.2	43.531	43.020	36.384
Mean absolute deviation		0.410	0.538	2.868
Standard error		0.484	0.716	4.046

If these models are compared with the 'moving average' approach of §4.7 we would normally find the latter performs less well as measured by a higher standard error and mean absolute deviation. Finally column (5) shows the results using the simplest of the models, $\hat{Y}_{t+T} = S_t$, which ignores both the seasonal and trend components and is, of course, highly inaccurate.

These forecasts in Table 7.1 have been calculated using smoothing parameters of $p = 0.2$, $q = 0.6$ and $r = 0.25$ which were chosen to minimize the standard error (or mean absolute deviation) of the model which included seasonal and trend components.

Table 7.2
The standard error and the mean absolute deviation for
different values of the smoothing parameter

p	q	r	*Standard error*	*Mean absolute deviation*
0.2	0.5	0.2	0.528	0.431
0.2	0.4	0.1	0.633	0.487
0.3	0.5	0.2	0.537	0.442
0.2	0.6	0.2	0.499	0.415
0.2	0.6	0.1	0.563	0.440
0.2	0.6	0.25	0.484	0.410

It does not necessarily follow that because the parameters were optimal for that model they were optimal for the other two.

Table 7.2 shows how the values of the standard error of the forecast, and the mean absolute deviation change for the trend/seasonal model as different values of the parameters p, q and r are used. The forecasts produced by the best model which includes both seasonal and trend are accurate with a standard error about 1½ per cent of the mean, though of course the relevance of this measure of accuracy depends on the end use of the forecast. The seasonal smoothing parameter is high at 0.6 and this is perhaps due to there being at most five observations used in calculating each of the four seasonal components F_{t-L} (L = 1, 2, 3, 4). With the data gathered so far the method has over-estimated the sales in the first quarter and underestimated them in the fourth. Some of this error could perhaps be eliminated by ensuring that

$$\sum_{i=1}^{L} \frac{F_{t-i}}{L} = 1;$$

that is the average of the seasonal factors is one.

The high value of the seasonal smoothing parameter points to a limitation in the method described here. If the seasonal fluctuations are unstable the error caused by this method of estimating the seasonal component is large. This conclusion is argued in a paper by Harrison (1965) where he states that the method described here performs reasonably well if there is little random fluctuation in sales. However, with large amounts of randomness it is quite possible for seasonal factors to be estimated when the data has already been deseasonalized; certainly an undesirable feature for the effect is to magnify the error considerably. Harrison recommends a method which eliminates some of the difficulties associated with seasonality. His primary idea is that after the trend has been removed from a time series the seasonal variation is smooth and wave-like, and can therefore be specified as a sum of sines and cosines. Each term in the given summation is a wave with a different amplitude, and the amplitudes are updated as each fresh observation becomes known.

Another popular method which has the same goal as Harrison's is called the Census

Method II which has been developed by the US Bureau of the Census (1965)†. It is considered the best method at present available, although it is expensive in computer time compared with the seasonal methods discussed in the earlier parts of this section. We recommend that when dealing with highly seasonal data (with a high pay-off if the forecasts are accurate) a number of methods for deseasonalizing the data are considered.

Looking back at the forecasts shown in Table 7.1 we see that not only is the seasonal component suspect but there is evidence that the trend is also changing. A smoothing value of 0.25 for the trend is somewhat high, 0.2 being more commonly found appropriate. Calculating the appropriate four-period moving average also gives some support for the idea that there is an increasing trend although from the limited data available no firm conclusion can be drawn. It may well be worth considering alternative smoothing models, each of which is based on a different generating model of the underlying time series.

Table 7.3 shows nine models which are variants of the smoothing models discussed in detail in this section. We have already discussed the case of additive trend/multiplicative seasonal, the forecast being $\hat{Y}_{t+T} = (S_t + T * R_t) * F_{t+T-L}$. The seasonal effect could as well be additive or the trend, multiplicative. The different combinations of these factors are shown in Table 7.3.

Table 7.3

Variations of the basic exponential smoothing model: each entry is the forecasting equation derived from the specification of the trend and seasonal components as either multiplicative or additive

	Constant	*Multiplicative trend*	*Additive trend*
Constant	S_t	$S_t * (R_t)^T$	$S_t + TR_t$
Multiplicative seasonal	$S_t * F_{t+T-L}$	$S_t * (R_t)^T * F_{t+T-L}$	$(S_t + TR_t) * F_{t+T-L}$
Additive seasonal	$S_t + F_{t+T-L}$	$S_t * (R_t)^T + F_{t+T-L}$	$S_t + TR_t + F_{t+T-L}$

Source: Pegels, 1969.

In summary, there are a large number of possible models, each of which has virtues in particular situations. For example, we might argue that because of the increasing trend suggested by the consumer product sales data of the previous example, a model including a multiplicative trend ought to work better than the model we used which included an additive trend. In practice while the initial choice of model is often arbitrary, by careful examination of the errors generated it is usually possible to improve the forecasting accuracy. However, with such a choice of methods, the reader

---

† The authors regret that the reference is not more accessible. For a technical discussion with necessary computer programs see: Salzman, L.

is entitled to ask where the simplicity that was stressed as a principal virtue of naive methods has disappeared to. The answer in practice is that it is only rarely necessary† to use the more complicated methods and the need to do so can normally be identified in advance. Thus it is customary to break down the products into three categories:

1. Those with either a high volume turnover, or those which are expensive to store.
2. Medium volume, or medium-cost products.
3. Low volume, or low-cost products.

It has been found that in many companies between 5 and 10 per cent of the items stocked represent about 70 per cent of the total company investment in stock. Only with the items in the first category is it necessary to design a fully responsive forecasting system, with attention being paid to each item individually. The medium volume/cost items require a fully automatic forecasting system, while all that is necessary in the low volume/cost category is a simple manual method. In the next section we go on to discuss the specialized topic of forecasting systems geared to meet the stringent needs of accuracy encountered by products in category 1 above.

7.3.3 *Monitoring the forecasting system*
In setting parameters to produce an optimum flexibility of response, we are seeking to balance the prospective costs likely to arise from two types of error in the forecasting system:

(*a*) a failure to transmit a true change in the behaviour of a time series;
(*b*) the transmission of a perceived change when no true change has occurred.

The smoothing parameters are chosen to balance these two types of error. The next problem, however, is in how to monitor the resulting performance of a forecasting system when it is in use so that neither type of error occurs persistently. Almost invariably a question will arise the first time the model generates an unexpected forecast. Is the assumed generating model wrong or is the world changing very quickly? In many situations a rapid re-check of calculations and some questions about the consistency of observations used may show that neither of these situations applies and that a simple correction produces a normal forecast. However, if no such obvious error has been made we need to consider just how extreme a given forecast is. This can only be judged against the forecasting models' existing record of errors between forecast and actual outcomes.

If at time period t we sum the last n errors $e_t, e_{t-1}, \ldots e_{t-n+1}$ we obtain the cumulative sums of error, s_n where

$$s_n = \sum_{i=1}^{n} e_{t-i+1},$$

and these sums should all fluctuate around zero when the errors generated by using the forecasting model are 'under control'. We can use this intuitive idea to calculate control limits for the series $s_1, s_2 \ldots s_n$ which are the limits within which these

---

† Harrison (1965) finds it is rarely necessary to use methods even as complicated as the smoothed seasonal and trend model discussed earlier in the chapter.

cumulative sums (cusums) should lie if the model is forecasting adequately. It has been found unnecessary to consider more than the last six errors i.e. $n \leq 6$. The usual formula for the control limits is:

$$L_n = \pm 0.4\hat{\sigma}(n + 3.5)$$

where $\hat{\sigma}$ is the standard error of the forecast. Note, for example, if $n = 1$, $L_1 = \pm 1.8\hat{\sigma}$ and that the limits spread as n increases. In using this method we expect the first sum $s_1 (= e_t)$, the latest observed error to lie within 1.8 standard deviations of the error mean of zero. Thus, we see that the control limits are similar to confidence limits. As a new data point becomes available the cusums are re-calculated and the new cusums checked to see if they lie within the control limits. If a cusum is outside its corresponding control limit this notifies the forecaster that this model is producing too large an error and an appropriate adjustment needs to be made to the forecast.

In normal circumstances a correctly specified forecasting model should produce cusums which lie within the limits a specified percentage of the time. If that percentage is too high because the value of L is large, then the method will be too insensitive to detect any real changes in the time series, while if it is too low because L is small it will result in the need to constantly investigate whether the series has truly altered its behaviour. Most of the time we would find that the alarm was false.

While the above method of calculating the control limits is not universal (various methods are discussed in: Coutie *et al.*, 1964, pp. 28–32; Harrison and Davies, 1964) all methods compare the limits with the calculated value of the cusums. A similar idea was proposed by Trigg (1964) who defined a tracking signal T_t which is updated afresh as each new error becomes known:

$$T_t = \frac{\text{smoothed error}}{\text{smoothed absolute error}}.$$

Suppose we take γ to be the smoothing constant then:

New smoothed error $= \gamma * (\text{error}) + (1 - \gamma) * (\text{old smoothed error})$ and

New smoothed absolute error $= \gamma * (\text{absolute error}) + (1 - \gamma) * (\text{old smoothed absolute error})$

T_t lies between ± 1 and its magnitude depends on whether there is a systematic error in the model. As with the cusum technique above, the tracking signal T_t is compared with a control limit L_t which as before, is similar to a confidence limit. Batty (1969) has calculated values of the control limit L_t and shows, for example, that for a smoothing constant $\gamma = 0.2$ the tracking signal $|T_t| < 0.5$, 90 per cent of the time. As before, when a signal is received which is outside the control limit the forecast is revised† to take into account the more recent data and any outside knowledge that the people working with the forecasts might have.

† An *ad hoc* adjustment used in ICI is to modify the calculated value of S_t by using the following formula which gives much greater weight to the three most current observations:

$$S_t \text{ (revised)} = 0.2 * S_t \text{ (calculated)} + 0.8 * (Y_t + Y_{t-1} + Y_{t-2})/3$$

One way of constantly revising the model in order to take into account the information implicit in the tracking system is to vary the value of p, the exponential smoothing parameter in the forecasting model. Suppose a variant of exponential smoothing which includes trend but no seasonal components, is in use where:

$$\hat{Y}_{t+T} = S_t + T * R_t;$$
$$S_t = S_{t-1} + R_{t-1} + (1 - p^2) * e_t; \text{ and}$$
$$R_t = R_{t-1} + (1 - p)^2 * e_t.$$

Instead of using a fixed constant p in the smoothing equation for S_t, Trigg and Leach (1967) and Shone (1967) suggest that p is replaced by $|T_{t-1}|$, i.e. the absolute value of the tracking system calculated one period earlier, while the smoothing equation for the trend factor R_t is left unaltered. The effect of this adaptive system is that when there is systematic error in the forecasts the increased value of the smoothing parameter $|T_{t-1}|$ ensures that the new forecasts quickly reflect this underlying change in the pattern of demand. The forecasting system has been made more responsive. Not only that: it now adapts to the changing situation, with $|T_{t-1}|$ increasing or decreasing depending on the stability of the time series.

In a sense all forecasting models are adaptive; the differences lie in the degree to which the monitoring and revision is an integral part of the model or whether it demands action from the operator. The most recent development in modelling (by Harrison and Stevens, 1971) have further extended the idea of an adaptive forecasting system and we would suspect this type of model building will become more common (for an interesting application of Harrison and Stevens, see Green and Harrison, 1973).

§ 7.4 General autoregressive models

(This section to be omitted on first reading. We are here concerned with the Box–Jenkins class of models, which are not yet easy to use. Thus we only give a brief introduction to the literature.)

The models we have discussed in the last two sections are particular examples of *autoregressive models* where the current value of a time series is determined by some combination of the historical values of the series. For example, in Chapter 4 we showed the basic equation of exponential smoothing may be written:

$$\hat{Y}_t = S_{t-1} = pY_{t-1} + p(1 - p)Y_{t-2} + p(1 - p)^2 Y_{t-3} + \ldots p(1 - p)^{k-1} Y_{t-k} + \ldots$$

As in the case above, the methods we have so far discussed place an arbitrary restriction on the weights attached to the historical values of the series.

Instead of approaching the problem by placing these restrictions on the parameters, we might start with the general kth order linear equation:

$$Y_t = \beta_0 + \beta_1 Y_{t-1} + \beta_2 Y_{t-2} \ldots + \beta_k Y_{t-k} + e_t,$$

and try and select just a few of the earlier values of Y which can then be used to form a good forecasting equation. For example, where the data shows a pronounced quarterly effect we would almost certainly include Y_{t-4} as one of the variables in the forecasting model. A simple indicator of the relevance of possible variables is provided by calculating r_k, the residual correlation between Y_t and Y_{t+k} after the trend component is removed from both series. Thus if we calculate the regression line $\hat{Y}_t = \beta_0 + \beta_1^t$ and define y_t as $Y_t - \hat{Y}_t$ then the autocorrelation coefficient of order k is defined by the equation:†

$$r_k = \frac{\sum\limits_{t=1}^{n-k} y_t y_{t+k}}{\sum\limits_{t=1}^{n} y_t^2}.$$

An alternative method uses the same formula but removes the trend by using first differences so that $y_t = Y_t - Y_{t-1}$. As an example we can use the data given in Table 7.1 (p. 157) for the quarterly sales of a consumer product in the years 1969−73. In this series the trend line is given by $Y_t = 34.2821 + 0.2108t$. With this formula it is possible to calculate r_k for different time lags. The results are shown in Fig. 7.2. As we were already well aware, the results show that the data contain a substantial seasonal component since r_4 and r_8 are large. (Our calculation of r_8 is unreliable as our sample is small.)

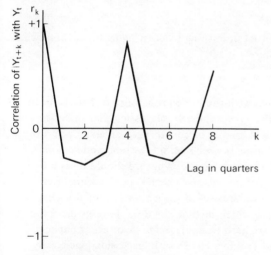

Fig. 7.2 *The coefficient of autocorrelation, calculated for the quarterly sales of a consumer product, 1969−73*

We could imagine developing a predictive equation using time and the value of Y, lagged to correspond to the season for which the prediction is being made. For quarterly data the model proposed is therefore

$$Y_t = \beta_0 + \beta_1 t + \beta_2 Y_{t-4} + e_t.$$

† There are alternative definitions of the kth order sample autocorrelation which take into account the different number of observations in numerator and denominator. Brown (1963) for example uses $r_k = [\Sigma y_t y_{t+k}/(n-k-1)]/[\Sigma y_t^2/(n-1)]$.

As we commented when we first introduced the idea of lagged variables, the estimation of the parameters poses some difficulties which we will discuss in Chapter 8.

An alternative and quite simple autoregressive method is to difference the time series, which usually has the effect of minimizing the trend component of the series. If we define $Z_t = Y_t - Y_{t-1}$ we can model the behaviour of the series by:

$$Z_t = \beta_0 + \sum_{j=1}^{p} \beta_j Z_{t-j} + \text{(error)}$$

where p has yet to be chosen. Newbold and Granger (1974) suggest that for quarterly series or monthly series with a comparatively small number of observations available p = 13 works well enough while for a longer monthly series p = 25 works satisfactorily. The parameters are then estimated by a step-wise regression procedure.

A more general approach to model building has been developed by Box and Jenkins (1962, 1970). They criticize the exponential smoothing approach because the models are chosen without reference to the data while they prefer to 'let the data speak for itself'. To illustrate the approach, consider the basic equation of exponential smoothing, where $\hat{Y}_{t+1}$ (equal to S_t) provides the one-step ahead forecast of Y_{t+1} according to the equation:

$$\hat{Y}_{t+1} = pY_t + (1-p)\hat{Y}_t.$$

Box and Jenkins show that the exponential smoothing forecasting model is 'best' when the underlying time series is generated by:

$$Y_{t+1} - Y_t = e_{t+1} - (1-p)e_t,$$

in which the errors are independent, each with the same probability distribution. In using the exponential smoothing model we are implicitly suggesting that the observations are generated by the above model. Normally of course, such an assumption is invalid and we have already introduced models which include a trend and seasonal component. Again the authors argue that this is *ad hoc*. What we should do is look at the data and choose from a general class of models the simplest model which fits. Their methods are complicated by the standards set in the earlier part of this chapter and while many computers have software which include the Box–Jenkins programs it is generally agreed that the methods are hard to implement. Two recent papers (Chatfield and Prothero, 1972; Box and Jenkins, 1973) with discussion give a case study of an attempt to forecast sales of a rapidly growing but highly seasonal product and as many of the commentators are much experienced with a wide variety of naive models, the papers are essential reading for any serious study of the subject.

Before leaving the subject let us sketch out the nature of the class of model Box and Jenkins propose for describing time series data. Consider first the simple case of the generating model for exponential smoothing mentioned above:

$$Y_{t+1} - Y_t = e_{t+1} - (1-p)e_t.$$

By introducing B (a so-called shift operator which has the effect of changing the index of the variable) on which B is 'operating', so that for example $BY_{t+1} = Y_t$, $B^2 e_t = e_{t-2}$

and more generally, $B^k Y_t = Y_{t-k}$, where B is operating on Y_t and e_t, we can re-write the above equation as:

$(1 - B)Y_{t+1} = [1 - (1 - p) B]e_{t+1}.$

Let $\theta(B)$ be a polynomial in B, defined as

$\theta(B) = 1 - \theta_1 B - \theta_2 B^2 - \cdots - \theta_q B^q,$

and it is of order q because the highest term in B is B^q. Each of the terms above has the effect of shifting the index of the variable on which $\theta(B)$ operates. To use the exponential smoothing example, if we take

$\theta(B) = 1 - (1 - p)B$, then

$$\theta(B)e_{t+1} = [1 - (1 - p)B]e_{t+1}$$
$$= e_{t+1} - (1 - p)e_t.$$

If we define $\phi(B)$ similarly as a polynomial of order p the authors claim that most non-seasonal time series may be represented by the equation:

$\phi(B)(1 - B)^d Y_{t+1} = \theta(B)e_{t+1}.$

Referring again to the exponential smoothing example, by taking $\phi(B) = 1$, $d = 1$ and $\theta(B)$ as above, we see that the exponential smoothing generating model is just a very special case of the above general class of models.

The first stage in deriving a working model is the choice of p, d and q, and this is equivalent to selecting the particular model to be estimated with the data from the general class of Box—Jenkins' models. The next stage is to estimate the parameters in the polynomials $\theta(B)$ and $\phi(B)$. Finally the adequacy of the model is tested, and if the model is unsatisfactory the process is repeated. We may think of the Box—Jenkins' procedure as relating two components, the autoregressive component $\phi(B)$ which operates on Y_t, and the moving average component $\theta(B)$ which operates on e_t. These two components give the process its acronym, the ARIMA (p, d, q) where ARIMA stand for 'integrated autoregressive-moving-average process' and p, d and q are the parameters of the model. Thus, exponential smoothing is an ARIMA (0, 1, 1) process.

The Box—Jenkins' methodology was developed primarily for use in designing control systems. It has recently attracted quite a lot of attention from forecasters, perhaps drawn by its complexity. In its more general form it can include seasonal factors, and also relate changes in Y_t to changes in an associated series X_t, when X is a leading indicator[†] of Y. The authors have described a class of models as well as the selection of a particular model from that class by reference to the data, a process which implies that the values of p, d and q are estimated from the data. It is not surprising that the model performs better, in general, than those discussed earlier in the section if the only criteria used are the mean absolute deviation and standard error, for in the earlier cases the model was specified on *a priori* grounds and with Box—Jenkins we may choose from a much wider class of models. In fact, many of the

[†] A series $[X_t]$ is a *leading indicator* for a series $[Y_t]$ if changes in Y_t are anticipated by changes in X_t.

methods discussed in §7.3 are just particular examples of the ARIMA (0, 2, 3) model:

$$Y_{t+1} - 2Y_t + Y_{t-1} = e_{t+1} - \theta_1 e_t - \theta_2 e_{t-1} - \theta_3 e_{t-2}.$$

Harrison in his 1965 paper comments that he has never found the complications of even this particular model necessary when forecasting sales.

To set against the increased accuracy and increased generality offered by this approach, there is:

(*a*) The cost and time required to produce a forecast;
(*b*) The skilled manpower necessary;
(*c*) The need for substantial historical data.

The forecaster is concerned with resolving the cost—accuracy payoff and evidence on the trade-off offered by the Box—Jenkins class of models is not yet definitive. Groff (1973) and Chatfield and Prothero (1972) have argued that the Box—Jenkins' models are difficult to apply and rarely produce better forecasts than the simpler methods of the earlier sections. While the first statement is undeniable, Box and Jenkins have replied convincingly that all that is required is an analyst familiar with the methodology (and fifty data points) to arrive at excellent forecasts. More recently a substantial contribution by Newbold and Granger (1974) shows through the analysis of some 100 varied time series the generally higher level of accuracy attainable using the Box—Jenkins' procedures.

As yet questions concerning:

1. The stability of the estimated coefficients as the behaviour of the time series alters;
2. The re-estimation of the coefficients as each new observation is gathered;
3. The type of series which most benefits from an analysis using this methodology,

remain unanswered. We doubt, in general, that the benefits as yet outweigh the costs of using the Box—Jenkins' methodology, although there are no doubt exceptional circumstances in which it is thoroughly justifiable. The analyst who recommends this should be prepared to argue its cost-effectiveness. The reader who wishes to understand the subject more thoroughly is referred with some trepedition, to the definitive book by Box and Jenkins, as well as a recent book by Nelson (1973) aimed at the mathematically inclined manager.

§7.5 Computer support in model building

The methods described in this section are conceptually simple. They are routinely used as part of the production/distribution/inventory system in most manufacturing companies. Every computer bureau and computer manufacturer offers a suite of programs developed from the models we have so far discussed. We have argued here that because we cannot make any 'best buy' recommendations as to which method to use, access to a suite of programs is desirable because this allows the user to investigate a time series in depth. In a decision situation where accuracy has a high value the analyst is then able to compare the results of using a wide variety of different forecasting methods. As we noted in the previous section we could expect Box—Jenkins to outperform the simpler models about 70 per cent of the time. However, because Box—Jenkins is more expensive and hard to use, the exponential weighted moving average technique of §7.3.2 is generally adequate. Thus, in considering which set of programs to have available, flexibility and choice are the primary criteria. If the suite of programs is interactive so much the better; certainly a fast turn-round time is important if the analyst is to benefit from a large choice of different models. While it is unlikely that the more complicated models just discussed will often be required, it is possible that certain critical forecasting situations may well require their added precision.

In summary, short-term naive forecasting models, though they vary in computational and mathematical complexity, are readily available and for the most part easy to use. As we pointed out in the introduction to these latter chapters in the book, they do not in themselves contain implications about the causes of the fluctuations in Y, and therefore the decision maker can only accept their predictions and take actions which will lead to his most favoured outcome, an outcome contingent on the forecast coming true. The causal models of the next chapter allow the decision maker to influence the forecast (and therefore the outcome of his chosen course of action) through his choice of strategic variables. To the decision maker it is obvious that a causal model is preferable, for it gives him more information on which to base his actions. Unfortunately, naive models may well be better at forecasting. Consequently, we see naive models as a particularly valuable part of the information system for besides their obvious and immediate use in the short term they are benchmarks by which to measure the forecasting performance of the more ambitious causal models.

§ 7.6 An introduction to long-term forecasting with naive models

Unlike short-term forecasting activities which tend to provide routine and continuing inputs for a monitoring and control process, long-term forecasts are associated with specific decisions which have important potential significance and require long lead times for implementation. Decisions that utilize long-term forecasts could be concerned with merger or diversification or perhaps with the type of factory expansion problem discussed in §3.3.2. All these decisions, however carefully we structure them, will depend to some extent on long-term forecasts.

The most common technique of naive long-term forecasting is by extrapolation of a trend curve. The underlying assumption made in using this technique is that the past history of a time series is a good guide to its future development and that an observed historical trend can therefore be validly projected. However, the longer we project ahead the less likely such an assumption is to be justified. Hutchesson (1968) for example discusses an example of two alternative trend curve models, both of which fit the data on bituminous coal consumption per head from 1820 to 1920 equally well. Ten years later they were already 100 per cent in error, as oil consumption rocketed. Unlike short-term models which are continually adaptive in response to errors, errors in long-term models are compounded by the mere process of extrapolation. One safeguard is to avoid using trend curves to predict narrowly defined variables. We are much more likely to be successful in predicting the total need for document reproduction than we would be predicting simply the growth in photocopying. This is because in the process of aggregation we can expect offsetting discrepancies in each component to cancel out. This, though, is only a partial solution. Since in long-term forecasting there is no formal corrective device built into the system, to ensure that the forecasts are not completely wild the forecaster's intuitions and knowledge of the industry is critical in the selection of a good forecasting equation, and the sensitivity of the decision to the forecast's accuracy needs to be thoroughly considered.

§ 7.7 Mathematical trend curves: long-term forecasting

As we stated in the previous section, a mathematical trend curve is a projection of the past history of a time series into the future. Since a large variety of models can be used to fit the same set of data, we propose to examine the properties of some of the more commonly used curves which, where a set of data is analysed by computer, will all be considered in the search for an appropriate model. As our first model we can describe a product's sales as a linear function of time:

$$Y_t = \beta_0 + \beta_1 t + e_t.$$

Figure 7.3 shows both a *linear* sales curve and its associated percentage growth rate for the particular linear model $Y_t = 5t$. The growth rate is generally $100 * (Y_{t+1} - Y_t)/Y_t$ and in the above situation of linear growth this equals: $100 * [5(t + 1) - 5t]/5t = 100/t$. We now see from Fig. 7.3 that in selecting a linear trend we are making an additional assumption that the percentage rate of growth in sales of the product is declining rapidly. In a situation where the rate of growth is declining, but the sales are not changing by the constant amount implied by the linear model, more flexible alternatives in the form of *parabolic* or *higher order polynomials* can be used. In particular Harrison and Pearce (1972) in a survey article comment that the parabola is often 'a

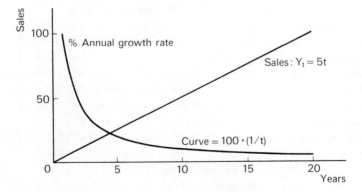

Fig. 7.3 *Straight line with per cent annual growth rate*

suitable trend curve for representing the growth of many products in their early or middle stages of development'. Unfortunately, it is often only with the benefit of hindsight that we know that products were in fact in those stages. A further obvious qualification of this statement is required where the curve is projected into the distant future. Here the use of any polynomial is unlikely to be satisfactory for its asymptotic behaviour (becoming very large, either positive or negative) cannot be a reasonable description of the eventual demand for any product. Such incautious extrapolation produces extreme predictions such as the one that every man and woman will have only two square feet to stand on by the year 2000. An *exponential* model of the form:

$$Y_t = \alpha(1 + \beta)^t,$$

carries this process further, since it implies a guaranteed constant percentage growth rate.† It is, of course, very unlikely that the demand for any product could increase at a fixed rate for more than a few years. However, the exponential is widely used and has figured prominently in the arguments concerning the Club of Rome's model of the world economy, *The Limits to Growth* (Meadows and Meadows, 1972). Figure 7.4

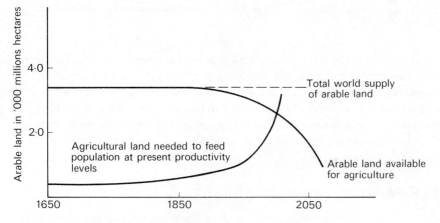

Fig. 7.4 Total world supply of arable land

provides an illustration of the use of exponential growth rates in the study. It shows that while the requirement of arable land for food grows exponentially with population the supply is exponentially reduced to provide the same population with houses, roads and so on. Where, as in sales forecasting, it is reasonable to assume extreme results are unlikely a *modified exponential* is often used:

$$Y_t = \alpha - \beta r^t,$$

with α and β positive, and $0 < r < 1$. In this curve as t becomes large r^t becomes small; Y_t then approaches a finite limit.

† The exponential model of Chapter 6 was: $Y_t = ae^{bt}$. The models may be shown to be equivalent by taking logarithms, and putting $\log(1 + \beta) = b$.

A similar result occurs when the *Gompertz* curve

$$\log Y_t = \alpha - \beta r^t$$

is used. Figures 7.5 and 7.6 illustrate the shape of these curves and their associated percentage growth rates. In sales forecasting if a trend curve gradually approaches a limit, this limit is the maximum market potential of the product. However, increasing GNP and increasing population both have the effect of increasing this potential.

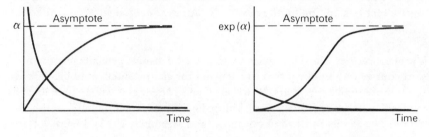

Fig. 7.5 *Modified exponential with per cent growth rate*   Fig. 7.6 *Gompertz with per cent growth rate*

Harrison and Pearce (1972) argue that either a plot of consumption per head or consumption per unit of GNP at constant money value overcomes this difficulty. It is obvious, however, that in an absolute sense there is a finite limit to world consumption, and this limit is not necessarily far distant. In the simple models provided by trend curves the unresolvable nature of what is suitable asymptotic behaviour in a time series points to the inherent limitations of a method which is merely extrapolative of the past.

§7.8 An example

In late 1971, as part of a comprehensive study into investment opportunities in the US chemical industry, a research team decided to make a preliminary forecast of sales for each major chemical product using trend curve analysis. These forecasts would then be used to select the most promising sectors of the chemical industry for further investigation using more detailed econometric methods, based on the expected technological development of the consumer and producer industries. Trend curve analysis was thus to be used to provide a number of benchmark forecasts, which would be useful as a comparison and focus of subsequent analysis. In the case of one of the initial products — chlorine — the time series data on production until 1969 are shown in Table 7.4.

An analysis of the chlorine production figures was made using the ICI long- and medium-term forecasting package.† First, however, the data are checked for extreme observations, or outliers which are replaced by averaged values. Using this smoothed

---

† The package may be obtained through Brown and Pearce Associates, Barnet, Herts. Our thanks are due to ICI and Dr Richard Munton for their help.

Table 7.4
Production of chlorine in US (short tons $* 10^3$)

Year	Production	Year	Production	Year	Production	Year	Production
1900		1915	31.0	1930	205	1945	1,192
1901		1916	41.3	1931	202	1946	1,165
1902		1917	48.5	1932	193	1947	1,443
1903	2.9	1918	55.6	1933	236	1948	1,640
1904	3.2	1919	55.6	1934	285	1949	1,767
1905	4.5	1920	61.0	1935	330	1950	2,084
1906	5.6	1921	48.0	1936	380	1951	2,518
1907	6.6	1922	64.5	1937	466	1952	2,609
1908	6.4	1923	77.7	1938	440	1953	2,797
1909	8.9	1924	81.0	1939	514	1954	2,904
1910	11.0	1925	100.2	1940	605	1955	3,421
1911	12.1	1926	122.0	1941	801	1956	3,798
1912	16.4	1927	135.5	1942	990	1957	3,948
1913	20.3	1928	165.0	1943	1,214	1958	3,604
1914	22.4	1929	219.5	1944	1,262	1959	4,347
1960	4,637	1965	6,517	1970	9,978	1975	13,155
1961	4,601	1966	7,205	1971	10,576	1976	13,840
1962	5,143	1967	7,654	1972	11,194	1977	14,538
1963	5,464	1968	8,500	1973	11,831	1978	15,248
1964	5,945	1969	9,400	1974	12,485	1979	15,967
1980	16,694	—		1990	23,851	—	

Source: Chemical Economics Handbook and Chemical Week

data the program fits six curves, the five already discussed together with the *log parabola*, log $Y_t = \beta_0 + \beta_1 t + \beta_2 t^2$. The program then calculates the curve giving the best fit, and prints out comparative measures for the fit of the other curves. In this example the log parabola, closely followed by the *Gompertz* came out best.† It is the experience of the program's developers that if a parabola or log parabola seem best at this stage a *modified Gompertz* curve will often greatly improve the forecasting accuracy. A modified Gompertz is similar to the Gompertz except its asymptote is increasing rather than horizontal, to reflect the underlying growth in GDP and/or population. If the original data is discounted by the growth rate of GDP (or population) and the transformed series fitted to a regular Gompertz, the result is that the asymptote of the original series grows (with GDP), and is therefore a modified Gompertz curve.

A modified Gompertz was fitted to the chlorine data but the results were similar to those obtained using the log parabola. With the parameters of the chosen curve estimated the residuals, $Y_t - \hat{Y}_t$, are analysed for any systematic variation. Three possibilities exist:

† Many of the models used, the Gompertz and the log parabola for example, are intrinsically non-linear: see §6.3, and require special estimation techniques.

1. An attempt can be made to relate the residuals to any additional variable which might seem relevant, using a least squares model:

$$Y_t - \hat{Y}_t = \beta_0 + \beta_1 X_t + e_t.$$

2. The residuals can be analysed to isolate any cyclical component.
3. The residuals errors can be smoothed using an exponential smoothing procedure, and the smoothed estimate (say E_t) used to predict future errors. Consequently the forecast $\hat{Y}_t$ is adjusted to incorporate the estimate of the error through the equation:

Final forecast $= \hat{Y}_t + E_t.$

Working through these steps, there seemed to be no significant linear relationship between the residuals and any other plausible independent variable. As a result the residuals were inspected for a cyclical component. A cycle of 13.5 years was estimated but failed to explain a statistically significant part of the variation in the residuals.

Finally the program smoothed the residual errors in an attempt to estimate any systematic component in the forecast errors. In fact the 'best' smoothing constant (see §7.3.1) was estimated to be one indicating that the smoothed error forecast E_t in 3 above was identical to the current observed error, e_t. After making the above adjustments to the initial forecasts the program graphed observed and forecast errors, combining the selected trend curve and the exponentially smoothed estimates of residuals to give point forecasts to the required time horizon of 1990. The final trend curve used to do this was a log parabola:

$$Y_t = \exp(\beta_0 + \beta_1 t + \beta_2 t^2).$$

The estimated parameters of the equation were:

$$\hat{\beta}_0 = 1.0383, \quad \hat{\beta}_1 = 0.1769, \quad \hat{\beta}_2 = -0.0008,$$

with a standard error of 137.

Using this equation and incorporating the last observed error for 1969 of 478.25 as the best estimate of future residuals the results shown in Table 7.5 and Fig. 7.7 were derived. Inspecting the results it appears from Table 7.5 that by 1980 the 90 per cent confidence limits, at ±12 per cent of the point forecast, are already rather wide and forecasting beyond this point on the basis of the trend curve alone is obviously hazardous.

To check the stability of the estimated trend curve an additional curve using data only between 1956 and 1969 was estimated and this resulted in a parabola being selected as the trend curve which best fitted the shorter data set. A cycle of 3 years in the residuals was also estimated. Comparing the forecasts of the original and new equations, considerable divergence was apparent with a forecast of 245,000 in 1990 from the shorter data base, almost ten times the forecast shown in Table 7.5. This shows that the estimated curves are neither stable nor reliable. Faced with this instability a check was made on earlier studies done in forecasting chlorine production and it was found that either a Gompertz or log parabola had proved excellent in

Table 7.5

The level and growth of chlorine production in the US together with 90 per cent confidence limits

Year	Forecast Lower Limit	Centre	Upper Limit	Growth (%)
1970	9,200	10,000	10,800	10.2
1971	9,700	10,500	11,500	6.0
1972	10,300	11,200	12,200	5.8
1973	10,800	11,800	12,800	5.7
1974	11,300	12,500	13,700	5.5
1975	11,800	13,200	14,600	5.4
1980	14,600	16,700	16,700	4.5
1990	19,200	23,900	29,600	2.9

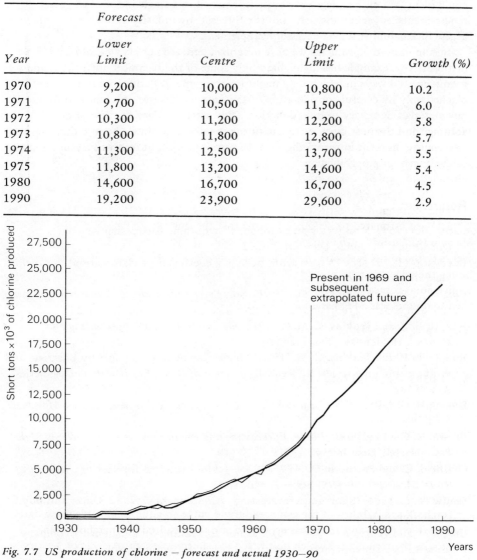

Fig. 7.7 US production of chlorine — forecast and actual 1930—90
———— *forecast*   ———— *actual*

estimating sales in 1969 to within 2½ per cent, with the data base 1903—50. This suggested that the parabola, which was selected when the shorter data base, 1956—69, was used and which produced such extreme forecasts, should not be considered further. In any case, given the instability of the 'best' trend curve to changes in the data base, it was thought necessary to seek external checks on the final forecasts produced by the log parabola. One possible method would be to try and forecast separately the trend in the sales of each major user of chlorine that the project team could identify and then aggregate these forecasts into a single index of chemical requirements. A general discussion of the forecasts by industry experts before their acceptance would also be a necessary supplement.

In summary, the problems we have described here are not atypical of trend curve methods. This example has highlighted only some of the technical difficulties, and we have suggested ways in which they might be overcome. A definitive forecast can be reached only by careful consideration of the product, its uses, its competitors and the raw materials necessary to its production. Only after considering the cost of inaccuracy and the possibility of restructuring the decision can we be sure that the uncertainty inherent in the method can be accepted without resort to a causal model of the demand—supply system.

References

Batty, M. (1969) 'Monitoring an exponential smoothing forecasting system', *Operational Research, Quarterly*, vol. 20.

Bliemel, J. (1973) 'Theil's forecasting accuracy coefficient: a clarification', *Journal of Marketing Research*, vol. x.

Box, G. E. P. and Jenkins, G. M. (1962) 'Some statistical aspects of adaptive optimization and control', *Journal of Royal Statistical Society*, Series B, vol. 24.

Box, G. E. P. and Jenkins, G. M. (1970) *Time Series Analyses, Forecasting and Control*, Holden-Day, San Francisco.

Box, G. E. P. and Jenkins, G. M. (1973) 'Some comments on a paper by Chatfield and Prothero and on a review by Kendall', *Journal of Royal Statistical Society*, Series A, vol. 136.

Brown, R. G. (1959) *Statistical Forecasting for Inventory Control*, McGraw-Hill, New York.

Brown, R. G. (1962) *Smoothing, Forecasting and Prediction: of Discrete Time Series*, Prentice-Hall, New Jersey.

Chatfield, C. and Prothero, D. (1972) 'Box—Jenkins seasonal forecasting', *Journal of Royal Statistical Society*, Series A, vol. 136.

Coutie *et al.* (1964) 'Short-term forecasting', *ICI Monograph No. 2*, Oliver and Boyd, Edinburgh.

Green, M. and Harrison, P. J. (1973) 'Fashion forecasting for a mail-order company using a Bayesian approach', *Operational Research Quarterly*, vol. 24.

Groff, Gene K. (1973) 'Empirical comparison for short-range forecasting', *Management Science*, Series A, vol. 18.

Harrison, P. J. (1965) 'Short-term sales forecasting', *Applied Statistics*, vol. 14.

Harrison, P. J. (1967) 'Exponential smoothing and short-term sales forecasting', *Management Science*, Series A, vol. 13.

Harrison, P. J. and Davies, O. L. (1964) 'The use of cumulative sum (cusum) techniques for the control of routine forecasts of product demand', *Operations Research*, vol. 12.

Harrison, P. J. and Pearce, S. F. (1972) 'The use of trend curves as an aid to forecasting', *Industrial Marketing Management*, vol. 2.

Harrison, P. J. and Stevens, C. F. (1971) 'A Bayesian approach to short-term forecasting', *Operational Research Quarterly*, vol. 22.

Holt, C. C. (1957) *Forecasting Seasonals and Trends by Exponential Weighted Moving Averages*, Carnegie Institute of Technology, Pittsburg.

Hutchesson, B. (1968) 'Market research and forecasting in the chemical industry. The state of the art', *Chemistry and Industry*, vol. 86.

Meadows, D. H., Meadows, D. L. *et al.* (1972) *The Limits to Growth*, Earth Island, London.

Nelson, Charles R. (1973) *Applied Time Series Analyses for Managerial Forecasting*, Holden-Day, San Francisco.

Newbold, P. and Granger, C. W. J. (1974) 'Experience with forecasting univariate time series and the combination of forecasts', *Journal of Royal Statistical Society*, Series A, vol. 137.

Pegels, C. C. (1969) 'Exponential forecasting: some new variations', *Management Science*, Series A, vol. 15.

Salzman, L. (1968) *Computerized Economic Analysis*, McGraw-Hill, New York.

Shone, M. L. (1967) 'Viewpoint', *Operational Research Quarterly*, vol. 18.

Trigg, D. W. (1964) 'Monitoring a forecast system', *Operational Research Quarterly*, vol. 15.

Trigg, D. W. and Leach, A. G. (1967) 'Exponential smoothing with an adaptive response rate', *Operational Research Quarterly*.

US Bureau of the Census (1965) 'The X-11 variant of the Census Method II seasonal adjustment program', *Technical Paper 15*, Washington, D.C.

Additional references

In the short term, naive models such as exponential smoothing or moving averages are discussed in most introductory texts. Perhaps

Lewis, C. D. (1975) *Demand Analysis and Inventory Control*, Saxon House, D. C. Heath Ltd, Farnborough, Hants

is the most complete, with a useful section on computer packages.

Benton, William K. (1972) *Forecasting for Management*, Addison-Wesley, Reading, Mass.;

Cantor, Jerry (1971) *Pragmatic Forecasting*, American Management Association, New York

are both introductory, and spend much of their time with basic methods examining their response in differing situations. Such books aim to give a feel for real problems and real data, an aim to which we also have adhered. They follow in the tradition of

Brown's first book (1959) and his subsequent, more theoretical work (1962), both of which are referenced above. The latter is essential reading for any theoretician, though we have tried to reflect some of his ideas for the practitioner's use.

The more advanced works of Box and Jenkins have already been referenced. A recent book, written for the ubiquitous practioner of intermediate mathematical abilities, which takes its own view of developments in the area of naive modelling is:

Kendall, M. G. (1973) *Time-Series*, Griffin, London.

Both Kendall and Brown in 1962 provide an introduction to an increasingly popular method among mathematicians, Spectral Analysis. An article by:

Jenkins, G. M. (1965) 'A survey of spectral analysis', *Applied Statistics*, vol. 14.

may provide a useful starting point for the operational researcher or economic statistician who is interested in learning the basic ideas. His aim was to present the techniques using the minimum of mathematics in order that the reader be able to apply it, a worthwhile though difficult exercise as the paper proves.

Fortunately, longer-term forecasting through trend curve analysis has not encouraged a substantial literature, the one basic reference so far omitted being the elementary:

Gregg, J. V. *et al.* (1964) 'Mathematical trend curves: an aid to forecasting', *ICI Monograph No. 1*, Oliver and Boyd, Edinburgh.

8
Causal models of cost and demand

§8.1 Introduction

Managers are interested in the help that forecasts can give them in controlling the future of their organization. The use of forecasts allows them to make decisions that are likely to generate attractive rather than unattractive outcomes. The intention in building causal models is therefore not just to predict what would happen if events developed according to a pattern discerned in previous observations, since this can often be done adequately using naive forecasting methods, but to predict what would happen in circumstances in which a deliberate management decision to alter the pattern of events is possible. To do this requires a causal model.

Before we can continue it is important to be clear about how we use the word 'causal'. In the last chapter we constructed models in which a variable Y was specified as functionally related to time. In doing this we do not suggest that changes in time 'caused' variations in Y_t. We intuitively construct a larger system in which time is just one of the variables affecting Y. Within this larger framework we understand that it is the systematic variations of these additional variables with time which produce a concomitant change in Y; not the ageing of the system. These intuitive considerations yield the following definition of causality adapted from Blalock (1964).

If outside influences, I, have no systematic effects on the relationship between the independent variable X, and the dependent variable Y, then a knowledge of both I and X does not alter the probability distribution of Y estimated when only X is known. Further, suppose that all other variables excluded in the causal model have been controlled or do not vary. We say X is a direct cause of Y if and only if a change in X produces a change in the probability distribution of Y. This definition of a direct cause may be extended to the notion of an indirect cause. If X is a direct cause of Z in system A we write $X \xrightarrow{A} Z$. We say X is an indirect cause of Z in system B if we can find variables U, V, etc., such that $X \xrightarrow{B} U \xrightarrow{B} V \ldots \xrightarrow{B} W \xrightarrow{B} Z$. The term 'intervening variable' is used to refer to variables such as U, V and W. Causation is thus a construct, developed by the experimenter to explain and predict changes within the system he has defined. If we change the system, for example by adding an additional variable in a regression equation, there is no reason why a direct causal relationship should not become indirect, or even spurious.

In constructing a causal model for forecasting the analyst therefore attempts to include those elements of a system which are important in determining the dependent variable's behaviour within the forecast time horizon. The system's definition implies that certain factors in the system are related in well-specified ways. For example, in forecasting demand for cars it is reasonable to expect that a comparative increase in real price will adversely affect demand, all other factors remaining constant. This assumed relationship translates directly into a testable hypothesis about the regression coefficient of price in a model for forecasting demand. If the assumptions from which a model is constructed are not supported by the estimated parameters of the model, however accurately the model has managed to duplicate the values of the dependent variable, it is no more powerful (and probably more dangerous) than the naive methods of the previous chapter.

The choice of variables to be included in a causal model of a system should be based on *a priori* assumptions about the functioning of the system. The basis of these assumptions is discussed more fully by Cox (1968, pp. 266—9) and includes:

(*a*) Conclusions from previous related studies;
(*b*) Relevant theoretical analysis;
(*c*) Known constraints on the system.

In addition it is desirable that the parameters of the models should:

(*a'*) have some physical interpretation.
(*b'*) be insensitive to changes in the data base or to minor changes in the model.

The validity (Naylor and Finger, 1967; Van Horn, 1971) of causal models is thus established as much by the reasonableness of the assumptions underlying them as by their predictive ability. This reduces the risk run in naive modelling of basing a model on an excellent but spurious correlation with the previous values of the series. Since causal models however, are more expensive to construct and validate than naive models they are normally only worth applying in situations where a sufficient time interval exists for the decision maker to benefit substantially from a partial control of the final outcome of the decision.

§ 8.2 Short-term control of production costs

Knowledge of the cost structure of production is one of the key inputs used in determining the most profitable price to set in selling output. However, in setting prices firms rely on accounting data as a source of cost information, without recognizing that accounting conventions are simply a convenient set of assumptions for allocating existing costs of current production and contribute very little information on the cost impact of changing the scale or mix of output.

The use of multiple regression techniques can often provide management with improved data on the cost consequences of changes in production, since it provides a method leading to statistical estimates of the breakdown of total production costs among the range of products responsible for generating those costs. Of course a full statistical analysis of cost data may not always provide the required answers. This would be the case, for example, where almost no variation in the pattern of production occurred over the period for which observations are available. Such an absence of variation is understandable given the system of pre-set budgets and targets under which most managers work. However, since multiple regression depends on isolating and explaining sources of variation, a series of production observations changing by only relatively small amounts from period to period contains information of only limited statistical value.

For example, it may be important to know what fuel savings could be achieved by reducing production by 20 per cent. If production had previously been constant over time there would be no data on which we could base our estimates of the consequences of such a cut. But in situations where production had fluctuated by 5 or 10 per cent a statistical relationship linking production level and fuel usage could be derived, although even here the projected cut of 20 per cent is outside the range of previous observations. Statistical cost analysis is particularly useful in situations where there are several products, perhaps even joint products, which use a number of similar, or shared resources, and where we have observations on a variety of product and input combinations. (A joint production process arises where two or more products are necessarily produced in fixed proportions. Meat and hide are typical examples.) Without statistical analysis, the amount of information available may mean that it is impossible to isolate the independent effect of a change in output on the level of overall costs. Using multiple regression techniques, however, such effects can be identified and once identified can be used as estimates in building a model to forecast production costs. Nevertheless the useful life of such a model in predicting production costs ends when the data on which it was based becomes unrepresentative of the latest production technology. Once technical change occurs it follows that some of the original output levels observed as data may no longer be feasible. Once such an irreversible change has occurred it is no longer valid to retain an unaltered short-run forecasting model.

8.2.1 The technology of the production process

The simplest process consists of a single product, made by using a relatively small variety of production resources. In a process of this kind observed output should be directly related to the level of observed resource inputs. This relationship can be expressed in the form of a production equation:

$$Y = f(X_1, X_2, X_3, \ldots, X_n),$$

where Y is the output level and where $X_1, X_2, X_3, \ldots, X_n$ are measures of the quantity of each type of resource used. In a simple situation of this kind, unless wastage or loss of any of the input resources has occurred the level of output, Y, may be assumed to be the maximum level that can technically be generated, given the mixture and levels of inputs that were in fact used. This would be most clearly the case for those industries where the relationship between inputs and outputs are almost totally linear. For many processes in the chemical industry for example, the mix of inputs and the prospective yield are governed by well understood physical relationships. The ideal proportions for inputs are thus known and total output can only change where total inputs, in their correct proportions, also change.

More often, the connection between resource inputs and production output is not linear. In many cases the same level of output can be produced from a variety of combinations of resource inputs, so it becomes desirable to respond to changes in relative prices of input by substituting more of those resources that have become comparatively cheap in exchange for those that have become comparatively more expensive. A very important example is that most production processes permit substitution between the use of capital equipment and the use of labour, so as labour costs rise relative to the costs of capital equipment, it becomes economical to replace as much of the labour as possible by machinery. A similar short-run example is of a manufacturer of chocolates who can increase or decrease the size of the centres of his chocolates to take advantage of relative shifts in the prices of sugar (the main ingredient for centres) and cocoa (the primary input for chocolate).

One conceptual difficulty, once we move away from linear production functions and permit substitution among inputs and outputs is to establish a distinction between short-run substitution and long-run substitution. In the long run, reliance on almost any resource can be reduced by a process of substitution, and equally a given set of resources can be used to make a wide variety of products. In the short run, however, production facilities require specific inputs and little, if any, substitution is possible. Thus the wide price fluctuations that are a characteristic for example of the market for non-ferrous metals such as copper, zinc and lead, arise because manufacturers are locked into production commitments that require specific materials that have to be procured almost at any price. In the longer run, however, substitution by both the manufacturers and their customers can contribute to a significant reduction in the demand for high priced inputs. The distinction between short-run and long-run adjustments to a production process can be made on the basis of the reversibility of the adjustment made. With a short-run adjustment it is possible to move back to the original production position. Where long-run adjustment has occurred, previous production patterns cannot be re-achieved because the technology and capital equipment employed have changed. For example a short-run response to the increasing cost of skilled engineers might be to reduce preventive maintenance and to accept a greater number of breakdowns. The long-run response would be to replace the equipment with more expensive but more reliable alternatives. The need to distinguish between short- and long-term adjustments becomes particularly important where industry-wide data is being used, since different firms in the industry will be at different stages of adjustment and will therefore react in different ways to changes in input and product prices.

8.2.2 Forecasting price levels for materials used
Statistical analysis of production data based on the technology in use allows the analyst to estimate the parameters in a model which relates production to the resource

inputs. Using such a model we can forecast resource requirements needed for any given output.

In order to forecast costs we need additional information about the future level of resource prices. Using these predictions and our knowledge of the substitution possibilities of the production technology used, it is possible to define both the lowest cost combination of resource inputs and the total overall cost of meeting any production target. For example, in Fig. 8.1, the economics of the choice of technology to be employed in an atomic reactor are shown to depend on the assumed relative costs of the two principal resources used — investment capital and nuclear fuel. The heavy-water system involves 10 per cent higher capital investment but generates twice as much electricity per unit of fuel used as does the alternative light-water reactor. If finance for the two projects was available on identical terms the cost of output of electricity for each system would then depend directly on expected fuel costs. The heavy-water reactor would be relatively more expensive at low fuel costs, given its higher capital charges. If the price of uranium rose to more than V however, the greater fuel economy of the heavy-water system would make it more attractive. The choice of reactor technology thus depends on the forecast of uranium prices.

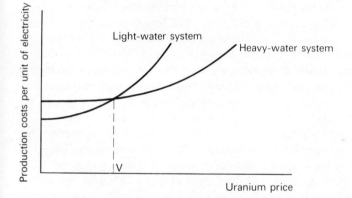

Fig. 8.1 *Cost curve of heavy- and light-water reactors*

For many products forecasting the price of inputs may present few problems because input materials are available under long-term contract at fixed or known prices. Airlines, for example, insist on a contract price procedure for maintenance and spare parts at the time they make the initial purchase of an aircraft. A very large proportion of the output of many commodities are sold on fixed contract terms, so that although we could attempt to predict the market price at which non-contracted supply was sold, such a price estimate would of course be substantially less reliable than would be the current rate for a contracted supply. This usually allows the producer to fix the price of the resource over the whole of the planning period. However, he may also have to pay above the market rate for the privilege of a contracted supply so a comparative forecast of the future price of the resource and its present contract price would give an idea of the cost to the producer of eliminating price uncertainty through the use of a contracted source of supply. Another source of information on future resource prices may be the existence of a 'futures' or forward market for the product. In this type of market, contracts to buy and sell a commodity at some determined future date are traded. For example on the 21 March 1975 the London Bullion market price for silver for immediate delivery was 182.5p per troy oz. The price quoted for delivery in 12 months' time was 204.3p, a clear indication that prices were expected to rise by about 12 per cent over the year.

However a more usual situation is where no organized futures market exists. Here price forecasts have to be made on the basis of estimated supply and demand conditions in each commodity market. Typical price behaviour in such markets will be discussed in §8.3.

a. Extractive materials. Extractive industries — mining, quarrying, oil production and so on — are usually capital-intensive depending on a substantial investment infrastructure, by which we mean railways, electricity supplies, roads and possibly pipelines, harbours and bulk handling equipment. As a consequence current supply capacity is almost totally determined by investment plans made perhaps several years ago.

With production capacity in the short- and medium-term determined, market prices depend almost entirely on demand. During 1972 and 1973 for example, it was physically impossible to expand raw material output at anything like the 7—8 per cent growth rate shown by world industrial output during those years. With raw material supplies expanding at a rate of only 3—4 per cent p.a. on the basis of earlier investment plans it was inevitable that demand would run ahead of supply, generating rapid price increases and overall scarcity. Any subsequent reduction in the rate of growth of world industrial output, coupled with more rapid investment in new raw material capacity under the stimulus of high prices would lead to a reduction in the pressure on supplies and an equally sharp reversal in raw material prices. This sequence of events is illustrated in Fig. 8.2, where the output of extractive materials is shown to grow steadily with little fluctuation. At times when industrial output accelerates intense demand for an almost fixed supply of materials forces prices up sharply. Equally, a cut-back in industrial output reduces prices rapidly. Without stockholding, material

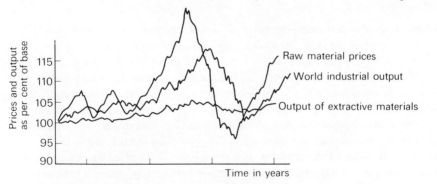

Fig. 8.2 Supply, demand and price — extractive materials

prices tend to move in advance of a change in the trend of industrial output becoming apparent, simply because raw materials are required at the beginning of the production cycle. Where widespread stockholding exists however, price shifts may lag behind output shifts.

b. Non-extractive raw materials. For some non-extractive raw materials, market behaviour is very similar to that of extractive materials. This is because they are only produced as a consequence of a long-term investment decision — for example current timber, rubber or olive oil output depends on decisions made between 5 and 50 years ago. Producers in these areas are locked into a product market on a long-term basis.

Other raw materials, however, are produced as a result of short-term decisions — less than one year — and from year to year it is relatively easy to substitute outputs. Farmers can switch from growing barley one year to growing sugar beet the next leaving whisky distillers with no raw materials and sugar refiners with an embarrassing surplus. Given this ease of substitution prices for these agricultural products depend on estimating fluctuating supply rather than on relatively stable demand. Since a production time lag of up to a year may be involved it is normally assumed that supply decisions this year depend on price conditions last year. An unusually low price one year might thus remove sufficient production capacity from the industry to produce a situation of low supplies and high prices for a product the following year. An additional variable which affects the supply of most agricultural materials is of course climatic conditions. As a consequence actual output may be higher or lower than intended, depending on whether climatic conditions are favourable or unfavourable. Because of these variations, any statistical examination of supply response to expected price should attempt to explain intended rather than actual output.

Where the supply conditions are unstable and the production is seasonal, substantial stockholding will be common. Market prices in this case do not reflect current supply conditions alone; they are also influenced by removals or additions to stock by buyers and sellers. Observed market price thus reflects not a point of equilibrium in production and consumption, but an equilibrium in total supply and demand including movements in or out of stock. This may be summarized by the equation:

$$\left.\begin{array}{c}\text{Current production (based on the supply}\\\text{response to previous year's prices)}\\+\\\text{Movements in or out of stock (based}\\\text{on response to current prices)}\end{array}\right\} = \left\{\begin{array}{c}\text{Consumption demand (based on}\\\text{current prices)}\\+\\\text{Movements in or out of buyers' stocks}\\\text{(based on response to current prices)}\end{array}\right.$$

Without data on movements in and out of stock, particularly in the case of products like coffee and cocoa where both buyers and sellers may hold stocks equivalent to a year or more of current production, it follows that a statistical explanation of price fluctuation based solely on current production and consumption would be unreliable.

c. Raw material supply — substitution possibilities. Any but the most short term of material price forecasts based on historical supply and demand relationships has to recognize the substitution process, whereby cheaper and readily available materials are brought in to replace scarce and expensive ones. Even in the case of an essential raw material – for example oil – the area of use in which substantial substitution is possible is very wide, even if no direct substitutes are available. For example, insulation materials are a substitute for oil, since they permanently reduce the demand. In the last resort, managerial skill can also be substituted since improved management of, for example, road transport distribution networks or improvements in the loading of facilities can easily reduce energy consumption by 15–20 per cent, with only a slight deterioration in the level of service and availability, as the airlines demonstrated, during the oil crises of 1973/74.

In forecasting, therefore, great caution is necessary in distinguishing between short-term, possibly violent price fluctuations, and the long-term influences on material prices once substitution factors are considered.

d. Conclusion. We can see that beyond a 1- or 2-year time horizon, within which stock movements, climatic conditions and temporary monopoly conditions exert a powerful influence on price, we rapidly become involved in predicting issues such as long-term productivity and substitution that are central concepts in technological forecasting (discussed in full in Chapter 10). Once we try to evaluate such factors, we not only have to consider supply and demand conditions in the market in which we are interested, but also the balance of supply and demand in the alternative markets to which buyers and producers may turn to in substitution. We rapidly become involved in a systems model of total material supplies. In many cases this could not be justified; instead it would be better to use a relatively cheap, naive model, perhaps of the Box–Jenkins type. Finally, we have not discussed the most important production cost, the cost of labour. One reason for this is the difficulty of doing so. Strangely enough, however, labour costs, although a big element in total costs, may not generate much variation so far as a firm's overall performance is concerned. This is because direct and indirect labour accounts for around 70 per cent of the total cost of all goods bought, so that changes in wage rates are rapidly reflected in product prices and vice-versa. Once costs are deflated by the changing value of money, the net effect of changes in the money cost of labour may be small. Because labour is a particularly flexible resource it is rare for major differences in the trend of wages rates in different industries to occur.

(For much more detailed discussion of the techniques of price forecasting see: Labys and Granger (1970) and Spencer *et al.* (1961).)

8.2.3 Estimating short-run cost changes – an example
The purpose of short-run cost models is to estimate the change in cost following a reversible short-run change in the pattern of production involving either a change in the mix of inputs or outputs. It is assumed in this example that no permanent or irreversible change is made to the production process, and that the forecasting model maintains its validity.

A firm produces three similar products that use a number of production facilities and processes in common. In the past the cost of energy used in the production process had been allocated by guesswork between the products. With increases in energy costs it becomes more important to relate energy usage directly to each product so that pricing and profitability can be reassessed. The available data is shown in Table 8.1.

Table 8.1

Energy consumption and production data

Month	Production Product A	Product B	Product C	Total energy consumption in kW/h
1	120	261	144	9,452.3
2	117	202	125	8,053.2
3	142	210	174	9,406.1
4	128	286	149	10,116.5
5	123	210	104	8,069.4
6	117	251	149	9,263.9
7	159	255	103	9,724.0
8	166	292	104	10,567.9
9	138	252	110	9,272.2
Total	1,210	2,219	1,162	83,925.5
Average	134.4	246.5	129.1	9,325.0

To estimate the independent effect that output of each product has on total energy consumption a model of the following form was estimated from the data.

Consumption of energy $= \beta_0 + \beta_1 \rho_A + \beta_2 \rho_B + \beta_3 \rho_C + \text{(error)}$,

where ρ_A: is output of product A, ρ_B output of B etc. The estimated coefficients for the equation are shown in Table 8.2. The calculated equation has an R^2 of 99 per cent, with each variable significant at the 1 per cent level, as is the overall F statistic. The Durbin–Watson statistic gives no evidence of autocorrelation.[†] We can therefore conclude that the model is statistically acceptable and that the calculated coefficients are reliable.

These coefficients provide a solution to the original problem because they allow us to identify the relative energy requirements for each product, and to assess the consequences of any given increase in energy prices on the total costs of production for each of the three products. If energy costs increase, the absolute effect on the costs of product A would be about 40 per cent greater than for product B and almost 100 per

† No formal test is possible with less than fifteen observations. A runs test can, however, be applied.

Table 8.2
Estimated coefficients

	Coefficient	Standard error	T value
β_0†	87.370	65.859	1.32
β_1	23.347	0.352	66.21
β_2	18.114	0.181	99.75
β_3	12.645	0.227	55.74

R squared	R-bar squared	Durbin–Watson	ANOVA
0.9998	0.9997	statistic	F value
		1.6413	7,982

cent greater than for C. Such a change therefore would require an analysis of both future selling prices and planned production levels for the three products. Using the same relationship it is also possible to calculate the best response to any reduction in energy supplies. Suppose the company was required to reduce energy consumption to 80 per cent of normal levels. Based on the observations we have used this would imply a reduction to 0.80 * 8,325.0 kW/h per period, or 7,460.0 kW/h. Without the derived equation and hence without information about the specific energy requirements of each product, a normal response would be to cut output of each product to 80 per cent of normal.

Assuming that each of the three products generated similar levels of contribution per unit we would thus expect total contribution to drop by 20 per cent and profits to drop even more. However, using the equation we can see that cutting output of product A would save much more energy than similar cuts in output for B and C. If average outputs were scheduled for products B and C then substitution in the calculated equation would yield the permissible output of A

$$7,460.0 = 87.370 + 23.347\rho_A + 18.114\bar{\rho}_B + 12.645\bar{\rho}_C$$

where $\bar{\rho}_B$, the average output of B = 246.5, and $\bar{\rho}_C$ = 129.1: Solving this equation

$$\rho_A = \frac{1,267.3}{23.347} \quad \text{or} \quad 54 \text{ units}$$

Thus we can meet the required savings using an altered product mix that still permits a total output of 54 + 247 + 129 units or 430 units, which is 84.3 per cent of normal production volume. If all products contribute identically this leaves us with 84.3 per cent of normal contribution, instead of only 80 per cent.

We should add one proviso to this example; cutting energy consumption by 20 per

† The constant term in the equation shows that 87.370 kW/h of energy per period cannot be associated with any of the production activities. Assuming this loss continued under reduced production actual output would have to be reduced to 79.8 per cent of normal.

cent leaves the firm producing below its previous minimum capacity of 8,053 kW/h. As long as production can be cut in the way recommended by the suggested solution without disturbing the production process and the start up energy costs (of 83.37 kW/h) the recommendation is valid. However, we have been forced to extrapolate somewhat beyond the range of the observed production data, and while we may be certain about the direction of the revised production decision it might be advisable to re-estimate the parameters of the equation once a lower level of production is established to check whether the new level is optimal.

8.2.4 Cost functions and technological change

The example in the previous section showed a method of analysing short-run costs. Because the observations were made for a single production unit over a comparatively short time interval we could be reasonably confident that no changes had occurred in the underlying technology. Production fluctuations were simply a consequence of demand fluctuation and were reversible.

Should, we be concerned either with a longer time span, or if our observations include data on several firms, we need to use a forecasting model which allows for the possibility of technological (irreversible) change. Thus we might collect data on short-run production costs for each of perhaps three plants (A, B and C) and then use this data to estimate the short-run cost relationship for each plant of the firm:

$$C = \beta_0 + \beta_1 V + \beta_2 V^2,$$

where C represents unit costs in £'s and V represents weekly production volume. However, it would be a mistake if we used these three short-run cost equations (illustrated in Fig. 8.3) to estimate future costs in setting up a plant to produce, for example, 3,800 units a week. Although the three plants on which we have observations could produce this output, the high indicated costs simply reflect the short-run diseconomies of working at an output other than the designed capacity of the plant. A more accurate estimate of costs under long-term adjustment would be provided by the envelope cost curve, CC' which connects up the minimum cost positions of the three plants studied. (The concept of the envelope curve is described in Stonier and Hague, 1972, p. 136.) Our estimate of production costs for a 3,800 unit plant would then be given by the intersection this output makes with envelope curve and would be £465 and not the £480 of plant B, the £550 of plant A or the £645 of plant C.

In analysing the possibility of technological change two separate factors are generally discussed:

(*a*) disembodied technological progress;
(*b*) embodied technological progress.

The distinction rests on whether the technological progress is achieved as a consequence of capital investment in new and more productive equipment (embodied change) or as a result of improved working methods, skills and management with existing capital equipment. In the case of embodied technological change one of the

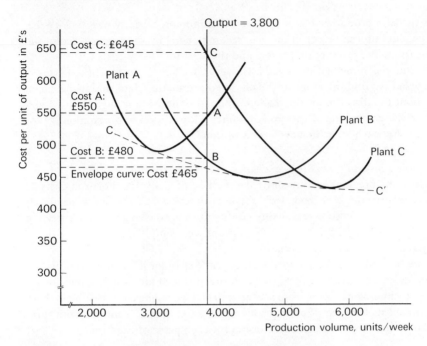

Fig. 8.3 Output volume per week: short-run cost functions and long-run envelope cost curve

principal explanatory variables in the cost equation is the level of investment in new equipment. In the case of disembodied change the main explanation is the build-up of product and production experience in the work force.

8.2.5 An example of disembodied technical change

An engineering firm accepted a contract to manufacture sets of guides and rollers as a major component of a new containerized air freight handling system. The total contract was for 5,000 sets. Each unit had to be made of a new light alloy that required special machining operations to provide accuracy of fit in the aircraft fuselage, to ensure matching tracking of the rollers and to eliminate excess weight. After 12 weeks' production the management of the company wanted to review their profit projection for this contract, which they had accepted at a unit cost of £125. Using the information in Table 8.3, they adopted and estimated a forecasting model of the form:

$$Y = \beta_0 + \beta_1 X_1 + \beta_2 X_2 + (\text{error}),$$

where $X_1 = \log_e$ [units of weekly output], $X_2 = \log_e$ [cumulative output] to date, and Y = unit cost.

The underlying assumption of the model was that variable X_1 would represent fluctuation in week to week output, and hence the short-run cost curve, while X_2 reflected the long-term learning of the particular skills and experience needed for this contract. A logarithmic transform was thought appropriate for both variables since this

Table 8.3
Contract costs and output

Week	Unit cost	Output	Cumulative output	Logarithm of output (X_1)	Logarithm of cumulative output (X_2)
1	175.6	10	10	2.30259	2.30259
2	168.9	8	18	2.07944	2.89037
3	165.7	11	29	2.39790	2.36730
4	158.8	15	44	2.70805	3.78419
5	150.0	16	60	2.77259	4.09435
6	146.8	20	80	2.99573	4.38203
7	153.6	18	48	2.84037	4.58497
8	137.2	29	127	3.36730	4.84419
9	136.3	29	156	3.36730	5.04986
10	135.4	33	189	3.49651	5.24175
11	135.3	35	224	3.55535	5.41165
12	132.3	40	264	3.68888	5.57595

reflected general opinion about the process of learning in assembly operation. The estimated coefficients for the equation are shown in Table 8.4. The calculated equation has an R^2 of 96 per cent with an overall F significant at the 1 per cent level. The t values for β_0, β_1 and β_2 are also significant. Our calculated equation is thus: $Y = 220.612 - 12.7005X_1 - 7.7436X_2$. Using this equation we can estimate that if production from week 13 on is stabilized, for example, at 45 units per week, estimated costs would be:

Unit cost, Week 13 = £220.612 − 12.7005 $\log_e$ 45 − 7.7436 $\log_e$ 309
                   = £127.842.

Table 8.4
Estimated coefficients

	Coefficient	Standard error	T value
β_0	220.612	6.5987	33.43
β_1	−12.7005	6.2592	−2.03
β_2	−7.7436	3.2180	−2.40

R squared	Standard error	Durbin−Watson statistic	ANOVA F value
0.965	3.06781	2.459	205.732

In other words the contract is currently at breakeven point. The future profitability of the product, for the same rate of weekly production, could be estimated say after 2,000 units have been produced using the same equation

Unit costs for 2,000th item = £220.612 − 12.7005 $\log_e$ 45 − 7.7436 $\log_e$ 2,000

$$= £113.410.$$

By this stage the contract looks quite profitable, given a contract price of £125.

8.2.6 Cost forecasting − embodied technical change

Short-run forecasting is largely concerned with the effective use of given resources. Once we start looking at changing costs resulting from new investment the main decision problem becomes one of selecting the investment offering the most effective combination of resources under anticipated future conditions. Of course these may or may not be realized, but that becomes a short-run problem once the investment decision has been made.

One of the central concepts in investment planning is that of substitution. A primary response to increasing labour costs, for example, is investment in labour-saving machinery. In other words, capital inputs are being substituted for labour inputs. Before we make labour-saving investments we need to know the substitution possibilities between the combinations of inputs required by each available technical solution. Where substitution possibilities exist in the configurations of alternative investments it is usual to adopt a production relationship of the form†:

Output = $f(X_1^{\alpha_1}, X_2^{\alpha_2})$,

where output is determined by the contribution of two inputs, X_1 and X_2. This type of model allows us to use observations on existing installations which embody an existing but not ideal technology to estimate a model that should point to the best future solution. The model itself can be estimated using linear regression techniques, simply by transforming the data observations to logarithms, as we showed in §6.3 and estimating the equation:

$\log_e$ output = $\beta_0 + \beta_1 \log_e X_1 + \beta_2 \log_e X_2$.

8.2.7 Optimal investment − an example

The capacity planning section of a chemical manufacturing company were investigating alternative investment proposals for a new production facility. The product they required could be manufactured using only one significant raw material − sulphuric acid. All other inputs were regenerated and recycled. The only other significant cost was related to capital expenditure. For any of the three processes considered (A, B or C) the level of capital expenditure involved rose (though not directly in propor-

---

† The best known application of this type of production function is the Cobb−Douglas model $Y = \alpha L^\beta C^{1-\beta}$ used by economists to estimate the productivity of labour (L) and Capital (C) in generating national output (Y). For an example examining electricity generating costs, see Lomax, 1952.

tion) as more sophisticated control processes were built in to increase the efficiency with which sulphuric acid was used. A productive function of the form: $P = \alpha v S^{\beta_1} K^{\beta_2}$ was fitted where P is 'production in hundreds gallons/day'; S is 'consumption of sulphuric acid in hundreds gallons/day'; K is 'the capital cost of installation in £'000'; and v is the error. The following equation was derived by taking logarithms of the production function:

$$\log_e P = \beta_0 + \beta_1 \log_e S + \beta_2 \log_e K + (\text{error}).$$

This equation was estimated separately for each of the three potential production processes using observations on the output, capital cost and sulphuric acid consumption characteristics observed for all currently operating installations of each of the three types. Each equation had significant coefficients and a standard small enough compared to the average output to make its use valid in the subsequent analysis.

Process A: $\log_e$ output $= 0.02 + 0.45 \log_e S + 0.47 \log_e K$

Process B: $\log_e$ output $= 0.08 + 0.58 \log_e S + 0.34 \log_e K$

Process C: $\log_e$ output $= 0.14 + 0.32 \log_e S + 0.56 \log_e K$

Using these equations it is possible to graph the possible combinations of resource requirements in terms of capital installation and sulphuric acid that would generate a daily output of for example 150,000 gallons from any of the three processes. This is done in Fig. 8.4. An inspection of the results in Fig. 8.4 shows that all three of the alternative technologies could potentially offer the cheapest costs, since parts of all three production curves lie below the remaining two curves at some combination of acid consumption and capital investment. As a result, we cannot dismiss any of the technologies on grounds of absolute inefficiency; we have to select on comparative cost grounds. This means we look for the process offering the lowest costs at the desired level of output.

To do this, forecasts of the costs of both sulphuric acid and capital are needed. Suppose the low grade acid required in the process could be secured on a long-term contract at £25 per '000 gallons and the daily cost of maintaining, depreciating and financing £1 of capital equipment was £0.0006 (equivalent to 18 per cent p.a., assuming a 300-day working year) we could evaluate the costs of all possible production situations for all three processes and pinpoint the cheapest. This process can be simplified using a graphical approach and allowing relative prices between capital and acid to be expressed by a slope. Thus it would cost £10 m. * 0.0006, or £6,000 daily to service £10 m. of capital equipment, while £6,000 would buy 240,000 gallons of acid at the contract price of £25 per '000 gallons.

By using 240,000 gallons and £10 m. as intercepts we can draw line PP_1 on Fig. 8.4 to represent all possible combinations of acid and capital equipment which would just cost £6,000 per day to buy, and this may be confirmed by costing any of the combinations of inputs lying on the line. Because PP_1 lies below all three production curves it follows that none of these combinations produce the desired output, of 150,000 gallons per day within the £6,000 per day budget constraint. However we can increase the budget while preserving price relativities between acid and capital by drawing new

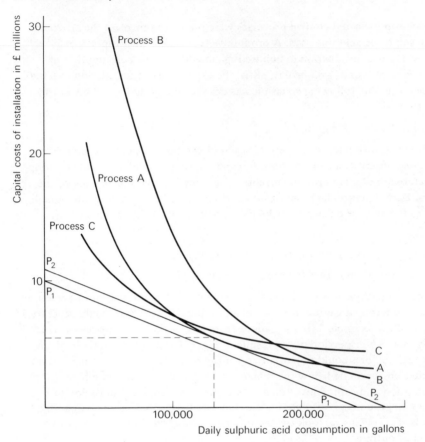

Fig. 8.4 Capital — sulphuric acid requirements for three production processes, at a production level of 150,000 gallons per day

price lines parallel to PP_1 but further out from the origin. In the example here the budget is increased until line PP_2 can be drawn tangential to the production curve of process A. This is the minimum cost production process for the forecast prices. At this point we would be buying a total of 132,000 gallons of acid daily and would have to invest £5,500,000. Total daily costs would be £6,600. Using technology C, on the other hand, would have required a daily budget for an identical output of about £6,720 and process B would have been even more expensive at £7,320.

   The final point is that the calculations above and the conclusion that technology A is cheaper relates only to that chosen level of output and the forecast level of costs used in the calculation. The three technologies have different scale characteristics so that the choice of the most economical process depends on the level of output even when costs remained unchanged. It is also apparent from Fig. 8.4 that a very small increase in acid costs relative to capital costs would be sufficient to make process C rather than process A the better one to choose.

8.2.8 Cost forecasting − a summary

The analysis of cost using forecasting models has relevance to two main issues. First, for short-term alterations in production volume or product mix, such models allow us to predict likely cost levels and resource requirements for situations which have not previously occurred. Secondly, in the long run where interest focusses on entirely new production technologies, forecasting models are useful in abstracting those key characteristics which we hope to develop in the new installation from the patchwork of observations we may have on existing installations and perhaps experimental data. In both cases cost models offer a basis for improved decision making.

§ 8.3 Forecasting models of market behaviour

8.3.1 Introduction

The prediction of future sales is one of the most frequently encountered forms of business forecasting and yet the area remains one of major uncertainty for business. Not only are the causal relationships connecting sales with the strategic and operational variables within the control of the firm poorly understood but also the conflicting activities of competitors mean that the environment within which they must operate is at least partially hostile.

Because market forecasts are essential to business planning, and have been developed for many different applications, a wide variety of models exist. Since sales forecasts are required so frequently it is not surprising that many of these models provide direct inputs into a decision process. Some even include decision variables within the model so that it can be used both to forecast and determine profitable management policy as part of the planning process in the firm. Before considering some of the more common models in greater detail, however, we intend to discuss the variables that tend to be used as basic components in most models.

8.3.2 The variables determining market behaviour

Price. Almost all models assume that the price of a commodity has a direct influence on the amount that is bought. Under conditions in which inflation is changing price levels in general it would be normal to measure price variables (for that matter all variables expressed in money values) in real terms, that is, after dividing money prices by a price index. Such an adjustment of course may result in loss of information because consumers may still respond, to some degree, to money rather than real prices. Whether or not real or money prices are used, we can specify a model which shows how price influences demand. Two possible assumptions are commonly considered.

1. The absolute level of price affects demand linearly. Neglecting other variables, this is written $Q_t = \beta_0 + \beta_1 P_t$ and consequently if we write ΔP for the price change, and ΔQ for the quantity change we have $\Delta Q = \beta_1 \Delta P$. Thus we see that whatever the level of price, an equal absolute change of price, ΔP, always has the same absolute effect on Q.

2. More often we assume that price effects are proportional and that a 2p price change on 20p affects demand in the same way as 4p on 40p. This can be described through the logarithmic model:

$\log Q_t = \beta_0 + \beta_1 \log P_t$.
By subtraction: $\log Q_t - \log Q_{t-1} = \log Q_t/Q_{t-1}$
$$= \beta_1 \log P_t/P_{t-1},$$

and we see that a fixed *proportionate* change in price always has the same effect on proportionate demand.

We can use these ideas to introduce the concept of price elasticity, defined by:†

$$e_p = \frac{\Delta Q}{Q} \bigg/ \frac{\Delta P}{P}.$$

It is the proportional change in quantity divided by the proportional change in price, and, in selecting a logarithmic model we implicitly assume the elasticity is constant. Price elasticity is a measure of the responsiveness of demand to a change in price. The higher the elasticity the larger the proportionate drop in demand produced by a given proportionate increase in price. The demand for a product is also affected by the prices of complementary or competing products. Where a pair of products, for example, records and record players, are complementary, a price reduction for records should generate a demand increase for players. For competitive products – records and cassettes – a price reduction in records should lower the demand for cassettes.

As before we have the choice of specifying either actual, or more normally real prices, and absolute or proportionate (logarithmic) price responses. If a logarithmic relationship is specified this results in a constant cross elasticity. For product A the cross elasticity of demand with respect to the price of product B is defined as:

$$\frac{\Delta Q_A}{Q_A} \bigg/ \frac{\Delta P_B}{P_B}.$$

When assumptions about direct, complementary and substitution price effects are made to justify including variables in the price equation, such assumptions should be supported by the coefficients actually measured. Thus the quantity sold should fall as its own real price, and the price of a complementary good increases, or as the real price of competing goods fall. Occasionally there are exceptions to this, for example where price is believed to be a primary indicator of quality. Skis, for example are impractical to test (except through consumer magazines) and therefore the buyer will accept that a high price means a correspondingly high quality. A second exception occurs when a price increase is a precursor of further increases. Demand here is a function not just of current price levels but also the expected levels they may reach in the near future.

---

† For the reader familiar with calculus, e_p is more correctly defined as $\dfrac{dQ}{Q} \bigg/ \dfrac{dP}{P}$. Consequently, with the logarithmic model $\log Q = \beta_0 + \beta_1 \log P$, differentiation shows the elasticity to be constant and equal to β_1.

Consumer attitude surveys may be useful in capturing this effect in modelling the behaviour of the market.

Income. The level of consumer purchasing power is also a powerful determinant of sales. Again, as with price levels, we would normally seek to adjust for inflation by transforming money income levels to real terms, using a price index. Income elasticity may be defined in the same way as price elasticity. When Y is income $e_Y = (\Delta Q/Q)/(\Delta Y/Y)$. As with the price variable, the relationship between sales and income is often described by a logarithmic model which also has a constant income elasticity over the range of observations. This would reflect an expectation that a given proportional increase in income would have the same proportional effect on demand. The income elasticity provides a convenient indicator of growth prospects for a product. An income elasticity below 1 indicates that the product will occupy a declining share of total consumer expenditure — it is called an inferior good — for as the consumer becomes richer he increasingly substitutes alternative purchases. An income elasticity above 1 indicates a growing proportion of consumer expenditure will be directed towards the commodity.

The growth consequences for a product are even more pronounced when the income variable chosen is itself growing more quickly than aggregate income. This might be the case if income was represented by disposable income or discretionary income (disposable income is defined as after-tax income; discretionary income is disposable income less all routine recurrent expenditures).

For major consumer durables such as cars or refrigerators, the concept of discretionary income is important since only above a given threshold income level would a consumer have enough left over, after meeting basic living costs, to contemplate the purchase of such an item. For this class of product the number of income earners crossing the threshold income level or acquiring an adequate discretionary income is an important variable. To convert straight income data to a threshold variable we would use a sample survey of the income levels of product buyers to establish the threshold level, and a distribution of incomes to indicate the number of income earners who are likely to cross the threshold for any given rate of increase in aggregate incomes. A widely used though approximate method for measuring the threshold effect is to include an income change variable as well as income itself in the regression equation in the expectation that roughly the same portion of the population pass the income threshold for each given increase in national income or average wage rates. To measure discretionary income a survey could again be used to first find average basic living costs for given consuming units. By deducting these costs from total income a measure of discretionary income is obtained.

While threshold effects and measures of discretionary income are one way of disaggregating total consumer income, another method is to use the distinction originally introduced by Milton Friedman between permanent and transitory income (see, e.g., Stonier and Hague, 1972, pp. 471–6; Houthakker and Taylor, 1970, pp. 255–9). Friedman hypothesized that both income and consumption could be divided into permanent and transitory components and that it was the permanent component which determined underlying demand. Thus a measure of permanent income should be used in empirical studies. One way of constructing an approximate measure of permanent income is by using a geometric average† of consumers' past income instead of simply a single observation of current income.

A final issue that arises is the identification of the appropriate consumption unit over which income is to be aggregated. While *per capita* income may be an adequate measure of the consumer's income for some products others for example, houses and perhaps cars tend to be family purchase decisions, so that family rather than individual income is the appropriate variable to use.

Once we have established appropriate measures of income we may easily combine them with price variables in a simple sales forecasting model. If, as is normal we assume that variables have a proportionate effect on demand then a logarithmic model (equivalent, of course, to a multiplicative model) is used, of the form:

$$\log Q_t = \beta_0 + \beta_1 \log P_t + \beta_2 \log Y_t + e_t,$$

where Q_t is the level of sales; P_t is the price of the good; and Y_t is income, all measured in time period t. The price coefficient in the model, β_1 provides a direct measure of the constant proportional effect on sales of changes in the price of a good, with β_2 similarly measuring the proportional effects of a change in income.

More formally we can call β_1 and β_2 the price and income elasticities of demand for the good. The value of calculating elasticities is that they provide a powerful summary of the nature of the relationship between an independent variable and sales. For example, if the absolute value of β_1, the price elasticity in the above equation, is greater than 1, we would immediately recognize that a change in price brought a more than proportional change in sales, whereas an elasticity of less than 1 would indicate that sales were relatively insensitive to price change. Similarly an income elasticity of greater than 1 indicates that as growth continues an increasing share of consumer purchasing power will be directed to the product.

Financial resources. Consumer purchasing power is a function of both income and the ability to borrow. Consumer durables involving major expenditures are frequently purchased on credit, and this borrowing is repaid from the income stream over future years. The availability and cost of credit is thus a factor in determining the level of consumption. For example, in a study of the demand for cars in 1965 in Great Britain made by O'Herlihy (1965) the effects of variations in hire purchase restriction were reflected by using as a variable the average life of a hire purchase contract. In tight monetary conditions this was as low as 1.5, but by 1959 had risen to 3 years. The longer this period the greater the effective purchasing power of the consumer. In the same way it is to be expected that mortgage interest rates have a considerable effect on the demand for houses.

Time. The inclusion of time as an independent variable in a demand forecasting model

† The geometric average of n observations $X_1 \ldots$ is equal to $n\sqrt{X_1 * X_2 * \cdots * X_n}$.

has two related functions. It is often postulated that the product itself is gaining acceptance in the market, through a process of communication with people who have previously bought the product or even by simple demonstration of the product in use. This process of diffusion can be approximated by including a time trend in the forecasting equation.

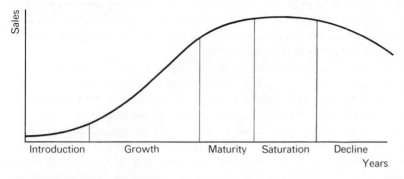

Fig. 8.5 The product life cycle

The appropriate form of time–demand relationship is dependent on where on the development cycle the product lies. It is convenient to divide the product life-cycle into five stages as shown in Fig. 8.5. The first two stages of introduction and growth are characterized by high percentage growth rates, and the analyst should consider the inclusion of exponential or quadratic terms, in forecasting for those stages. Similarly when the product is in decline, its function being superceded by superior alternatives, a quadratic term might well be useful, while through maturity and saturation a linear relationship suffices. Despite the appeal of the concept, supported by the statistical argument of §6.8, where by including time in a forecasting model the parameters of the model were more readily interpretable, the possibility of confusing two causal mechanisms arises. It is difficult to discriminate between the movement along the product life cycle and increases in, for example, income as the two variables are often collinear. Consequently it is better (though difficult) to try to measure consumer taste and its relationship to technological change directly rather than to use the product life cycle concept with time as a proxy variable for measuring the movement along the cycle. (Both Robinson, 1971, pp. 53–5 and Palda, 1969, pp. 50–1, 238–44, give interesting discussions of the effect of taste on demand. They do not directly concern themselves with its measurement and subsequent inclusion in demand models.)

Quality. The correct measurement of product quality poses great difficulties, not least because product quality and product price are very closely connected. For some industries it is reasonable to assume that the output from all firms is homogeneous and that all firms have equal access to a homogeneous market, but for most industries we know there are significant differences in product design and distribution which differentiate the product offered to the consumer by different manufacturers.

The same situation may occur in comparing the products of an industry over time. A car manufactured this year is considerably more expensive than one manufactured 5 years ago, but part of this increase is represented by the inclusion of new features — electrically-heated windows, disc brakes, safety equipment or radial tyres. The problem is to deduct the price changes due to an alteration in quality from total price change to leave an estimate of price change at constant quality. If we do not do this we could well find that our regression equation shows that consumers increase their purchases as unit price rises when the real situation is that after deducting the cost of quality changes the constant quality price is falling.

A number of avenues exist for handling quality changes in regression models. In some cases it may be possible to obtain a direct estimate of the extra cost incurred in making a quality improvement and this cost can be used as an indicator of quality. For cars this is usually possible because most quality changes are available as an option before they become standard equipment. We would thus be able to deduct the cost of an electrically-heated window from any revised price once this new feature became standard. An alternative approach is to estimate qualitative differences by surveying consumers to establish the price differential they attach to given qualitative variations and adjusting price variables by a commensurate amount. In some circumstances the qualitative differences between products can be estimated more directly from physical performance. Frequency of overhaul for machinery, protein content of animal feed-stuffs or nicotine content of cigarettes (see e.g., Telser, 1962) are all capable of being measured directly and such measurements can be included as a variable in the regression equation in the normal way.

Of course where quality differences are the major dimension of competition elaborate methods of estimating quality are justified and in Appendix 5 we describe the compilation of a hedonic (Cowling and Cubbin, 1972) quality index that can be derived where there are several important dimensions to product quality.

Stock variables. So far we have considered a number of variables that often appear in models used to forecast sales. It is more accurate, however, to suggest that price, income and quality variables affect consumption rather than sales and that in turn sales result from a chosen level of consumption, a situation of indirect causality. This distinction may seem pedantic, and in practice for many products, sales and consumption are virtually contemporaneous and hence may be used interchangeably. However, where the product is relatively durable the consumption derived from a given sale continues over several periods. We therefore cannot assume that sales levels from period to period are independent. A consumer who had just bought a new car, for example, is demonstrably less likely to buy a new car the following month than is a consumer with a similar income and set of commitments who bought his last new car 2 years ago. While the car consumption level of these individuals is not dissimilar, in relation to income and other variables, it is apparent that the sales likelihood is considerably different. Since we normally are only able to observe sales levels, the forecasting ability of the equations we would seek to employ would be relatively poor, unless a specific variable measuring stock level was included as an independent variable in the equation. In measuring such a variable, either we might observe the level of stocks directly, or else construct an artificial stock variable.

The need for a constructed stock variable occurs particularly in the case of capital equipment and long-lived consumer durables where, although we can physically identify stock levels in terms of numbers of machine tools or cars, we know that year by year the effectiveness of the stock is being reduced by depreciation and technical obsolescence. To adjust for this a specific calculation reflecting the age structure of the observed stock of goods needs to be made. In making this calculation both an initial stock level and a depreciation rate may have to be assumed.

Table 8.5
Construction of a stock variable using historic sales and a given depreciation rate

Time	Sales in constant prices	Deprecia- tion rate (%)	Stock at the beginning of year	Depreciation	Starting stock − depreciation + sales
$t-6$	95.6	25	320.5	80.13	336.0
$t-5$	112.7		336.0	84.0	364.7
$t-4$	130.2		364.7	91.2	403.7
$t-3$	117.6		403.7	100.9	420.4
$t-2$	114.9		420.4	105.1	430.2
$t-1$	125.4		430.2	107.5	448.0
t	136.1		448.0	112.0	472.1

Thus in Table 8.5 we show how, given an original assumption of depreciation rate and starting stock, it is possible to construct the estimated stock. By calculating stock over a long enough series most of the bias that would be introduced by assuming an incorrect starting stock can be eliminated before we need to use the stock variables in the forecasting equation. The choice of a depreciation rate is more difficult since an inappropriate rate will generate continued bias in estimated stock levels. Ideally the depreciation rate† should ensure that the residual variation in consumption, after price, income and other effects have been removed, is minimized even though this implied ratio may not match either taxation allowances or expert opinion on actual depreciation.

Thus the final forecasting model is of the form

$$Q_t = \beta_0 + \beta_1 S_t + \beta_2 P_t + (\cdots) + e_t$$

with S_t, the stock variable depending on an arbitrary depreciation rate δ. The equation is then estimated. A further value of δ is then used to give a new set of estimates. The value of δ finally chosen is the one maximizing R^2.

† New purchases during a year should be adjusted for depreciation by the end of that year, so a smaller depreciation rate should be used to reflect the shorter period of usage compared with the stocks which have been held through the whole year.

Two further approaches to stock-holding may also be encountered. In some instances the problems of initial stock and possible variations in depreciation rates are handled by explaining current sales using previous sales levels as independent variables in a forecasting equation. The coefficients of these variables should automatically reflect the negative impact of previous sales variation on current sales and also the diminishing (depreciating) nature of such an influence. Another approach is through the so-called stock adjustment model, where sales are to be determined by both the amount consumed in previous time periods as well as the stock level the consumer needs to hold to service his intended level of consumption. The adjustment model is based on the hypothesis that purchases in time period t will be determined by a desire to bring his actual stock into balance with his desired stock.

Such models have received wide application in forecasting the purchase of consumer durables, as well as the demand for industrial capital goods where investment expenditures are motivated by a desire to equalize desired and actual production capacity. (Two particularly famous studies of consumer durables are: Chow, 1957; Stone and Rowe, 1954, 1956. These studies have initiated further articles, e.g. Chow, 1960, and Stone and Rowe, 1960. O'Herlihy, 1965 uses this approach in forecasting the demand for cars. Houthakker and Taylor, 1970, use an effective variant in their study of some commodities.)

The concept of a stock variable to cover the situation of habit formation has been extended by Houthakker and Taylor (1970). They argue that there is a carry over effect from one period to the next for many goods which do not fit the stockholding category. For instance, if a consumer has established a habit of smoking or visiting the cinema, the influence of the habit will carry over into current consumption. His consumption pattern reacts to changed income and price coefficients as if he were still drawing on a psychological stock of the product bought under the old price and income condition. For expenditure on many non-durables we would therefore expect the stock coefficient to be positive. The greater the habit the larger the amount consumed.

In summary, stock models are a flexible method of modelling the consumption of all types of commodities and although extra care is necessary in estimating and interpreting the resulting forecasting equation any serious attempt to model the process of consumer behaviour cannot neglect the stocks concept.

Marketing expenditure variables. In 1971 marketing expenditure accounted for more than 1 per cent of UK GNP (Crutchley, 1973) and in the United States the proportion is even higher. Despite the amount of money spent it is not altogether clear what effects marketing has. Ostensibly it is intended to raise market share and perhaps total sales. However, since advertising and marketing expenditures are in the nature of investments from which payoffs are distributed over time it is often difficult to associate any given expenditure with a direct return. Another difficulty is that marketing is not a homogeneous expenditure. A pound spent on a television advert is not identical with a pound spent on a special discount offered to a retailer or for that matter, a pound spent sponsoring a Grand Prix car racing team, yet all these marketing activities may well take place simultaneously and have a joint effect on observed sales.

In using marketing expenditures to predict sales there is therefore, a choice in the extent to which the marketing budget is decomposed into the separate components of expenditure. Before attempting such a decomposition, however, there should be some indication that a relationship between aggregate advertising expenditure and sales can exist. To check such a relationship the central problem of linking advertising expenditure to subsequent sales has to be tackled. A variety of approaches have been used to transform a series of marketing expenditures into a variable that can be linked to sales at any point in time. A general assumption made is that advertising expenditures are subject to decay in their influence on sales. Although the effect of a given expenditure may persist for several periods its influence diminishes. By using moving or exponential averages on marketing expenditures it is reasonably easy to generate a single marketing variable which reflects current and past marketing expenditures. A more common situation is to find that the lagged effect of advertising is measured directly in the forecasting equation. If we assume that the effect of advertising expenditure on sales decays at a constant rate then the basic sales equation is:

$$Q_t = \beta_0 + \beta_1 Y_t + \beta_2 (A_t + \lambda * A_{t-1} + \lambda^2 * A_{t-2} \ldots) + (\text{error})_t,$$

where Q_t is the sales level; Y_t income level; A_t, A_{t-1}, etc. advertising expenditures; and t indicates the time period of each observation.

As is shown in §6.5 by algebraic manipulation we can modify this to give an equation in which the parameters can be estimated directly:

$$Q_t = \beta_0(1 - \lambda) + \beta_1 Y_t + \beta_2 A_t + \lambda Q_{t-1} + (\text{error})_t.$$

Making appropriate assumptions about the error term now allows the parameters to be estimated. (More correctly we should also include the term $-\beta_1 \lambda Y_{t-1}$ but this is rarely done because it then poses the same estimation problems that exist with autocorrelation. Some difficulties also arise from the form of the error term resulting from this transformation. We discuss the problem briefly in §8.3.5.)

A well-known study using this type of model was made by Palda (1964) using data on the advertising strategy of the Lydia Pinkham Patent Medicine Company, which was a monopoly supplier of a particular patent medicine. The equation derived was:

$$Q_t = -3,649 + 1,180 \log_{10} A_t + 774 D_t + 32t - 2.83 Y_t + 0.665 Q_{t-1}$$
$$\quad\quad\quad\quad (243) \quad\quad\quad\quad\quad (107) \quad (5.9) \quad (0.67) \quad\quad (0.063)$$

$R^2 = 0.941$ Durbin–Watson statistic = 1.59.

(Figures in parentheses are standard errors.)

where both sales Q and advertising A are in thousands of dollars; Y is total personal disposable income in millions of dollars; and D is a dummy variable taking a value 1 in the halcyon days before 1925 when the Food and Drug Administration insisted on some factual support for advertised claims.

The equation can be interpreted to show that at average levels of sales and advertising ($\bar{Q} = 1,828$ and $\bar{A} = 934$), an extra \$10,000 spent on marketing would lead to an immediate sales increase of $1,180 * (log 944 − log 934) = $5,074 and a long-term increase of $5,074/(1 − 0.665) or $15,146.

The logarithmic transform of the advertising variable is justified on the reasonable assumption that advertising effectiveness declines as saturation levels are reached, and the negative income variable is not unexpected given the nature of the product. Before we can accept the model as 'correct' we need to assure ourselves that the omission of a price variable is unimportant. Secondly, for this particular product an approximately constant per cent of sales revenue was spent on advertising which suggests that revenue and advertising were simultaneously determined signifying a fundamental failure of the regression assumptions. The effect of such a failure is discussed in §8.4.

In general few attempts to measure advertising effectiveness are completely success-ful (Schmalensee, 1972 gives a critical review of the effectiveness of advertising literature). Consequently instead of attempting to develop better measures of the quality of advertising expenditures, or to select a more appropriate lag structure, com-panies and researchers have tried cross-sectional experimentation to find the optimal advertising strategy for the firm. But in forecasting, the difficulties to be faced are many and Quandt (1964), in a clear and well-argued paper, lists some of these pitfalls.

8.3.3 Model building and the marketing environment
So far we have described the variables and their transforms that are normally encoun-tered in sales forecasting. In combining a number of these variables into a sales fore-casting model the intention is to reflect the total interaction of all the factors affecting the market place and to do this we need to think in terms of the total marketing system within which sales are generated (Kotler, 1972, provides an expanded descrip-tion of the marketing system). For example in Fig. 8.6 the total distribution process for coal is illustrated. Total sales are split between sales to final consumers and indus-trial sales. A total sales forecast depends on consumer purchases of coal itself, but also indirectly on consumer expenditure on cars and refrigerators and all the other products in the production of which coal is absorbed.

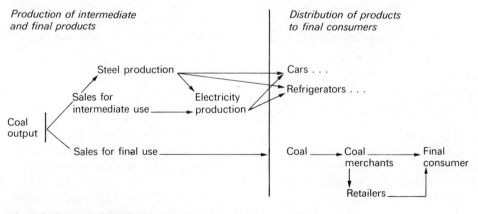

Fig. 8.6 The total distribution system − coal

202

The stock policies and delivery delays characteristic of each channel of distribution also play a key part in sales forecasting. We have already discussed how stock adjustment by consumers plays an important role in determining sales levels. In turn retailers have a level of stock in relation to sales that they try to normalize and fluctuations in this stock position can often obscure the sales relationships unless it is specifically recognized. For example a car dealer with an exceptionally large stock of cars will take advantage of higher sales to run down stocks. His orders to the manufacturer will for a time grow more slowly than retail sales. When he has almost no stock, however, he might order at a rate far in excess of current sales. In either event the manufacturer's orders would not reflect retail sales. In building a sales forecasting model it is apparent that the level of disaggregation between channels, between final markets, between different regional areas and so forth is an important consideration.

So too is a decision about the relevant boundary we draw around the marketing system. In the last analysis the sales of every product is affected by the sales level achieved by every other product, not least because of their competition for each pound of consumer expenditure. However, it would be totally impracticable to include prices of all possible products as independent variables in any forecasting model, since we know that given normal data limitations only a very small number will be shown to have any important or significant role in determining sales. Instead we are forced to specify a forecasting model which includes only variables that *a priori* are thought to be important and to leave the less important variables to the error term. Among the important variables, some, like income and population growth are general to most models, but prices of competing and complementary goods are specific to each sales equation. It is helpful, however, to judge competitiveness and complementarity in relation to the uses of products rather than their physical characteristics.

8.3.4 Industry models
In this section we will give a particular example of a model of industry sales to show how the variables discussed in the previous section are integrated into a forecasting equation.

A forecasting model for household appliances. Carman (1972) has used models containing three of the basic determinants of demand — price, income and time — to forecast the sales of appliances in Northern California. His general model is of the form:

$$Q_t = \beta_0 + \beta_1 P_t + \beta_2 Hs_t + \beta_3 Ht_t + \beta_4 Y_t + \beta_5 Ps_t + \beta_6 t + \beta_7 t^2 + e_t,$$

where P_t and Ps_t were the average installed prices for the appliance and for any substitute appliances; Hs_t and Ht_t were new single-family and total new housing units connected to utilities, and Q_t, Y_t and t are numbers of units sold, total income and the time trend respectively. Table 8.6 shows the estimated sales equations for two appliances: clothes dryers and refrigerators. The figures in parentheses are t statistics. No substitutes were considered possible for these two appliances so the variable Ps was not included in the equations.

The demand equation for clothes dryers has a high $\bar{R}^2$ and the standard error is 4½

Table 8.6
Estimated sales – clothes dryers and refrigerators

Appliance	n	β_0	P	Hs	Ht	Y	Ps	t	t^2	$\bar{R}^2$	Standard error	Average sales	Durbin–Watson
Clothes dryers	19	39,585	−263 (−5.98)	0.26 (3.12)		12.25 (2.99)	−	3,297 (8.34)		0.99	2,304	55,498	2.11
Refrigerators	22	236,740	−148 (−1.53)		0.52 (3.01)	−74.41 (−2.62)	−	−	535 (4.19)	0.89	11,602	118,190	1.44

per cent of average sales. The Durbin—Watson statistic suggests that there is no serial correlation in the residuals and the coefficients of price, housing and income have their expected sign. The equation should provide useful forecasts. In the second equation for refrigerators $\bar{R}^2$ is lower and the income coefficient is negative, although refrigerators are not obviously inferior goods. Carman notes that there are 'serious problems of multicollinearity between the income and trend variables, so no statements can be made about the separate influence of the two variables'.

As we have remarked earlier, multicollinearity is common with time series data because price and income variables, particularly if these are undeflated, can be approximated by a simple trend. This obviously leads to confusion if we also wish to include a separate time trend, as in this case, to account for changes in replacement demand, increased multiple ownership, and the diffusion of the appliance through the State. A possible solution to this problem is to estimate income elasticity using cross-sectional data. Klein (1962, pp. 61—74) describes in detail an appropriate method for incorporating cross-sectional evidence which we sketch out here. (Houthakker and Taylor (1970, pp. 254—80) gives a conceptually advanced discussion of some of the problems.) Observations are taken on the purchases, and corresponding income of a sample of households, and the model:

$$\log Q = \alpha_0 + \alpha_1 \log Y + (\text{error}), \text{ t fixed}$$

is fitted. The coefficient of the income variable, α_1, represents income elasticity and can be used as a direct external estimate for the income elasticity in a logarithmic time series model.

However, Carman in modelling refrigerator demand, used a non-logarithmic time series model. Thus the income coefficient on the equation is not an elasticity, since it expresses a direct relationship $\dfrac{\Delta Q}{\Delta Y}$ instead of the proportional elasticity relationship $\dfrac{\Delta Q}{\Delta Y} \Big/ \dfrac{\bar{Q}}{\bar{Y}}$. To use $\hat{\alpha}_1$ as an external estimate of the income coefficient β_4 we need to transform it from the proportional elasticity to the direct measure. We therefore multiply by $(\bar{Q}/\bar{Y})$, i.e.:

$$\hat{\beta}_4 = \hat{\alpha}_1(\bar{Q}/\bar{Y})$$

and we may then use this external estimate of $\hat{\beta}_4$ to deduct income effects from sales before re-estimating the parameters of the other independent variables, i.e.:

$$(Q_t - \hat{\beta}_4 Y_t) = \beta_0 + \beta_1 P_t + \beta_3 Ht_t + \beta_7 t^2 + e_t.$$

When Carman made this adjustment the new equation provided a worse fit than the old one. This confronts the analyst with an unfortunate choice between using the collinear equation complete with perverse income coefficient and hoping that collinearity does not break down, or adopting the second equation which not only fits the data less well but is also a problematic way of destroying the multicollinearity. The method nevertheless is generally quite successful and is recommended in the situation of multicollinearity. The solution to the difficulty is ideally to abandon the trend term responsible for the collinearity and estimate the variables for which it was a proxy using direct observation. In the case of refrigerators a stock adjustment model would appear to be more appropriate, and we will discuss an example of this in the next section.

8.3.5 Market share models

The value of forecast information is a direct function of the way in which it can be related to decision making. In forecasting sales it follows that predictions of a company's own sales are likely to be a more useful input to decision making than aggregate sales of the whole industry of which a company forms a constituent part.

In order to relate the sales of a product or brand of an individual company we need to know not only overall market sales but also the market share of that particular product or brand. Thus:

$$BJ_t = Q_t * MSJ_t$$

where BJ_t are sales of brand J; MSJ_t is it's market share; and Q_t the total market demand, all in period t.

Forecasts of brand sales may be made using a single model of the behaviour of BJ or else the forecasting model may be split into two parts — estimation of the total market and estimation of the brand's market share. If only a single equation is used it will be similar to a total market demand equation:

$$BJ_t = f(PJ_t, PC_t, AJ_t, AC_t, Y_t, ZJ_t, ZC_t) + (error),$$

where PJ is the price of brand J, and PC is the price of competing brands,† AJ and AC are similarly measures of advertising expenditures‡ for the brand and for its competitors; Y is the income variable, and ZJ and ZC are other measures of competitiveness, perhaps in distribution, not associated with price or marketing. Such an equation would normally require the addition of lagged dependent and independent variables to capture the dynamic characteristics of the sales process.

Schmalensee (1972, pp. 190–211) and Rao (1972) have studied brand sales of cigarettes using models of this form as shown below:

$$BJ_t = CJ + \beta_1 BJ_{t-1} + \beta_2 Y_t + \beta_3 PJ_t + \beta_4 AJ_t + \beta_5 AC_t + \beta_6 H_t + \beta_7 QJ_t + e_t.$$

In this equation PJ, BJ, AJ, AC and Y represent the variables described for the previous equation while CJ represents an independent constant term for each brand.¶ H_t is a dummy variable representing publicity given to the cancer—smoking link with a

---

† PC may be a straightforward average price of competing brands or a price index usually weighted by market shares. Sometimes, where relatively few brands exist, the price of each competitor might be entered directly.

‡ Measuring advertising expenditure presents problems. We noted earlier that advertising is not generally homogeneous. For an example where a great deal of care has been taken in constructing suitable measures, see Schmalensee, 1972, pp. 245–64.

¶ This is achieved using n − 1 dummy variables for the n brands. The dummy variables then measure the average differences in market share between brands while the constants CJ measure the average level of sales of brand J.

value 0 before the cancer health scare and a value 1 subsequently. QJ is a measure of the relative quality of brand J compared with its competitors.

Schmalensee offers a thorough discussion of some of the difficulties involved in this type of study; in particular his comments on the measurement and incorporation of advertising into the model are informative. Rao argues that the specification of the dependent variable is important and that market share rather than brand sales is easier to forecast. This presumably occurs because in a single equation model of brand share variables act in often conflicting ways. An increase in competitor's advertising, for example, both increases total market and decreases our market share. The overall effect is thus unpredictable. A general approach to this problem is to make a clear distinction between the factors which affect total market sales — average price, aggregate advertising, total consumer income and so on, and those factors such as relative advertising and relative price which govern the distribution of total market sales between competing brands.

The kind of models used to predict total market sales have already been discussed. Here we consider some of the models used to allocate total sales across brands. One of the simplest of these models is the probabilistic brand switching model, based on observations of the individual consumer. (For a summary of what are called stochastic models of consumer choice, see: Montgomery and Urban, 1969; Ehrenberg, 1972, Chs 1 and 2.) Thus, the probability of buying brand j in time $(t + 1)$, $\text{Prob}_j (t + 1)$ may be modelled by:

$\text{Prob}_j (t + 1) = \alpha_j + \beta_j \, \text{Prob}_j (t)$:   If brand j was purchased in interval t;

$\text{Prob}_j (t + 1) = \gamma_j - \delta_j \, \text{Prob}_j (t)$:   If brand j was not purchased in interval t.

In the equations the probability of purchasing brand j is predicted on the basis of a set of constants α_j, β_j, γ_j and δ_j which differ from brand to brand, and on the brand-buying history of that individual. These probabilities of purchase are not related to any marketing variables. They are naive models which describe rather than explain buyer behaviour and as such are useful primarily in providing a benchmark against which changes in the environment can be measured. Unfortunately they do not meet the criteria of a good naive forecasting model nor can they be easily adapted to include the decision variables which are used as competitive weapons in the determination of market share. However, we can describe a similar model used to predict market share directly which can easily be adapted to include causal variables:

$$MSJ_{t+1} = \alpha MSJ_t + \beta J$$

where, as before, MSJ is the market share of the Jth brand and βJ is the dummy variable for the Jth brand.

Because by definition all market shares must sum to 1 the values of the constant α and the βJ's are subject to the following constraints:

$$1 = \sum_J MSJ_{t+1} = \alpha \sum_J MSJ_t + \sum_J \beta J$$

$$= \alpha + \sum_J \beta J$$

and a similar constraint should properly apply to the coefficients of any other market share equation. (The problems of constraining the coefficients of market share models are discussed in Schmalensee (1972), pp. 104–13. Kuehn and Weiss (1965) and Weiss (1969) have also considered the problem. There is little evidence on the problem's importance.)

To explain market share in a way which aids decision making we need to include marketing policy variables directly in the estimating equation. A simple stock model developed by Lambin (1970, pp. 231–45) to study brand share in the small electrical appliance market did use this approach in specifying a general equation of the form:

$$MSJ_t = \beta_0 + \lambda MSJ_{t-1} + \beta_1 RQJ_t + \beta_2 RPJ_t + \beta_3 AJ_t + \beta_4 AC_t + (\text{error}),$$

where λ is a Koyck lag, RQJ and RPJ are relative quality and price measures and AJ and AC are own and competing advertising. All variables in the equation are logarithmic transforms of the original variables. The use of absolute advertising in the equation means that it could produce a total of estimated market shares either below or above 1. To overcome the difficulty Lambin modified his equation to use relative rather than absolute marketing. Lambin (1972) also developed an adaptive model of petrol marketing which focussed on the model's integration into the decision-making process of the firm. To increase management acceptance of the model he made provision for the equation coefficients to be modified to take account of subjective views about the effectiveness of an advertising campaign or alternative point of sales promotion activity. The coefficients were adjusted until the model could explain historic values of the dependent variables with an acceptable level of accuracy. The section on simulation (§8.6) discusses this type of approach in more detail.

An investigation of market share in the motor industry produced a similar model to the one used by Lambin. Cowling and Cubbin's (1971) reported market share equation was:

$$\log MSJ_t = -0.0233 + 0.7237 \log MSJ_{t-1} - 1.9497 \log QAJ_t + 0.1889 \log RAJ$$
$$(9.836) \qquad\qquad (-3.802) \qquad\qquad (2.400)$$

(Values in parentheses are t statistics.)
$R^2 = 0.936$;   Durbin–Watson = 2.145

QAJ is the quality adjusted price of brand J and RAJ is brand J's share of advertising. (The construction of the quality adjusted price measure is discussed in Appendix 4; p. 273.)

The validity of the model is confirmed by the parameter estimates having their expected signs and magnitudes. In this equation the coefficient for MSJ_{t-1} is λ, the Koyck lag, and we can use it to convert the short-term (one period) price and advertising responses to long-term measures reflecting a permanent shift. This is done by adjusting the respective short-term coefficients, -1.9497 and 0.1889 by the estimate of the Koyck lag, λ, to give $-1.9497/(1 - 0.7237)$ or -7.06 as the long-term price response and $0.1889/(1 - 0.7237)$ or 0.684 as the long-term advertising response.

In their model Cowling and Cubbin also suggest a second equation for advertising;

current advertising is determined by current market share and market share of the previous period, i.e.:

$$\log AJ_t = \gamma_0 + \gamma_1 \log MSJ_t + \gamma_2 \log MSJ_{t-1} + e_t.$$

They use the two equations to test whether market share and relative advertising are determined simultaneously. We consider this approach briefly in the next section.

To summarize this discussion of market share models it is clear that they are more difficult to build than industry models. Not only do they include variables such as quality and perhaps distributive efficiency that are difficult to measure but they are also designed to discriminate between very close substitutes so that the relationships established are inherently less robust. While many analysts have been quite successful it is important to remember that for forecasting applications a good explanation of past history is not enough. Thus no matter how well relative advertising explained past variations in market share the forecasts such a model produces depend as much on our simple ability to predict competitors' advertising outlay as they do on the statistical elegance of the forecasting equation.

Nevertheless decision makers do find information on market share and its response to changes in policy particularly useful. Such models are valuable as a means of combining the subjective knowledge of the decision maker with the objective history of sales experience and are thus a powerful addition to the decision-making structure of the firm.

§8.4 Estimation problems in demand models

(This section to be omitted at first reading.)

The errors made in forecasting are of three kinds:

1. Errors of model structure.
2. Estimation errors due to the random nature of the data.
3. Errors in forecasting the future values of the independent variables.

In building a causal model the intention is to minimize errors of the first kind. Two particular problems arise which limit the ability of an ordinary least squares model to do this.

1. Autocorrelation. Autocorrelation usually results from the omission of an important explanatory variable. If this cannot be remedied directly the analyst is forced to adjust the autocorrelated residuals until they satisfy the assumption of independence. This is done by estimating the first-order autocorrelation coefficient (see §6.6.1) and using it to make *a priori* adjustments to the variables in the equation. Unfortunately in sales models where a lagged dependent variable is used as an explanatory variable we may not recognize the need for this simple adjustment because the Durbin–Watson test which alerts us to the existence of autocorrelation fails to pick up the full extent of the autocorrelation. The remedy when a lagged dependent variable is used is to extend the rejection region for the null hypothesis of zero autocorrelation to include values that would normally fall within the indeterminate region.

Hopefully, even applying the modified test for autocorrelation the equation used should still be acceptable. However, if there is an indicated autocorrelation problem, correction is not easy, although Johnston (1972, pp. 307–20) does discuss the problem. In these circumstances, if accuracy of the model is thought to be paramount, specialist advice is indicated.

2. Simultaneity. A more serious weakness of sales models lies in the possible break-down of the model's causal structure.

Thus we might encounter a situation in which a firm decides their advertising budget by reference to expected sales. If this occurs we cannot then use a model which reverses the causality by defining sales as a function of advertising. If we do so the least squares estimates are only usable within the limited conditions described in the next section and the coefficients themselves are uninterpretable. To minimize struc-tural errors in this situation we need to model the complete sales–advertising system just as Cowling and Cubbin (1971) did in their model of price–quality demand relationships in the car industry. Palda's study of patent medicine advertising suffered from exactly this problem of simultaneity. The error could have been discovered either by monitoring the actual decision-making process of the firm, or else by observing the high correlation between advertising and sales lagged one period. Either would have indicated the need to use a systems model to capture the intricacies of the sales–advertising relationship.

§ 8.5 Models of systems and identification problems

So far in this chapter we have discussed production and sales forecasting as separate and independent activities. In many situations such a separation may not be possible because the levels of production and sales are simultaneously determined.†

Such a situation may be expressed by the following pair of relationships:

(Quantity demanded)$_t$ = f(Price$_t$);
(Quantity supplied)$_t$ = g(Price$_t$).

These equations model a situation where both buyers and sellers respond within a single market period to price. In this situation the only equilibrium price than can occur is at the level where the demand function (of price) interacts with the supply function (of price).

In practice we need to handle more complicated situations than this in which both the supply and demand functions depend on factors other than price. Even this com-

---

† The discussion here considers a situation where two variables are simultaneously determined by two equations. Situations in which many variables are simultaneously determined do, however, exist. In modelling market share each firm's share affects the share of the others. All shares are thus simultaneously determined, with as many equations as there are firms in the model.

plication is not too difficult to handle if only one of the functions, in this case demand, depends on an additional exogenous† factor:

(Quantity demanded)$_t$ = f(Price$_t$, Weather$_t$)

(Quantity supplied)$_t$ = g(Price$_t$)

because when this occurs all observed prices and quantities lie approximately along the function not subject to this exogenous influence. Thus in Fig. 8.7 if the demand curve shifts between observations due to changes in the new exogenous variable and the supply curve remains unchanged the observation allows us to estimate the parameters or identify the supply curve (the topic of identification is the subject of an early definitive paper by Working, 1927). The demand curve remains unidentified.

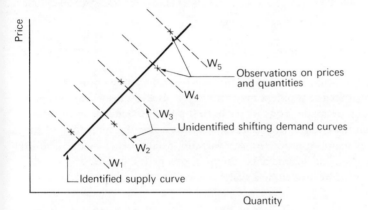

Fig. 8.7 *Identification of supply curve; demand curve, unidentified*

More often we might find that both demand *and* supply functions depended on factors other than price and that both curves therefore shifted:

(Quantity demanded)$_t$ = f(Price$_t$, Z_{Dt}) + e$_{1t}$

(Quantity supplied)$_t$ = f(Price$_t$, Z_{St}) + e$_{2t}$

where Z_D and Z_S are sets of exogenous variables other than price and e$_1$ and e$_2$ are error terms. In this situation the observations do not permit the easy identification of either supply or demand functions and any attempt to run a regression model with one dependent variable and its corresponding exogenous variables would generate a misleading equation as Fig. 8.8 shows. Since this problem of identification is encountered quite frequently particularly in modelling demand, where not only supply and demand but also sales and advertising expenditures may be simultaneously determined, it follows that a statistical method of modelling the total system is necessary before the component parts can be identified.

† An exogenous variable is one whose value is determined outside the system being modelled. An endogenous variable is determined within the system.

211

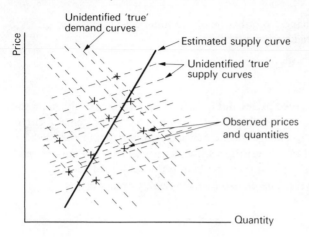

Fig. 8.8 Shifting demand and supply curves

Before considering statistical solutions to the identification problem though it is worth investigating whether the problem may arise solely as a result of the frequency with which observations are made. Thus where both supply and demand are in equilibrium over time period t, we might find as a result of increasing the frequency of the observations that the demand response to price was still instantaneous over this shorter period but the supply response depended on the price one period earlier. The simultaneity has been destroyed by modelling a system based on more frequent observations.

$$\text{Simultaneous} \begin{cases} \text{(Quantity demanded)}_t = f(P_t) \\ \text{(Quantity supplied)}_t = g(P_t) \\ \text{t measured in years, for} \\ \text{example} \end{cases} \quad \text{Non-simultaneous} \begin{cases} \text{(Quantity demanded)}_t = f(P_t^*) \\ \text{(Quantity supplied)}_t = g(P_{t-1}^*) \\ \text{t measured in quarters, for} \\ \text{example} \end{cases}$$

In the original version of the system P_t is endogenous, but in the revised system P_{t-1}^* is predetermined and acts as an exogenous variable in determining current supply. The intersection of current supply and the demand function then determines current price, P_t^*, which in turn serves as a determinant of supply in the next market period. Such a system is called *recursive* and the parameters of the two equations in the system can be estimated using ordinary least squares, and can be used for forecasting. We could encounter a recursive situation in sales forecasting where advertising expenditure was fixed as a proportion of the previous quarter's sales. However, with only annual observation of this situation available we would have to describe it by a simultaneous model, because the current annual advertising budget would be determined by three quarters of current sales and only one quarter of the previous year's sales. This brings us back to the need to develop methods to handle simultaneous systems.

Indirect least squares (see Kane, 1968, pp. 325–7 for more detailed discussion). Suppose that an annual sales forecast is needed where the supply of the product, QS, depends on both price and an additional exogenous variable while demand, QD, depends solely on the simultaneously determined level of price. The system may be described in terms of two equalities:

$$QD_t = \alpha_0 + \alpha_1 P_t + e_{1t},$$
$$QS_t = \beta_0 + \beta_1 P_t + \beta_2 W_t + e_{2t}.$$

Since our observations on this system are of market equilibrium, where supply equals demand we can solve the two equations to specify equilibrium price and equilibrium quantity solely in terms of the exogenous variable:

$$P_{equilibrium} = \gamma_1 + \gamma_2 W + v_1$$

$$Q_{equilibrium} = \delta_1 + \delta_2 W + v_2$$

where v_1 and v_2 are random variables depending on e_1 and e_2 in the original equation and γ_1, γ_2, δ_1 and δ_2 depend on the α's and β's. These so-called *reduced form equations* can then be estimated from the original observations using ordinary least squares methods. Because in this system the shifts in the supply curve caused by movements in W are sufficient to identify the demand curve we can use the parameters γ_1, γ_2, δ_1 and δ_2 to calculate its parameters. The supply curve remains unidentified, however.

Similarly, if a further exogenous variable (other than W) in a two-equation simultaneous system affected the demand curve, both the supply and demand curves would be identified and their parameters could be estimated from the coefficients of the reduced form equation. This method of estimating the structural parameters from the reduced form equations is called *indirect least squares*. It can only be used in estimating an equation which in its specification omits n − 1 of the total of endogenous and exogenous variables appearing in the system of n equations, from which it is drawn.

In the equations above three variables were used: one exogenous, W; and two endogenous, P and Q. The supply equation contained all three and was unidentified while the demand equation omitted one, W, which is sufficient to allow it to be identified in a two-equation system (n − 1 = 1).

Over-identification (see Walters, 1968, pp. 177–97 for simple extension of basic ideas given here; Johnston, 1972, pp. 408–20 for hard but not inaccessible discussion of how to treat the problem of over-identification). An equation in a simultaneous system is over-identified when its specification omits more than n − 1 of the total of exogenous and endogenous variables appearing in the system of n equations from which it is drawn. This situation is likely to occur where equations use large numbers of exogenous variables not included in other equations in the system. The consequence of this would be that the reduced form equations provide several estimates for the parameters of the structural equations. To overcome the difficulty a number of methods exist, and if the reader is primarily interested in estimating the parameters of the structural equation he should consult a recommended text. However, if the main purpose is to forecast and the analyst is willing to dispense with the guidance the parameters of the structural equation can provide in validating his model, least squares methods can still be used as we show in the next section.

Forecasting in simultaneous systems. Although we can derive and use the structural equations for validation, predictions can be made from the reduced form equations.

If the problem is to predict Y_1, from a structural equation in which Y_2 is a further endogenous variable and X is a set of exogenous variables, we may write the model as:

$$Y_1 = \alpha_0 + \alpha_1 Y_2 + \alpha_2 X + \text{(error)}.$$

The parameters of such an equation can be estimated by ordinary least squares and the equation used to forecast Y_1, given values of Y_2 and the set of variables X. If Y_2 itself is unknown then the reduced form equation

$$Y_1 = \gamma_0 + \gamma_1 X + \text{(error)}$$

is again estimated by ordinary least squares and used, given values for X, in forecasting. Johnston (1972, pp. 418–20) calling this method 'least squares no restriction', argues that it is not the 'best' method even for prediction. It, nevertheless, seems adequate in most circumstances.

In summary ordinary least squares remains useful for forecasting purposes (though not for estimating structural coefficients) in a system of equations. It is also appropriate in the case of recursive systems.

§8.6 An introduction to simulation

At the beginning of this chapter the construction of a causal model was described as an attempt by the analyst to break into the black box connecting input with output. Once we have constructed such a model it becomes possible to feed in the past values of the exogenous variables and replicate the observed behaviour of the endogenous variables. A causal model can do more than this because by specifying different values of the exogenous variables we can investigate the properties of the model under conditions which may not have occurred during the original operations. Such a model allows us to *simulate* reality. In doing this we are able to experiment with the model in the same way in which we might like to experiment with the real system if such experiments were not too expensive, too dangerous and too time consuming. This allows us to answer the 'what if' type of questions that have to be answered by any decision maker. This is particularly advantageous where the decision maker controls a number of the exogenous variables in the system, because he can examine the consequences of alternative levels for each of these decision variables and then set them in a way that ensures that the behaviour of the endogenous variables is as favourable as possible for his organization.

A second use is to examine the sensitivity of a possible policy to changes in the environment. For example, a particular production/inventory policy may only be cost effective for a limited range of sales forecasts. By changing the parameters of the operating environment the analyst is able to test whether this is the case.

A final benefit is that a simulation approach provides a useful framework to integrate different types of forecast. There is a limit to the amount of causal modelling that is worthwhile and external estimates of variables, derived from naive models or, as in the case of Lambin's market share model (in §8.3.5) subjective judgement are acceptable. A simulation model connects up these disparate sources of information in a way that provides constructive support for decision making.

A model of the petroleum industry. In the medium term, forecasting and control are not easily separated. We have argued throughout that a forecast is not just a constraint within which a company has to operate, but a direct commentary on likely policy outcomes and hence crucial in determining the direction a company takes in its attempt to satisfy and reconcile its many goals. Because a forecast may lead to the revision of these goals, and because of the feedback between the forecast, associated policies and the organization's goals forecasting systems have developed into large-scale models of a firm, an industry or even of a nation state. In this way it is hoped to develop an understanding of the complex inter-relationships involved.

Naylor (1971) has described many of these attempts, stressing the use of simulation as an experimental technique for understanding the effects of policy, and Guetzkow *et al.* (1972) contains a number of articles, each presenting an overview of simulation applied in a particular subject area (Kotler and Schultz's article, reprinted from the *Journal of Business*, 1970, is particularly interesting). In the remainder of this section we will describe in skeleton form a recent model of the petroleum industry, with the aim of demonstrating the range and power of simulation as part of the control system of the organization.

The model. The simplified version of Adams and Griffin's (1972) model for the US petroleum refining industry, shown in Fig. 8.9 was developed to 'provide a medium-term perspective over the business cycle and to serve as a framework for long-term projections. It can also be used as a tool for simulation under alternative assumptions about economic conditions or policies.'

The economic environment in which the petroleum industry is operating is seen as a crucial factor in determining demand for the range of products, produced as a result of the refining process. In keeping with this assumption the level of GNP appears as an exogenous variable in most of the demand equations. Price on the other hand does not have much effect on demand, since in the short term the scope for substitution between different refined products and other sources of energy is low, and so is omitted in many of the equations.† Typical of the estimated demand equations for the five products is that for kerosene, the product being used as a heating and industrial fuel as well as a fuel in jet aircraft.

$$DK = 40.72 + 0.0212DDD + 1.87Xm + 0.2661\ JET - 10.1\ TIME$$

where DK = Demand for kerosene; DDD = A measure of the sensitivity of heating usage to temperature; Xm = Activity in mining and manufacturing at constant prices; JET = Number of commercial jet aircraft. The equations were statistically 'satisfactory' measured in terms of R^2 etc.

† The experience of 1973 supports this assumption, since a trebling in the price of petroleum products has resulted in relatively little change in demand and most of this change can be explained as a response to altered rates of GNP growth.

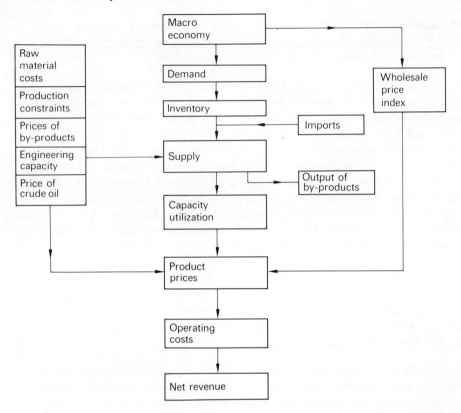

Fig. 8.9 A recursive model of the US petroleum industry

Inventory levels are assumed proportional to demand and imports are exogenous. Costs are then calculated using a linear programming model to select the feasible product mix which has minimum cost and yet meets demand. (Baumol, 1965, Chs 5, 11 and 12, provides a clear discussion of cost control using linear programming in a multi-product industry.) Price in the industry is set as a mark-up over production costs; the mark-up determined through a regression equation of the form:

Price = f(crude oil price, price index, production costs, inventory levels, demands).

Figures 8.10(*a*) and (*b*) show how the model compares with the industry's actual performance for two of the endogenous variables, gasoline price and kerosene production. The simulated results are calculated by using actual values of the exogenous variables throughout the simulated time period of 1955–68. The starting values of any lagged endogenous variables are also real, but after the first iteration the model is able to recursively calculate the values of the endogenous variables. The forecasts are calculated using the same method, although the forecast values of the exogenous macro-economic variables have to be derived from other sources, in this case one of the many US economic forecasting models.

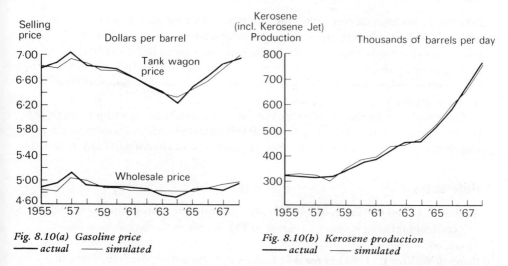

Fig. 8.10(a) Gasoline price
—— actual   —— simulated

Fig. 8.10(b) Kerosene production
—— actual   —— simulated

Results from the simulation model. The model's objectives, specified by the authors, were to provide a framework for long-term projections, and as a vehicle for experimentation with the effects of different economic conditions, and these were successfully achieved. Exogenous variables representing alternative futures, can be processed by the model and the dynamic effects traced through the whole industry. The authors, for example, produced basic forecasts of the dynamic effects of the introduction of government restrictions on the use of lead additive as well as certain changes in the refining process. They also considered the effect of a change in the price of crude oil on such a vertically integrated industry.

Two critical assumptions were made in the model's construction that make the model less useful than would otherwise be the case and it is only knowledge of the changes in the industry in 1973 that permits us the criticism. While it was true that incremental increases in price have little immediate effect on demand, it cannot be assumed that no long-run changes in the consumption patterns would occur. However, the range of variation of relative price data from which the model was constructed was inadequate to take into account such major changes in the price of crude oil as those of 1973/74. With prices stabilizing again around the new high level the equations might perhaps be revised to take this quantum jump into account. The second important assumption made lay in the omission of industry capacity (and capital investment), a key variable in 1973. Without the addition of this sector (currently exogenous) to the model the model is of limited value to decision makers within the oil companies. Despite these drawbacks the model does demonstrate the results of an ambitious attempt to simulate a complex vertically integrated industry operating with multi-product production plans.

Summary. While no model can provide a total representation of reality the model of the petroleum industry provides forecasts which illuminate the policy alternatives available to decision makers within the industry and within government and it is perhaps a little specious to argue about the completeness of a forecasting model when one knows that the output of such a model is in any case an input to a decision-making process which is comparatively coarse in its application. (It is worth repeating a basic tenet underlying the writing of this book. A forecast is 'satisfactory' only as it relates to its use.)

Generalizing from this example we can see that a simulation model provides a convenient framework for combining formal and informal models in a way in which its ability to represent the overall system rather than its constituent parts can be tested.

References

Adams, F. C. and **Griffin, J. M.** (1972) 'An economic-linear programming model of US petroleum refining industry', *Journal of the American Statistical Association*, vol. 67.

Baumol, William J. (1965) *Economic Theory and Operations Analysis*, 2nd edn, Prentice-Hall, New Jersey.

Blalock, H. M. (1964) *Causal Inferences in Experimental Research*, University of North Carolina Press, Chapel Hill.

Carman, H. (1972) 'Improving sales forecasts for appliances', *Journal of Marketing Research*, vol. ix.

Chow, G. C. (1957) *Demand for Automobiles in the United States*, North-Holland, Amsterdam.

Chow, G. C. (1960) in Harberger, A. C. (ed.) *The Demand for Durable Goods*, University of Chicago Press, Chicago.

Cowling, Keith and **Cubbin, J.** (1971) 'Price, quality, and advertising', *Economica*, vol. 38.

Cowling, Keith and **Cubbin, J.** (1972) 'Hedonic price indices for UK cars', *The Economic Journal*, vol. 82.

Cox, D. R. (1968) 'Notes on some aspects of regression analysis', *Journal Royal Statistical Society*, Series A, vol. 131.

Crutchley, R. A. (ed.) (1973) *I.P.C. Marketing Manual of the United Kingdom*, International Publishing Corporation, London.

Ehrenberg, A. S. C. (1972) *Repeat Buying Theory and Applications*, North-Holland, Amsterdam.

Guetzkow, H., Kotler, P. and **Schultz, R.** (1972) *Simulation in Social and Administration Science*, Prentice-Hall, New Jersey.

Houthakker, H. S. and **Taylor, L. D.** (1970) *Consumer Demand in the United States: Analysis and Projections*, 2nd edn, Harvard University Press.

Johnston, J. (1972) *Econometric Methods*, 2nd edn, McGraw-Hill, New York.

Kane, E. J. (1968) *Economic Statistics and Econometrics*, Harper and Row, New York.

Klein, L. (1962) *An Introduction to Econometrics*, Prentice-Hall, New Jersey.

Kotler, P. (1972) *Marketing Management: Analysis, Planning, and Control*, 2nd edn, Prentice-Hall, New Jersey.

Kuehn, A. A. and Weiss, D. L. (1965) 'Marketing analysis training exercise', *Behavioural Science*, vol. 10.

Labys, W. C. and Granger, C. W. J. (1970) *Speculation Hedging and Commodity Price Forecasts*, Heath Lexington, Mass.

Lambin, Jean-Jaques (1970) 'Advertising and competitive behaviour', *Applied Economics*, vol. 2.

Lambin, Jean-Jaques (1972) 'A computer on-line mix model', *Journal of Marketing Research*, vol. ix.

Lomax, K. S. (1952) 'Cost curves for electricity generation', *Economica*, vol. 19.

Montgomery, David B. and Urban, Glen L. (1969) *Management Science in Marketing*, Prentice-Hall, New Jersey.

Naylor, Thomas H. (1971) *Computer Simulation Experiments with Models of Economic Systems*, Wiley, New York.

Naylor, Thomas H. and Finger, J. M. (1967) 'Verification of computer simulation results', *Management Science*, Series B, vol. 14:2.

O'Herlihy, C. St. J. (1965) 'Demand for cars in Great Britain', *Applied Statistics*, vol. 14.

Palda, Kristian S. (1964) *The Measurement of Cumulative Advertising Effects*, Prentice-Hall, New Jersey.

Palda, Kristian S. (1969) *Economic Analysis for Marketing Decisions*, Prentice-Hall, New Jersey.

Quandt, Richard E. (1964) 'Estimating the effectiveness of advertising: some pitfalls of economic methods', *Journal of Marketing Research*, vol. 1.

Rao, Vithala R. (1972) 'Alternative econometric models of sales—advertising relationships', *Journal of Marketing Research*, vol. ix.

Robinson, Colin (1971) *Business Forecasting*, Nelson, London.

Schmalensee, R. (1972) *The Economics of Advertising*, North-Holland, Amsterdam/London.

Spencer, H. S., Clarke, C. G. and Hoguet, P. W. (1961) *Business and Economic Forecasting*, Richard Irwin, Homewood, Illinois.

Stone, R. and Rowe, D. A. (1954, 1966) *The Measurement of Consumer's Expenditure and Behaviour in the U.K.*, 1920—38, vols 1, 11, Cambridge University Press, London.

Stone, R. and Rowe, D. A. (1960) 'The durability of consumer's durable goods', *Econometrica*, vol. 28.

Stonier, A. W. and Hague, D. C. (1972) *A Textbook of Economic Theory*, 4th edn, Longman, London.

Telser, L. G. (1962) 'Advertising and cigarettes', *Journal of Political Economy*, vol. 70.

Van Horn, Richard L. (1971) 'Validation of simulation results', *Management Science*, Series A, vol. 17:5.

Walters, A. A. (1968) *An Introduction to Econometrics*, Macmillan, London.

Weiss, D. L. (1969) 'An analysis of the demand structure for branded consumer products', *Applied Economics*, vol. 1.

Working, E. J. (1927) 'What do statistical demand curves show', *Quarterly Journal of Economics*, vol. 41. (Reprinted in Townsend, H. (1971) *Price Theory*, Penguin, Harmondsworth.)

Additional references

Cost models
Cost models have remained the preserve of the economist. Two texts which have helped us substantially with our ideas are:

Johnston, J. (1960) *Statistical Cost Analysis*, McGraw-Hill, New York;
Johansen, L. (1972) *Production Functions*, North-Holland, Amsterdam.

While Johnston's text is only slightly more advanced than our own, Johansen's is difficult. On an elementary level

Hague, D. C. (1969) *Managerial Economics*, Longman, London,

develops the basic ideas we draw on.
In addition to the two references given in this section on price forecasting,

Granger, C. W. J. (ed.) (1974) 'Trading in commodities', *Investor's Chronicle*, Woodhead-Faulkner, Cambridge

offers an introduction to the commodity markets while,

Labys, Walter C. (1973) *Dynamic Commodity Models*, Heath Lexington, Lexington, Mass.

describes systems models for commodities.

Demand models
While most of the work on demand has already been referred to, a book orientated toward marketing decisions, which includes economic models of demand set in contrast to those of sociology, demography and psychology is:

Hughes, C. David (1973) *Demand Analysis for Marketing Decisions*, Irwin, Homewood, Illinois.

It contains a useful appendix on data sources, as well as a large bibliography. However, in most parts it is not sufficiently detailed to provide any more than an overview.
To convey some of the basic ideas of demand forecasting to middle level executives with little time to absorb the detail contained in this book we recommend a clear article on the benefits of the causal approach to modelling demand:

Parker, George and Segura, Edilberto (1971) 'How to get a better forecast', *Harvard Business Review*, vol. 49:2.

System models
Systems models have, over the last few years, developed substantially. **Guetzkow** *et al.*

and **Naylor,** our two cited references, both contain extensive bibliographies.

Wheelwright, Steven and **Makridakis, Spyros** (1972) *Computer-aided Modelling for Managers*, Addison-Wesley, Reading, Mass.

provides a basic introduction, while

Meier, Robert C., Newell, William T. and **Pazer, Harold L.** (1969) *Simulation in Business and Economics*, Prentice-Hall, Englewood Cliffs, New Jersey

adds to these preliminary ideas. The particular model we discuss of the petroleum industry is developed from:

Griffin, J. M. (1971) *Capacity Measurement in Petroleum Refining*, Heath Lexington, Lexington, Mass.

which is a difficult book.

For a survey of forecasting as part of a particular company's decision making (Corning Glass) an interesting and clear presentation may be found in:

Chambers, J. C., Mullick, S. K. and **Smith, D. M.** (1971) 'How to choose the right forecasting technique', *Harvard Business Review*, vol. 49 : 4,

and this we again use to help management understand the basics of forecasting in a system.

9

Forecasting the business environment: the national economy

§ 9.1 Introduction — the firm and national economic forecasting

The individual business firm making forecasts of the conditions likely to affect their selling, purchasing and investment activities will rely on external estimates of most of the variables that are beyond the firm's immediate environment. Among these variables are usually series that are recognized as being central indicators of the behaviour of the national and international economy. Obviously, the likely national levels of unemployment, consumer expenditure, interest rates and investment are key factors in determining the outcome of a firm's policy decisions, but it is rare to find an individual firm attempting to forecast these variables on an independent basis. This type of aggregate forecasting is normally left to national and usually official sources for a number of reasons:

1. The number of variables that have to be considered in preparing forecasts of the national economy are typically large. And since these variables are part of a consistent economic system they are also interrelated. This means that the independent analysis of any given segment would be unreliable unless cross-checked against similar analyses of those sectors to which it was related.
2. All forecasts, including forecasts of the national economy, are conditional on the continuing validity of their underlying assumptions. Since the appearance of a national economic forecast may be sufficient to prompt an alteration in policy making, the validity of such assumptions may be short lived. Unless as an outsider we were in a position to second-guess the government's response in our original assumptions, our forecasts would rapidly become misleading.

For this reason it is essential that national forecasts are reviewed and updated at regular intervals both to take into account the effect of new policy changes by changing assumptions, and hence outcomes, but also to check the validity of the model by establishing how well the model would have predicted current events if accurate assumptions about policies had been built into the model. For most firms, with an occasional rather than a continuous need for information about the economy, such a substantial expenditure of effort is not worthwhile.

§9.2 Forecasting and planning

National economic forecasts are prepared as an essential input in the process of planning the management of the economy . They, therefore, appear to be simply a byproduct of the planning process.

In fact the relationship between forecasting and planning is altogether more complex than this. The planning process at either firm or government level basically involves forecasting the consequences of a range of alternative policies and then comparing these consequences with previously desired objectives. A government, for example, might have the following objectives:

1. To keep unemployment below 3 per cent.
2. To maintain the growth rate in the economy at 2 per cent.
3. To secure a balance on the non-oil external trade account.

The government would begin by forecasting how the economy would be likely to develop over the planning period if there were no changes in existing government policies. Suppose this exercise produced a forecast of a rate of unemployment of 2.5 per cent, a growth rate of 3 per cent, but a deficit on the external trade account of £400 m. If there were no policy changes the government could then achieve the first two of its objectives, with reasonable ease, but at the cost of an unacceptable balance of trade deficit. Its response might be to examine policy instruments – personal and company tax rates, investment incentives, monetary policy, international exchange rates and so on. It would then select those measures that seem most likely to counteract the imbalance in the external trade account. Forecasts are then reworked to reflect the consequences of these policies and the new results checked once again against the national objectives. Suppose the government, for example, chose to increase the income tax rate by 2 per cent because they felt it would reduce consumers' demand for imports at the expense of a slight reduction in the rate of economic growth. Using this new tax rate the reworked forecasts might then indicate that the external trade accounts would be in balance, but that the expected growth rate of the economy might have slipped back to 2.5 per cent, with projected unemployment at 2.8 per cent. Even so, this outcome satisfies all three of the prior objectives, and would thus be an acceptable outcome in national terms.

A forecast outcome that is acceptable in terms of the original objectives may not, however, always be possible, since the original objectives may have been too optimistic in relation to constraints outside the government's control. This would be revealed when all available government policies had been considered and in no case did the forecast of expected consequences permit all objectives to be attained. This would indicate that the objectives, desirable though they might be, were not realistic and, in the circumstances, it would be necessary to revise the objectives so that they fall within the feasible distribution of outcomes.

The relationship between planning and forecasting can be summarized in the flow diagram in Fig. 9.1. The diagram shows the planning process, starting with a definition of objectives. To achieve these objectives a set of plans – planned outcomes and policies – are devised. Thus in the example just discussed the objectives related to

223

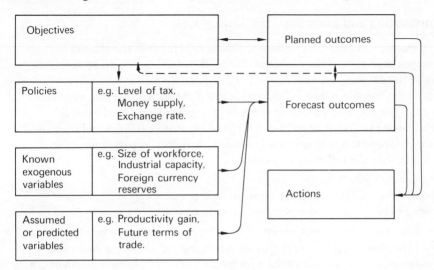

Fig. 9.1 Planning and forecasting in government

employment levels, economic growth and equilibrium in the balance of payments. A set of policies and planned outcomes consistent with these objectives would then be devised.

Taking the plan's policies, together with known or assumed values of other exogenous variables, a forecast outcome, based on a 'most likely' criterion can be constructed and compared with the planned outcomes which were based on a 'preferred' criterion. If plans coincide with forecasts, action to implement proposed policies can be taken, since planned outcomes would be not only desired but also objectively likely. Where planned and forecast outcomes do not coincide, first policies and then objectives have to be altered until the coincidence occurs. If actions are taken where planned outcomes differ from forecast outcomes, then it is unlikely that plans will be realized, and this will also be the case where a discrepancy between plans and forecasts is resolved by arbitrary changes in the assumptions used in the forecasting process.

9.2.1 National planning — the UK experience
In the United Kingdom there have been three major attempts to present coherent and reasonably detailed medium-term plans for the national economy: the National Economic Development Council's *Growth of the United Kingdom Economy to 1966* (N.E.D.C., 1963); the *National Plan* (Department of Economic Affairs, 1965); and *The Task Ahead — Economic Assessment to 1972* (Department of Economic Affairs, 1969).

Of these three exercises only the last, 'The Task Ahead', corresponds to a planning document, as we have defined it, in the sense that the policies outlined in it, taken together with the known or objectively predicted conditions against which they operate, produced forecasts that corresponded fairly closely with the planned outcomes and stated objectives. The earlier documents started with a set of objectives, and attempted to find a set of policies and conditions that would permit these set objectives to be met. In essence this was a feasibility study, since unless appropriate measures to generate the required conditions and to implement appropriate policies followed, there was no reason to suppose that the probable, or even likely outcome would bear any resemblance to the planned outcome. Since neither the National Economic Development Council study nor the 'National Plan' were forecasts, in the sense that the plans contained in them were not the most likely results of the proposed policies under expected conditions, the forecasting spin-off from them was limited. As feasibility studies they generated some idea of the bottlenecks that were likely to occur if the growth rate were to be increased, and perhaps indicated possible areas of shortage and hence opportunity, but without any expectation that this quickened growth rate would follow it was not clear when, if ever, these bottlenecks and shortages would be likely to appear.

'The Task Ahead' was a considerable step forward from these earlier attempts, in that it was based on assessments of the most likely attainable changes in important areas — the central one being the expected increase in labour productivity. 'The Task Ahead' forecast that the most likely rate of growth in the period 1967–72 was 3¼ per cent p.a., but also considered the implications of two alternative rates of growth (4 per cent and just under 3 per cent) that might arise, if some of the basic assumptions made about changes in productivity turned out to be, respectively, over-pessimistic and over-optimistic. Such a 'multiple' plan, that is predicting several alternative outcomes, each generated by a set of assumptions made about a central input, make it much more effective as a forecasting document because it goes some way towards acknowledging the uncertainties that are inevitably inherent in any forecasting exercise. In 'The Task Ahead' an increase or decrease in the actual growth rate could be accomodated within the framework of the planning model, simply by shifting to consider the higher or lower projection available in that model. The 'National Plan' on the other hand was completely undermined by an immediate deviation between the expected growth rate of 4 per cent and the actual growth rate of around 2½ per cent. All the calculations and assumptions in the Plan became immediately invalid, because they were all geared to a growth rate that was an objective but not an expected outcome. This lead to the 'National Plan's' early demise.

9.2.2 Consultation and national planning

Any effective national plan has to make provision for extensive consultation with decision takers in industry. In 'The Task Ahead' this process of consultation and coordination is given particular prominence. The process of consultation is a necessity in all planning exercises, not only to allow decision takers to comment on the feasibility of the underlying planning assumptions, as much in a social as a technological sense, but also to provide them with an opportunity to re-examine their decision-taking in the light of the additional information available about policy intentions and possible outcomes. The decision taker will inform the planners of the modified decisions, and the planners can then use the information gained to prepare new forecasts based on the direct and indirect effects of the revised decision taking. In this way individual firms relate their forecasts to national figures, confident that the national forecasts embodied in the plan were attainable and consistent, not only in national terms, but also for their industry and firm.

This process of consultation currently occurs through informal channels, through the regular information-gathering operations of government, and also through the industry sub-committees of the National Economic Development Organization. In addition, control of investment and output decisions in the nationalized industries gives a government considerable powers of direct intervention.

§9.3 The methodology of national forecasting

Predicting the future course of the economy in any worthwhile detail is a task that is much more demanding than would be apparent from inspecting the relatively small number of hard forecasts that finally emerge.

Before any forecasts can be made, an enormous amount of preparatory work has to be done. As a first step a large volume of data needs to be assembled, and then standardized by eliminating the effects of seasonal variation and changes introduced by depreciating money values. Following this the economic behaviour of the various sectors has to be estimated from the data available, normally by econometric methods, and assumptions have to be made about those variables entering into the model, such as defence expenditure and the growth of world trade, that are either not estimated by the model or are determined on a non-economic basis. Only after these steps have been taken can the overall economic model be assembled, and forecasts of the results of alternative policy choices be made.

The scale of the task virtually dictates the use of computers. In fact one of the primary explanations for the gap of 30 years between the development of overall economic models at the theoretical level of Keynes and the translation of these models into practical tools for analysis lies in the absence during the period of any suitable method either for estimating the complex relationships involved or for resolving the interactive consequences of these relationships. The computer is invaluable because not only can it readily store the large quantities of data required for investigation, and perform the appropriate statistical analysis, but in addition it can be used to record the whole forecasting model in a way that permits the implication of altering any of the assumptions and policies built into the model to be calculated almost instantaneously. For example a set of plans may be based on a taxation policy which generates a surplus of taxation over expenditure of £800 m. Using this assumption a set of fore-casts might indicate an unacceptable level of unemployment. Altered tax policies lowering the planned surplus to £400 m. can then be substituted and an alternative set of forecasts generated. By comparison of the forecasts the expected change in employ-ment brought about by the taxation change can be obtained.

The previously mentioned facility is also available when changes are expected in parts of the economic environment not directly estimated in the model. For example, the development of the economy might be forecast on the assumption that world trade would expand at 9 per cent p.a. This value would then be fed into the model to allow estimates of overall growth and sector by sector forecasts of imports and exports to be calculated, together with an estimate of the resulting overall trade balance. A subsequent revision of international trade treaties resulting in lowered tariff barriers might increase the expected growth in world trade from 9 to 11 per cent p.a. This obviously changes the basis on which exports, imports, the trade balance and the level of economic activity are estimated, so it is fed into the computer model, and revised estimates for the economy are generated. A change of this latter type is a change in an 'exogenous' variable. World trade growth is a variable that is determined outside the system being modelled, and hence differs from both 'endogenous', variables such as GDP which are estimated within the model from equations and from identities.† In economic models there is a further distinction between exogenous variables that are states of nature and those that represent policies. Thus the rate of growth of international trade is a state of nature, since it could not be significantly altered by any single government acting alone.

Policy instruments, on the other hand, are decisions taken outside the model, in anticipation of certain consequences within the model, but subject to revision if these consequences are not achieved, or cease to look desirable. For example, the quantity of money, or the level of defence spending could both be altered by the government, and such an alteration would have an effect on the forecasts of the model.

The completed national income model thus consists of a set of exogenous variables, a set of policy instruments and sufficient relationships to define, directly or indirectly, all the endogenous variables that we wish to forecast.

In developing the relationships used in such a model we will often find that independent variables used in one relationship will also be defined as dependent variables in other relationships. For example we might analyse the time series data of sales of a consumer product, Y, and evolve a satisfactory equation to predict them:

$$QY = \beta_0 + \beta_1 X + \beta_2 PY + \beta_3 PZ + (\text{error}),$$

where QY is the *per capita* consumption of good Y at constant prices, X is the level of real disposable income per head, and PY and PZ are the deflated prices of the good itself and a close substitute.

In turn, real disposable income itself might be defined in terms of employment: E, a trend in productivity; t, and the tax rate T:

$$\text{Disposable income} = X * (\text{population})$$
$$= (\beta_0 + \beta_1 E * (1 - T) + \beta_2 t * (1 - T) + (\text{error})) * (\text{population})$$

and employment in turn might depend on total consumer purchases, among which we would naturally include good Y.

Thus while it is relatively straightforward to estimate individual equations, when they are put together as parts of a jigsaw we find that a good many of the equations have to be solved simultaneously rather than recursively. This simultaneity simply

---

† An identity arises when, for example, n − 1 equations are used to define components of an aggregate of n variables. For example, if we have an equation to determine pre-tax incomes, Y, and an equation to determine tax, then post-tax income N, is given by an identity N = Y − T.

reflects the interdependent nature of relationships within an economy, but it neverthe-less adds to the statistical problems of estimation. (Simple examples of the estimation of simultaneous systems were given in §8.5.) For this reason most national income models only seek to explain the generation and disposal of national income at a fairly aggregate level, while an input—output (see Ch. 10, §§ 10.3 and 10.4) model is used as a convenient way of disaggregating product groups.

§9.4 National income models

Mathematical models of national income generation differ in the complexity and dis-aggregation attempted in the model. At one extreme the Brookings model (Duesen-berry *et al.*, 1965) has more than 500 equations; at the other, simple models represent-ing the economy with only eight equations exist. The Treasury model falls in an intermediate position.

A simplified version of the general structure of a national income model is shown in Fig. 9.2. It shows that Gross Domestic Product can be defined in three ways — total income, total expenditure and total production. This arises because in aggregate, a nation, neglecting international transactions, has to consume all it produces. This means that for an equilibrium to occur the wages, salaries, profits and interest charges paid out by producers of goods and services in order to produce a given level of output must be sufficient to generate a level of demand among consumers that exactly absorbs that output. As we move away from this simple model by adding more variables, the equilibrium condition becomes more complicated but the basic principle, that the supply and demand for each factor of production and for all goods including monetary assets must be in balance, remains unchanged.

If we introduce a government sector that both produces some goods and services and absorbs others in fulfilling its functions, it follows that there must be a new equili-brium at which the wages and salaries paid out by producers of goods and services, less taxes, must be just adequate to generate demands that would absorb all output, including the government sector, less the amount of goods and services being absorbed by the government to fulfil its objectives. In adding a government sector to the model the alternative effects of fiscal and monetary policies may thus be made a subject for investigation. In the same way we can move nearer to reality by opening the economy to international trade using international demand and supply relationships. The equili-brium that would then arise would be when the final demand generated by the wage, salary and interest earners, the government and foreign customers, exactly balanced the supplies made available domestically, together with imports from abroad. This equilibrium, of course, could occur even though there was a net deficit in the balance of trade provided balancing capital transactions occurred.

As such a model approaches reality it necessarily increases in complexity, with new relationships to be estimated for each additional sector, together with inter-relation-ships to link it to all the existing sectors. At some stage of complexity the available data becomes insufficient to resolve the number of relationships involved and this sets a limit on the amount of detail that can be incorporated in the model. Nevertheless

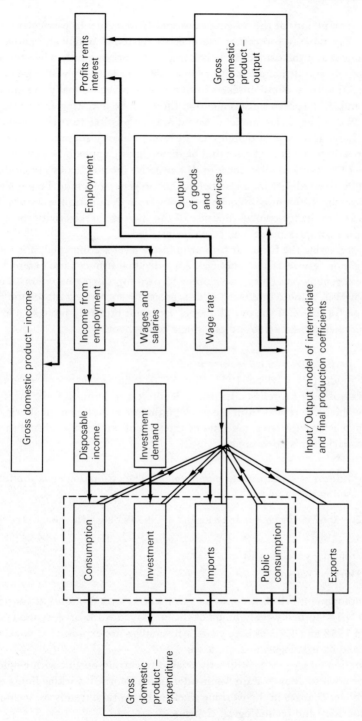

Fig. 9.2 Representative national income model

increasing the complexity of the model brings specific benefits. In particular disaggregation makes it possible to forecast at a level easily related to policy alternatives both at the government and the firm level. This is important because only when forecasts refer to the supply and demand conditions in a particular industry will there be any immediate reaction from decision takers in that industry. Additionally the more complex the model the greater discrimination there can be in testing alternative policy instruments. With an aggregate model it would only be possible to test for aggregate policies such as fiscal surplus or deficit and the level of money supply. As the model becomes more complex tax changes could be differentially applied. For example, the consequences of investment allowances or of a negative income tax or tax credit system could be assessed. It would also be possible to generate a model complete enough to show the different consequences arising from devaluation, as opposed to import levies and exchange control. Because of this increase in selectivity the extra expenditure on a complex model will often be justified.

So far as forecasting the future at firm or industry level is concerned, it is not clear that disaggregation is necessarily beneficial. An individual firm can use external estimates as exogenous variables in developing its own forecasting equation. A central forecaster, however, is more interested in disaggregation so far as it allows him to improve the performance of the overall model. He is not primarily interested in the accuracy of prediction as it relates to any single component.

9.4.1 Some equations from the Treasury model
The Treasury model (see Maclean, 1964; Roy, 1970) is an aggregate one, producing little in the way of sector forecasts. Its principle interest to business forecasters is in the extent to which the results from the model influence government in altering the parameters such as interest rates, tax rates or the level of public expenditure that directly affect each firm's operations.

The supply of resources — output and employment. The estimating equation for employment used in the model is:

$$\log E_t = 0.6226 + 0.6219 \log Q_t + 0.3818 \log E_{t-1} - 0.1491 \log NH_t - 0.0131 t_1 - 0.007 t_2$$
$$(4.7) (1.9) (0.5) (2.6) (3.1)$$

(Figures in parentheses are t statistics.)
$\bar{R}^2 = 0.96$;   Durbin—Watson = 1.78

where E = employment, full-time equivalent workers; Q = total output at constant factor prices; NH = normal weekly hours of the employed workforce; t_1 and t_2 are time trends in 1958 and 1963 as base years. All variables are expressed at constant factor prices and natural logarithms are used.

In this equation employment is directly related to current output with employment last period included to allow for any lag in adjustment. Normal working hours are included to reflect changes in the working week, and two time trends are included to pick up productivity and technological changes.

In the model the validity of the relationship is based on the assumption that in general (though not for individual industries) prices always react fully to changes in wage rates and that employment is not affected. This assumption is convenient in that it allows the wage rate to act as an exogenous variable on employment in defining total money wages. By adding money wages calculated in this way to employment-related employer payments, and armed forces' pay the total wage and salary bill in current prices is obtained. Adding equations or estimates of other sources of income — rents, profits and self-employed income and adjusting for stock appreciation, defines Gross Domestic Product in terms of total current incomes.

To convert this estimate to the constant price basis necessary to estimate consumption and investment in real terms, money values have to be deflated by a price index. If the intention is to measure the impact of price control measures, then an assumed price index is used as an exogenous estimate. Otherwise the price level is treated as an endogenous variable and estimated by an equation of the type:

$$\Delta PC_t = 0.823 \ \Delta WC_t + 0.692 \ \Delta WC_{t-1} + 0.777 \ \Delta MC_t + 0.348 \ \Delta MC_{t-1}$$
$$\quad\ \ (5.61) \qquad\quad (4.60) \qquad\qquad (6.52) \qquad\quad\ (2.47)$$

(Figures in parentheses are t statistics.)

$\bar{R}^2 = 0.96$ Durbin–Watson = 1.99

where Δ represents that first differences of a variable are in use; PC = the consumer price index; MC = value of imports divided by total final output at 1963 factor prices; WC = the total wage and salary bill divided by total final output, at 1963 prices. Similar price equations are used in determining separate price change estimates for inventories, investment goods and goods bought by public authorities. Using these price indices for components of total output all values can be converted to a constant price basis before estimating investment and total consumption. The investment by manufacturers in plant and machinery, in 1963 prices, is for example given by an equation:

$$\Delta IM_t^{P\,\&\,M} = 5.58 \ \Delta GM_t + 8.46 \ \Delta GM_{t-1} + 2.23 \ \Delta GM_{t-2} - 5.97 \ \Delta GM_{t-3}$$
$$\qquad\qquad\ \ (2.0) \qquad\quad (2.8) \qquad\qquad (0.8) \qquad\qquad (2.2)$$

(Figures in parentheses are t statistics.)

$\bar{R}^2 = 0.56$ Durbin–Watson = 1.57

where Δ indicates first differences for the variables are being used, and where GM stands for manufacturing output (itself a function of real Gross Domestic Product) in 1963 prices, while $IM^{P\,\&\,M}$ is real investment in plant and machinery. The equation indicates a multiplier relationship for investment. At zero growth no investment is made, while a 3 per cent growth in manufacturing output triggers an investment growth of 3 * (5.58 + 8.46 + 2.23 − 5.97), or 10.30 per cent.

The three equations from the Treasury model we have chosen to discuss illustrate both the simplicity of the relationships used and the aggregate nature of the exercise. This arises because the model is principally designed for testing the outcomes of alternative policies, in assisting in a judgement about what is and what is not feasible within given resource constraints and policy alternatives. In the next section we do, however, consider the problem of expanding the basic forecast to the industry level.

§ 9.5 Disaggregating national income forecast with input—output

A national income model will generally produce relatively aggregate forecasts of demands and supplies of goods and services. The role of input—output analysis, reflecting as it does the technological conditions under which production is undertaken, is to translate these aggregate estimates into industry-by-industry estimates of overall production and resource requirements. This task is a necessary one because a list of goods and services required for final consumption gives only a partial impression of the required overall pattern of economic activity in the economy. For example, only small quantities of steel enter into final consumption, but when consumers buy a washing machine they are buying, indirectly, a considerable amount of steel, together with rubber, copper, plastic and so on. In addition the steel industry itself, in providing the steel needed by the washing machine industry, is itself using considerable quantities of coal, iron ore and electricity; and to make matters worse, in providing that coal, iron ore and electricity, the mining and electricity industries are probably using considerable quantities of steel.

Fortunately, the use of input—output models provides a means of breaking down any list of commodities entering final consumption and translating them into required production levels, sector by sector. In this way estimates of the investment and manpower needs of intermediate producers can be derived and matched to existing and planned availability of these resources. In the event that the resources are not available it follows that an unchanged pattern of consumption would produce bottlenecks and shortages. Once warning is given it may be possible to apply appropriate corrective actions — either through altering the pattern of final demand or adding to the resources available to overcome the potential bottleneck. Thus the government may encourage and subsidize training programmes for particular classes of workers whose skills may be shown to be in short supply. Because such models are complex it is not possible to provide more than this outline of their construction and operation. More detailed accounts of input/output modelling are, however, available (see, e.g., Barker and Woodward, 1972, pp. 37—55 and §10.4).

§ 9.6 Published medium-term forecasts

Several forecasts concerning the prospects of the economy over the next year or two are regularly prepared and updated. The coverage of these forecasts is broadly similar, so that a direct comparison between them can be made. We have already discussed the indicators published by the Treasury. In addition series are prepared by the National Institute for Economic and Social Research and by the London Business School.

The methodology of these forecasts lies in the combination of econometric analysis, trend projection and subjective judgement. Some element of informality is necessary simply because of the severity of the fluctuations in the basic statistical

Table 9.1

Forecast and actual GDP growth rates 1970—73

	Actual GDP growth	Treasury forecast	National Institute forecast	London Business School forecast
1970	2.0	2.8	3.4	3.2
1971	1.3	1.2	−0.3	1.4
1972	2.4	4.7	3.5	3.6
1973	5.4	6.5	6.9	5.8

Sources: National Institute Economic Review, May Issues; Sunday Times, May 3 1970, April 28 1974, August 18 1974; Financial Statement and Budget Reports (HMSO). (Comparable forecasts are published by the Sunday Telegraph and by OECD.)

series used, where, for example the monthly trade figures may be distorted by the impact of a dock strike or by the shipment of several large airplanes within one month.

In Table 9.1 a comparison between forecasts from the three previously mentioned sources for the growth of Gross Domestic Product are shown. These forecasts not only vary for the aggregate GDP estimates shown but also in their estimates of the components of GDP. Some details from recent National Institute forecasts are shown in Table 9.2. Figures shown are the February estimates from the NIESR Economic Review and are in £ millions, at 1970 prices.

In part, some of the discrepancies between forecasts from alternative sources arise from differences in the timing of the exercises producing them, as well as differences

Table 9.2

NIESR forecasts 1972—74, £ millions, 1970 prices

	1972		1973		1974	
	Forecast	Actual	Forecast	Actual	Forecast	Actual
						(Estimate)
GDP	11,223	11,116	11,909	11,706	11,363	11,764
Consumer expenditure	8,330	8,529	8,927	8,917	8,575	8,879
Public Authority current spending	2,055	2,446	2,169	2,525	2,577	2,580
Gross fixed investment	2,401	2,345	2,600	2,486	2,375	2,424
Exports of goods and services	3,091	3,102	3,255	3,370	3,355	3,592
Imports of goods and services	3,121	3,137	3,488	3,419	3,403	3,514

in the methodology used. Taking these into account a major remaining source of difference is variation in the supporting assumptions. Since we argued that the assumptions are as important a part of a conditional forecast as the predicted outcomes it follows that by examining the assumptions made in preparing alternative forecasts many of the discrepancies can be ironed out. Beyond this, remaining discrepancies do indicate the relative imprecision of forecasting. However, as we showed in Chapter 2, uncertainty in information does not necessarily exclude it from being valuable. Probably the areas in which perfect forecasts are possible are areas where few changes occur, and where, as a consequence the likely value of a forecast is low.

9.6.1 Evaluating medium-term forecasts

The required accuracy from forecasts depends on the use for which they are intended, so it is misleading to assess forecasts on purely statistical grounds. In fact because all the forecasts, except the *Sunday Telegraph*'s, are presented in seasonally adjusted form and in real prices considerable work may be needed before any forecasts capable of contributing to a firm's financial production and sales planning can be generated.

Even allowing for the fact that modifications have to be made, we still face problems in evaluating forecasts. The central one is that forecasts are made on a conditional basis but may provoke a government response which changes the basis on which the forecast is made and hence invalidates it. There is some evidence to indicate such a response, even an over-response, in government economic management. To the extent that the response is predictable it can be taken into account. Even so, there is evidence that the available forecasts do on balance predict the future considerably better than a naive assumption that all existing levels will re-occur in the immediate future (Ash and Smyth, 1973). There is also evidence that some of the error in the forecasting is consistent, so that a routine adjustment to remove this bias would improve forecasting performance. Part of the bias arises because the models are demand oriented and tend to set GDP growth in line with projected demand without reflecting the effect of production constraints. As a consequence GDP growth tends to be overestimated.

§ 9.7 Other indicators of the trading environment

9.7.1 Business indicators

So far in this chapter most of the attention has been devoted to models which attempt to provide a causal explanation for economic variations, and we have commented on the ability of systems of equations to do this. However, not all business decisions are best helped by this type of forecast. In particular where a forecaster is primarily concerned with the direction in which a time series moves rather than the amount it moves, he may often be prepared to sacrifice the relatively better quantitative accuracy of a causal forecast.

As an example, a firm intending to replace a large overdraft with a fixed interest debenture would find it opportune to make this switch when long-term interest rates were at a minimum, irrespective of whether that minimum is at an interest rate of 8 or 12 per cent. In such circumstances forecasts that predict turning points are widely used.

The most common way of predicting turning points is to identify a leading indicator series whose behaviour consistently anticipates the behaviour of the series that has to be forecast.

In Fig. 9.3 we show how an indentification of series B and C as leading indicators for series A could lead to a forecast of the minimum (turning point) for series A. If series B leads series A by an average of 6 months and series C leads A by 2 months then the recognition (which, because it depends on the behaviour of the smoothed series, lags somewhat behind a change in the raw data) that series B has reached a turning point alerts the forecaster to a possible turning point for A. The turning point observed for series C confirms the forecast of an imminent change in A. Thus we might observe that the *Financial Times* Ordinary Share Index and the index of retail sales regularly precede an improvement in investment expenditures. As a producer of capital goods we might respond to such indications by manufacturing for inventory when these leading indicators have reversed from previous minimum levels.

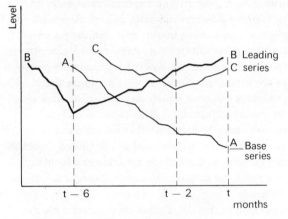

Fig. 9.3 Leading indicators and forecasting

In the United States considerable attention has been given to the concept of business indicators as they relate to the general business cycle, and the methodology developed assumes that for the lead (or lag) between series to be stable the two series must be causally related, even though such a relationship cannot be accurately specified. The National Bureau of Economic Research has described a method for evaluating lead and lag relationships between variables based on the length of the lead time and the consistency, in terms of standard deviations in lead time, in the association of turning points. (For a review of this material see Gordon, 1962. A complete description is given in Moore and Shiskin, 1967.)

In summary leading indicators offer a different approach to forecasting and their simplicity has made them a popular method of forecasting the national economy in the US. They supplement the more formal methods discussed in the earlier part of the chapter but may not perform particularly well in the UK mixed economy situation where economic intervention by the government on grounds of policy is more frequent than in the US. (Recently published work offers evidence on this, see O'Dea, 1975. *Economic Trends*, London, HMSO will, in future, publish suitable indicators and for comment, see the issue of March 1975, No. 257, pp. 95—110.)

9.7.2 Business surveys

Instead of trying to forecast the behaviour of an economic variable over the next two years or so by a process of quantification and model building, an alternative approach is to survey a sample of all the decision makers who have influence on the relevant economic outcome. Their opinions and perhaps intentions may then be used as the basis of a forecast.

An example of an anticipatory survey designed to provide forecasting information by collating individual opinion is provided by the Confederation of British Industry Survey (CBI). Information is collected and published tri-annually on expectation about sales prospects, price levels, business activity and exports. Similarly the US Department of Commerce survey businessmen quarterly on expected sales and inventory levels, and in the *Survey of Current Business* they also publish future invest-ment plans. Since survey techniques are widely used in market research the potential and limitations of the technique are well understood (see e.g., Ferber and Verdoorn, 1962, pp. 267—77). The relative importance of issues such as the respondent's invest-ment intentions or sales expectations are sufficiently important to minimize the problems of non-response or worse, spurious response which may affect the findings of surveys collecting information on less important variables. Despite the additional problems of survey design, administration and interpretation that are inherent in collecting information in this way, such surveys are widely used in the United States as an indicator of the future trading environment, and are made available as a regular component of official statistics (for example the data on *Consumer Buying Indicators* published by the US Bureau of the Census).

While no equivalent exercise is conducted in the UK, Gallup do conduct a much more limited private survey aimed at measuring the same phenomenon (Heald, 1971). Such a survey, by asking well-tried questions such as: 'Looking a year ahead do you think you will be better off financially, or worse off, or about the same?', can produce an index that reflects consumer confidence in the economy, and such an index can be interpreted as a leading indicator of the growth in the economy (Katona, 1969).

As well as questions to establish general consumer confidence, more direct questions on consumer buying intentions for given products over a chosen time interval ahead can be included, and techniques have been developed to process verbal answers into probability estimates (Juster, 1966). Whether the information obtained from a survey is general or specific the resulting indices can be used as variables in a normal sales forecasting equation, for example in a model of the form:

$$Q_{t+1} = \beta_0 + \beta_1 P_t + \beta_2 A_t + \beta_3 Z_{t+1} + \text{(error)},$$

where P is for example a weighted probability of purchase index, A is an index of con-sumer confidence, Z stands for other objective variables such as stock variables, relative prices, etc. and Q is the forecast sales of a given product.

236

Research into the performance of forecasting equations including non-objective variables suggests that without objective variables in the equation such series do provide an acceptable explanation of variation in the expenditure variable. However, inclusion of normal economic variables both improves the performance of the equation and makes the contribution of survey variables insignificant. This indicates that the 'intentions' variables measure much the same factors as does a direct objective forecast of GDP. Klein and Schapiro confirm this impression (in Strumpel *et al.*, 1972) by showing that 'intentions' survey data can itself be explained in terms of lagged values of objective economic variables.

This suggests that while 'intentions' surveys measure factors which are also taken into account in making macro-economic forecasts, their use as an alternative produces a worse forecast while introducing a more complex set of causal relationships on which the validity of a model is judged. If, as in the UK, they have to be privately commissioned we suggest their performance be rigorously compared with an objective model.

§ 9.8 Conclusion

Most of the models discussed elsewhere in this book recognize that the behaviour of the economy within which a firm competes for resources and sales is a critical determinant in the success or failure of alternative policies. For this reason many of the models use GDP as an exogenous variable, while even more use components of GDP — for example consumer income, investment expenditure — in the same way. This presents few difficulties in estimating the forecasting equation, since only known values of exogenous variables are required. However, forecasts made from such equations depend on the future values for exogenous variables and such future values have themselves to be forecast.

In this chapter we suggest that access to published forecasts of these variables means that independent estimation is not justified, although substantial adaption may be. The discussion given to the errors arising in such forecasts reflects a view that equations that require their use should be evaluated on their predictive power over the appropriate time interval using forecast values of the exogenous variables, rather than on their historic explanatory power using observed values for these variables.

The need for policy evaluation tends to limit the use of non-causal models in forecasting macro-economic variables even when survey data or Box—Jenkins techniques statistically perform well (for a comparison using Box—Jenkins see Nelson, 1972). This is because these methods do not permit easy modification of their underlying assumptions, for example concerning government economic policy changes; nor do they permit the forecaster to learn about the model's structure, from which a gradual improvement in the performance of causal models can be expected.

References

Ash, J. C. R. and **Smyth, D. J.** (1973) *Forecasting the U.K. Economy*, Saxon House (D. C. Heath), Farnborough.

Barker, J. S. and Woodward, V. H. (1972) 'Inflation, growth, and economic policy in the medium term', *National Institute Economic Review*, No. 60, May.

CBI, *Industrial Trends Survey*, Confederation of British Industry. (Discussed in Glynn, D. R. (1969) 'The C.B.I. industrial trends survey', *Applied Economics*, vol. 1.)

Duesenberry, J. S. Fromm, G., Klein, L. R. and Kuh, E. (eds) (1965) *The Brookings Quarterly Econometric Model of the United States*, North-Holland, Amsterdam.

Ferber, R. and Verdoorn, P. J. (1962) *Research Methods in Economics and Business*, Macmillan, New York.

Gordon, R. A. (1962) 'Alternative approaches to forecasting – the recent work of the National Bureau', *Review of Economics and Statistics*, vol. 44. (Reprinted in Haynes *et al.* (1973) *Readings in Managerial Economics*, Business Publications, Dallas, Texas.)

Heald, Gordon (1971) 'Consumer confidence and its effect on expenditure for the British economy', *Journal of the Market Research Society*, vol. 13.

Juster, F. T. (1966) 'Consumer-buying intentions and purchase probability', *Journal of the American Statistical Association*, vol. 61.

Katona, G. *et al.* (1969) *1968 Survey of Consumer Finances*, Survey Research Center, University of Michigan, Ann Arbor.

Maclean, A. A. (1964) in Worswick, G. D. N. and Blackaby, J. J. (eds) *The Medium Term*, Social Science Research Council/National Institute of Economic and Social Research, Heinemann, London.

Moore, Geoffrey H. and Shiskin, Julius (1967) *Indicators of Business Expansion*, National Bureau of Economic Research, New York.

Nelson, Charles R. (1972) 'The prediction performance of the FRB—MIT—PENN model of the U.S. economy', *American Economic Review*, vol. lxii.

O'Dea, D. J. (1975) *Cyclical Indicators for the post war British Economy*, Cambridge University Press for the National Institute of Economic Social Research, London.

Roy, A. D. (1970) in Hilton, K. and Heathfield, D. (eds) *The Economic Study of the United Kingdom*, Macmillan, London.

Strumpel, B., Morgan, J. N. and Zahn, E. (eds) (1972) *Human Behaviour in Economic Affairs: Essays in Honour of George Katona*, Elsevier, Amsterdam.

Additional references

For an alternative view of forecasting problems in the National Economy see:

Robinson, C. (1971) *Business forecasting*, Nelson, London, Ch. 3;

Butler, W. F. and Kavesh, R. A. (eds) (1966), *How Business Economists Forecast*, Prentice-Hall, Englewood Cliffs, New Jersey. Parts 2 and 4.

For a full discussion of one particular non-mathematical approach used successfully by a consulting group:

Morrell, J. (ed.) (1972) *Management Decisions and the Role of Forecasting*, Penguin, Harmondsworth, Middlesex, England.

For a description of 'opportunist' forecasting; that is, gathering data, information, and insight of any relevant kind and synthesizing it into a quantitative model, see:

Lewis, J. P. and Turner, R. (1967) *Business Conditions Analysis*, McGraw-Hill, New York, 2nd edn.

For further ideas on econometric methods for forecasting the economy see:

Suits, D. B. (1962) 'Forecasting and analysis with an econometric model', *American Economic Review*, vol. 52.

Two books which give a detailed discussion on macro-economic forecasting, built around an econometric model, are:

Evans, M. K. (1969) *Macro-Economic activity*, Harper and Row, New York;
Kuh, D. and Schmalensee, R. L. (1973) *An Introduction to Applied Macro-economics*, North-Holland, Amsterdam.

A general discussion of problems in modelling the UK economy is in:

Hilton, K. and Heathfield, D. (1970) *The Econometric Study of the United Kingdom*, Macmillan, London.

We have already mentioned Klein's essay in Strumpel *et al.*, 1972 (see reference above). The whole of Part V on 'Predicting consumer behaviour' is particularly valuable.

An interesting research study using survey data which investigated the impact of forecasting error on inventories and production was made by:

Hirsch, A. A. and Lovell, M. C. (1969) *Sales Anticipation and Inventory Behaviour*, Wiley, New York.

Two technical studies concerned with the evaluation of forecasts are:

Zarnowitz, V. (1967) *An Appraisal of Short-Term Economic Forecasts*, Occasional Paper 104, National Bureau of Economic Research, New York;
Mincer, J. (1969) *Economic Forecasts and Expectations. Analysis of Forecasting Behaviour and Performance*, National Bureau of Economic Research, Columbia University Press, New York.

In an attempt to improve national forecasts in the US the American Statistical Association and the National Bureau have instituted a survey to record economists' forecasts of future trends, and these are published regularly by *The American Statistician*; see:

Zarnowitz, V. (1969) The New A.S.A.–N.B.E.R. survey of forecasts by economic statisticians', *The American Statistician*, vol. 23.

10

Long-range forecasting and technological change

§ 10.1 Introduction

Forecasting exists to generate relationships that link future conditions with currently known variables. Whether the relationships used by the forecaster are derived by a process of historical analysis or are simply the expression of expert opinion it is inevitable that the further ahead the relationships are projected the less accurate they become. This decay in the validity of relationships as they are extrapolated further and further into the future arises because at the time the forecasts are made it is virtually impossible for the forecasting model used to take account of every element of change in the environment.

In practice, therefore, no model based on current data and relationships will ever be general enough to be indefinitely applicable under future conditions. Altered production methods, technology, markets, legislation and a thousand and one other changes conspire over time to ensure that the model becomes increasingly obsolete and non-representative under future conditions. As projections are made further and further ahead of existing data the sources of change specifically recognized in the forecasting model become a smaller and smaller component of the total change to. which the forecast variables are exposed. Even those relationships in the forecasting model that continue to be relevant get less useful, since the projection of observed errors usually generates confidence limits that are so wide that they encompass all the alternative futures we wish to choose between. In long-run forecasting the emphasis thus tends to be on defining the bounds of the possible rather than predicting a single most likely outcome.

§ 10.2 Generality and model design

Because forecasting models become less and less accurate the further ahead they are used to project, it is important that this built-in obsolescence is kept to an unavoidable minimum. This can be done by improving the generality of the forecasting model.

One method of increasing generality is to raise the level of aggregation in the fore-

240

cast, since an aggregate is invariably more stable and more predictable than its component parts. It would be foolhardy, for example, for a clothing manufacturer to try and predict sales of women's dresses 10 years ahead, since the clothing market is largely dependent on short-run changes in fashion. However, he could expect to predict the total expenditure on women's clothing 10 years ahead with reasonable accuracy, and provided the premises and equipment he buys are flexible enough to make a reasonable variety of articles this aggregate forecast would be useful in formulating investment plans.

The generality of forecasting models can also be improved by ensuring that the relations are calculated in relation to the variables we actually want to predict rather than for surrogates of these variables that happen to be more easily available. Frequently equations might be set up that use money values for all variables as surrogates for the underlying physical transactions. Any change in the value of money, or the rate at which money can be converted into any of the physical variables involved, inevitably undermines the validity of the measured equation and hence of the forecasts it produces.

A forecasting model can also be made more general for long-term applications by combining statistically derived relationships with subjective judgements. Some elements in any situation may be amenable to statistical analysis — technological relationships perhaps, and long-run economic trends, whereas other elements we believe to be significant cannot be reasonably predicted. In this situation the forecasting model might reasonably combine both conventional statistical methods and subjective judgements.

§ 10.3 Forecasting and long-range planning

The key purpose of long-range planning is to prepare the way for future decisions which may be required as conditions change. Forecasts help in this process to the extent that they predict future conditions. However, since long-term forecasts do little more than indicate an area of probabilities within a field of possibilities the planning process should aim to speed the reaction time of the organization to a range of possible futures rather than to prepare specific action to suit a single 'best estimate' of future conditions.

The more difficult forecasting becomes and the more uncertain the resulting forecast the more important it is that this approach is adopted. Producers and users of capital equipment — ships, aircraft and process plant for example, make major current commitments against their estimates of future conditions. Most of the time their forecasts cannot be right yet by building sufficient flexibility into the planning process the investment commitment can still produce a moderately successful outcome. This concept of planning flexibility reaches its ultimate development in circumstances where it is almost impossible to generate remotely reliable forecasts. Such situations might occur because no current precedents exist, or because we are facing many outcomes each having only a small probability of occurrence or else because the situation is interactive.

To counter these difficulties an approach called contingency planning is used (see Stern, 1974 for an example describing 'protection' of computer-installations). Instead of considering most likely outcomes, contingency planning focuses on extreme outcomes irrespective of their probability of occurrence in order to test planned policies for their flexibility and performance. In defining a future strategy contingency planning relies on collecting, by suggestion and search, a reasonably exhaustive set of possible 'futures' which can be used as scenarios to measure the effectiveness of alternative policies. A possible scenario, for example, could involve a 5-year period within which contingencies such as a 2-month internal labour dispute, a shut down of Middle East oil fields, devaluation of the pound and a major war in Southern Africa all occurred. Each alternative strategy can then be evaluated against this range of possible future events, to give an indication of its profitability and survival potential.

10.3.1 An example of contingency decision making under uncertainty

Company B has developed a new safety device which may be made compulsory for all cars. Company A, a much larger company, is researching the same area and has three alternatives. They could buy company B; they could acquire a licence from company B, or they could ignore company B's development and pursue their own independent research in the expectation that a device superior to company B's would be produced in due course. The major contingency influencing the desirability of the alternative strategies is whether the device made by company B is made compulsory by the government, thus pre-empting sales for any device A may subsequently develop; whether it is simply recommended by government or whether the government decides to take no action for the time being.

To investigate the implications of alternative strategies, their profitability under each of the alternative government policies are calculated (Table 10.1). Inspection of strategy alternatives indicates that there is no single policy that is best whatever action the government takes. Thus acquiring company B is a good idea if B's device is recommended or made compulsory, but very bad if the government takes no action. In these

Table 10.1
Profit payoff to company A of alternative strategies (£'000)

	Government action		
		B's device made compulsory	B's device recommended	No action
A's strategies	1 Buy licence from B	150	50	20
	2 Continue R & D	−50	100	250
	3 Acquire B	200	150	−100

circumstances some other grounds have to be found for selecting the preferred strategy alternative.

One criterion that could be considered is the *maximin criterion*. For each possible strategy the decision maker picks out the worst that could possibly happen, and then picks the strategy which is 'least worse' — the strategy whose most unattractive contingency is least disastrous.

Inspecting the outcomes in Table 10.1 the worst outcome for strategy 1 is a profit of £20,000, while strategies 2 and 3 involve worst outcomes of —£50,000 and —£100,000 respectively. On the maximin criterion strategy 1 is thus best because it offers the least bad of the 'worst' outcomes.

This maximin criterion might be an attractive one in some circumstances — notably where contingencies were selected with deliberate malice, perhaps by an opponent or competitor. It might also be attractive where the decision taker was judged solely on his skill in avoiding disasters rather than for his overall performance. For example, more resources will tend to be devoted to avoiding 100 vehicle crashes on motorways than to avoiding a similar number of independent vehicle crashes off the motorway, simply because mass accidents attract much more adverse publicity than individual accidents. In the same way a firm's personnel manager would tend to avoid a short-term but major strike with his workforce even where this was cheaper than the longer-term but less dramatic costs involved in avoiding the strike.

In our particular example, however, the maximin criterion is too conservative since we have no reason to suspect that the government is deliberately trying to minimize A's gains, nor are the other outcomes so disastrous that A would want to avoid them at all costs. In these circumstances an alternative criterion, the *Bayes—Laplace* criterion is often recommended. This approach suggests that in a situation of complete uncertainty we simply assume that each of a set of exhaustive and exclusive outcomes is equally probable, and use this equiprobability assumption to weight the outcomes for each strategy. On this basis the strategies have expected values of;

Strategy 1: $\frac{1}{3} * 150 + \frac{1}{3} * 50 + \frac{1}{3} * 20 = 73\frac{1}{3}$,

Strategy 2: $\frac{1}{3} * -50 + \frac{1}{3} * 100 + \frac{1}{3} * 250 = 100$,

Strategy 3: $\frac{1}{3} * 200 + \frac{1}{3} * 150 + \frac{1}{3} * -100 = 83\frac{1}{3}$.

Thus strategy 2, pursuing independent R & D, is the most attractive. Whatever basis we choose in selecting the strategy, most of the benefit in contingency planning is generated in the exercise of defining strategies and evaluating alternative outcomes, in a way that leads to consistent if not optimal decision making.

§10.4 Input—output as a forecasting technique

One requirement in long-term forecasting is for generality in the forecasting model. Because input—output techniques are designed to predict the behaviour of an integrated system rather than the behaviour of a single isolated variable they offer the opportunity to develop forecasting models that are general enough to be readily applied to national- and firm-level planning. They are particularly appropriate where questions of technological interdependence and complementarity arise, for instance as a result of inter-trading between the divisions of a large company, and they also provide a powerful tool for assessing the indirect as well as the direct consequence of any planned change in output or sales levels.

The basic building block in constructing an input–output model is a record of the pattern of transactions occurring in the area of interest. For example we might be interested in the trading relationships between two industries who both supply and buy from each other, as well as selling to other final buyers. Using records of the purchases and sales made involving these two industries it is possible to construct a matrix of transactions (Table 10.2). Reading from Table 10.2 we can see that industry 1 achieved gross sales of £1,600,000. Of these (reading along the first row of the table) £200,000 were sales made within industry 1; £400,000 were sales made to industry 2; and £1,000,000 were sales to final customers. Naturally the £400,000 of sales industry 1 makes to industry 2 also appear as purchases by industry 2 from industry 1 (column 2, line 1).

Table 10.2
Table of transactions (£'000)

Sales by	Purchases by			
	Industry 1	Industry 2	Final buyers	Total output
Industry 1	200	400	1,000	1,600
Industry 2	600	100	2,000	2,700

While in the table the presentation of only two industries means that the interdependence is unrealistically high, in fact sectors do interface quite extensively. Thus in 1968 the electronics and telecommunications industry bought £16.3 m. of inputs from the electrical machinery industry and, in turn, made sales of £12.8 m. to that industry (CSO, 1973).

Information of this type, on inter-sector transactions, can be used to construct an input–output model provided two assumptions can be justified.

1. An assumption of linear homogeneity in production, under constant technology.
2. An assumption that each industry produces a single homogeneous product.

Taking these assumptions in turn, the assumption of linear homogeneity simply requires that the inputs of materials will always be directly proportional to output — there will be no economies or diseconomies of scale.

The second major assumption made in input–output analysis is that of product homogeneity. This means that each industry produces a single standard product and that, for example, all cars are identical. In practice, virtually every industry produces a variety of products. The motor industry, for example, produces family saloons, commercial vehicles and sports cars and each of these products tends to require a differing amount of steel. However, provided the mix of products produced by an industry remains more or less unchanged, the assumption of product homogeneity may not be too far-fetched.

If these two assumptions can be made for the industries generating the transactions flows shown in Table 10.2, it is legitimate to derive technical coefficients from the transactions information. To do this we simply calculate the purchase requirements of each industry as a proportion of its total output. Thus in Table 10.2 industry 1 buys £600,000 from industry 2 in making £1,600,000 of output. To make £1 of output industry 1 would require £600,000/£1,600,000 or £0.375 of output from industry 2. We can repeat this calculation for the other transactions in Table 10.2 to give Table 10.3. The technical coefficients shown in Table 10.3 are simply the coefficients of two equations that could be written:

$$0.125X_1 + 0.148X_2 + C_1 = X_1,$$

and

$$0.375X_1 + 0.037X_2 + C_2 = X_2,$$

where X_1 and X_2 are the total outputs of industries 1 and 2 respectively, while C_1 and C_2 are the sales to final buyers.

Table 10.3
Technical coefficients

	Purchases by	
Sales by	*Industry 1*	*Industry 2*
Industry 1	200/1,600 = 0.125	400/2,700 = 0.148
Industry 2	600/1,600 = 0.375	100/2,700 = 0.037

10.4.1 An example of input—output analysis
A manufacturer of electronic and electrical equipment has two divisions, one making semi-conductors and printed circuits, the other electronically controlled production and scientific equipment. Last year's shipments to final customers amounted to £600,000 from division 1 and £1,500,000 from division 2 (the direct requirements matrix is shown in Table 10.4). However, next year it is anticipated that a new contract will raise the final sales of division 2 from £1,500,000 to £2,300,000, although sales from division 1 will remain constant. The problem is what effect would this have on division 1. It is not sufficient simply to raise the output of division 2, since this division relies on materials produced in division 1, and a unilateral expansion in division 2 would absorb division 1 output which is required to meet its own planned

245

Table 10.4
Table of transactions for electric equipment manufacturer

Sales by	Purchases by			
	Division 1	Division 2	Sales to outside customers	Total output
Division 1	£100,000	£300,000	£600,000	£1,000,000
Division 2	£100,000	£400,000	£1,500,000	£2,000,000

sales. Because of the close relationship between division 1 and division 2 the inter-actions of any change in production volume have to be considered. As a first step the transactions matrix in Table 10.4 can be converted into a technical coefficients matrix shown in Table 10.5.

Table 10.5
The technical coefficients — electrical equipment manufacturer

Sales by	Purchases by	
	Division 1	Division 2
Division 1	100,000/1,000,000 = 0.10	300,000/2,000,000 = 0.15
Division 2	100,000/1,000,000 = 0.10	400,000/2,000,000 = 0.20

Using C_1 and C_2 to represent the quantities available for final sales from division 1 and division 2 respectively, and X_1 and X_2 the associated gross outputs, we can set X_1 to the old capacity of £1,000,000 and C_2 to £2,300,000 and solve two equations for C_1 and X_2:

$$£0.10 * 1,000,000 + 0.15 * X_2 + C_1 = 1,000,000$$
$$£0.10 * 1,000,000 + 0.20 * X_2 + 2,300,000 = X_2$$

$$0.15 * X_2 + C_1 = 900,000$$
$$0.8 * X_2 = 2,400,000$$

Thus

$$X_2 = £3,000,000; \quad C_1 = £450,000.$$

The solution to the example shows that the expansion of final sales in division 2 from £1,500,000 to £2,300,000 would require an expansion in capacity in this division to bring up total gross output to the level of £3,000,000.

At the same time this expansion places increased demands on the output of sector 1, so that the amount left for sale to final customers declines from £600,000 to only £450,000. The issue to be decided is whether it is more valuable to sell the limited output from division 1 directly, or indirectly as a component part of the output from division 2.

10.4.2 Input—output and environmental forecasting

Input—output analysis is a descriptive model that relies for its usefulness on an assumption of a relatively stable set of relationships within a system, for example an economy. Using this assumption the model provides an indication not only of the direct consequences of any change, but also the indirect ones. For this reason input—output models are useful in converting general environmental changes into specific forecasts relevant to a single firm.

The importance of this can be illustrated by considering, for example, the effects of legislation designed to achieve equal wages for women workers. At first sight this would have little direct impact on a firm employing few or no women workers. However, if the position of suppliers and customers who may employ women is altered it follows that substantial indirect adjustments have to be made. A firm using exclusively male labour to make textile machinery, for example, would find that demand for its products would be affected with any reduction in the profitability of the textile industry, relying as it does on female labour. Exactly the same issues arise if the problem is to forecast the consequence for an individual firm of selective import controls. The obvious step to take is to consider the tariff changes that apply to the firm's own product and those of its potential competitors. However, this ignores the facts of a situation in which the firm is part of an overall system, and where the indirect effect of changes in the tariffs affecting suppliers and customers may be just as important as the more obvious direct effects. These indirect effects can be evaluated on an industry by industry basis using figures provided in the national input—output tables (CSO, 1973. A full explanation of source and calculation of the figures used in this section is provided in the text of the study.). Suppose, for example, we were interested in expanding the machine tool industry. From Table D in the CSO UK input—output tables this industry acquired a total £229.5 m. of direct inputs in 1968. However, it would not be sufficient simply to multiply each item of direct input by a required expansion factor because this does not take into account the increased resources required in their turn by each supplying industry. In fact Table E, the table of inverse coefficients, allows an assessment of direct and indirect requirements to be made automatically, because it presents the total (direct and indirect) requirements generated by an additional gross output of £1,000 from any given sector. Reading directly from the table each £1,000 of output from the machine tool sector requires for example £139.5 of iron and steel products and £12.7 of coal. If the capacity of the machine tool industry is to be expanded it follows that iron and steel, as well as coal output would have to expand too, and at a rate not just proportionate to their direct sales to the machine tool industry but by an additional amount to increase supplies to all the other industries supplying machine tool inputs.

10.4.3 Input—output in market forecasting

Firms selling direct to final consumers have an advantage in forecasting demand because their sales level is a direct function of consumer demand for their product. As a consequence we could expect to predict a reasonable proportion of the variation in such demand in terms of conventional variables such as the growth in consumer incomes, population change and price and competition effects.

For firms engaged in selling to other producers rather than to final buyers the problem is more complex because the demand for their product is a derived demand. There is no consumer demand for steel, as such, but consumers buy large quantities of steel in the form of cars, washing machines and other consumer durables. The sales of steel thus depend on the sales performance of steel-based products rather than on the direct efforts of steel manufacturers themselves. One response to this problem is to utilize input—output data to identify the ultimate destination of intermediate outputs. Using inverse-coefficients it is possible to identify how demand for steel alters as demand for cars or domestic appliances change. By multiplying these inverse-coefficients by projected final demand, product group by product group, it becomes possible to forecast derived demand for steel.

In a sense this is only transferring the forecasting problem down the line, and still leaves us with the need to develop forecasts for all relevant final demands. Fortunately this does not mean that intermediate goods producers have to be expert in forecasting each of their customers' markets. Because intermediate goods typically contribute to several categories of final product quite adequate forecasts of *total* derived demand for an intermediate good can be obtained simply by using trend curves to predict each final demand category. Input—output techniques are thus useful in predicting longer-term growth prospects for particular industries such as energy, packing materials, containers and so on, where fluctuations in levels of demand tend to be produced as much by changes in the distribution of sales between sectors supplied as they do on changed levels of sales within any sector.

§ 10.5 Collective inputs in decisions under uncertainty: the Delphi approach

The Delphi technique is used because it provides a mechanism for coordinating forecasts of the future from a variety of sources in a way that focuses attention in a constructive manner on discrepancies between forecasts. The Delphi method is specifically designed to overcome the disadvantage of face-to-face committee discussion, in which the pressure to conform, concepts of status and the bandwagon effect tend to produce an artificial and misleading outcome.

The Delphi process has three attributes:

(*a*) anonymity;
(*b*) feedback;
(*c*) group response.

Anonymity is ensured by the use of questionnaires or other media, under the administration of a non-participant. This anonymity reduces the influence of dominant individuals on a forecast.

The controlled feedback is obtained by conducting the forecasting exercise in a series of rounds, with each participant informed of the summarized forecasts of the group as a whole. Such feedback continues until forecasts emerging from the questionnaire are stable. In this way a group response is made in which the opinion of every participant reflects what he knows of the opinion of other participants — a true group forecast emerges.

The assumptions of the Delphi technique, that with repeated rounds the range of estimates will narrow and converge on the 'true' value, are not always fulfilled. However, residual disagreement, reflecting genuine uncertainty is often a good indication of the complexity and variability inherent in the issues under consideration.

10.5.1 The application of Delphi techniques

Delphi techniques have been used in a variety of applications though the expense of the undertaking generally means it will only be directed to eliminating major uncertainties. However, problems of new product selection (Parker, 1971), organizational design and manpower planning (Milkovich *et al.*, 1973) and technological forecasting (North, 1968) have been handled using Delphi techniques. In using the approach one of the problems is in selecting an appropriate membership for the participating panel. In many instances the obvious expert has already taken a committed position, so that anonymity disappears. Often also the expense in terms of fees may be prohibitive. Fortunately, there is little evidence that 'experts' are any better at long-term forecasting than people only partially exposed to the problem's complexities.

The method can also prove cumbersome and lengthy, particularly where several rounds of questionnaire are required. Against this it is possible to involve a far wider, perhaps international participation in a Delphi study than would be feasible where a straightforward committee system was adopted. Finally the deliberations may not result in an output that is easy to interpret. In the same way that diplomats have a facility for discovering forms of words that are open to diametrically opposed interpretations the Delphi study may conceal basic disagreements behind an ambiguous facade.

§ 10.6 The impetus to technological change

The direction and pace of technological change is largely a consequence of decisions taken not as a result of directly expressed scientific or economic needs, but as a result of planned efforts to satisfy social needs, or normative goals. An understanding of the processes by which these needs and goals arise and are translated into action can therefore contribute to an understanding of the way in which choices between alternative avenues of technological endeavour are made (Dunckel *et al.*, 1970).

An example of the importance of these non-economic and non-technological goals in dictating the whole progress of technological advance is provided by the programme to put a man on the moon by 1970 (the Apollo Project). Within 5 years of this commitment, taken on purely political grounds, NASA had control of the second largest scientific budget in the world, without any attempt to justify the expenditure being made in terms of scientific or economic priorities. However because technology and the social values underlying goals change over time it is necessary to modify goal oriented development as additional information becomes available. This process of continuous feedback is a common feature of several long-range forecasting techniques. At this level the technique of forecasting social goals (predicting needs to be met) and technological forecasting (analysing the methodology and pace of progress) interact to determine jointly a continually changing matrix of possible methods and possible outcomes.

One approach to the identification of this matrix is a technique called PATTERN (Planning Assistance Through Technical Evaluation of Relevance Numbers) (Sigford and Porvin, 1965, pp. 9—13; Esch, 1969, pp. 197—210). PATTERN is a procedure developed by Honeywell Inc., using relevance trees to relate social, economic and political forecasts to technical forecasts. In using this approach forecasters first prepare a scenario describing broad objective and shorter-term goals within the forecast area.

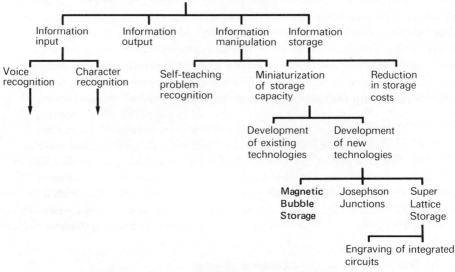

Fig. 10.1 *A section of a relevance tree for processed communication*

The completed scenario then forms the basis for the preparation of a relevance tree of the form shown in Fig. 10.1 in which objectives are broken down, level by level, into all the disaggregated components from which they might be achieved. This has the effect of setting out the relationships between objectives and existing technological capabilities. Once this is done experts are asked to assign relevance numbers to each element in the tree on the basis of their subjective assessment of the relative importance it would make in achieving the change to which it directly contributes. At each node the sum of weighting for all contributing factors is thus one.

Finally the relevance tree and relevance numbers are transferred to a computer and the overall relevance number for each technological change is estimated by evaluating the product of all the relevance numbers at each level down that branch of the tree.

At any level of the tree the size of the relevance number attached to alternative research problems provides a forecast of the value of researching that area given the initial importance attached to the various objectives. By altering the relative importance of overall objectives the forecaster can also see from the changed values of the relevance numbers how stable his recommendations are.

As an example a computer manufacturer† might be considering research strategy over the next few years. A relevance tree is constructed to show the link between company objectives and desired technology (Fig. 10.1). As a first step the company defines its objectives as continued pre-eminence in processed communications — in handling communication transactions involving manipulation, storage and recovery. This definition therefore excludes primary communication systems — television, telephone, film and so on. Having selected this objective an investigation of the consequences can follow.

To evaluate the relevance tree it now has to be considered in relation to the social, economic and political changes which might arise during the planning horizon. The increasing cost of energy, public concern over the growth in data banks and the availability of given skills through the educational system are all factors which might be considered in evaluating the alternatives in the development pattern shown in the relevance tree.

§ 10.7 Structuring technological forecasting problems

There are several ways in which the problem in decision making caused by the basic uncertainty in technological forecasts can be lessened.

As a first step the firm can consider its longer-term objectives and then identify a relatively small number of alternative ways in which these objectives could be achieved. Once this is done technological forecasts are not used to make absolute predictions but to choose between identified alternatives. In this way even if the forecast is subject to considerable error it is still likely that the best of the available alternatives will be selected.

This approach can be illustrated by considering a chemical company that has a primary objective of maintaining its market share in an expanding market. Given this objective the company identifies two alternative methods of providing the required additional capacity — either by building a plant using the existing technology, (A), or postponing expansion until research on a new and more economical process (B) is completed. Before making any technological forecast the company could compare the production and sales consequences of the two technologies to find a breakeven date representing the longest delay on process B which would still enable it to match the returns secured by immediate adoption of process A. If it is calculated that process B could never catch up if delayed beyond 4 years, but would be highly profitable if available before then, the technological forecaster can be asked to calculate the probability that process B would become available within 4 years. As a forecasting

† The material for this example is drawn from David Fishlock 'I.B.M. peers into the computer's future', *Financial Times*, 31 May 1973.

task this is much easier than requiring an exact date for the availability of process B, yet still allows a decision to be taken on the form of the additional capacity.

In specifying alternative solutions in this way the critical path method outlined in Chapter 3 not only helps to define alternatives in time but also ensures that an unnecessarily long lead time does not constrain the forecaster. A second way in which decisions can be made less dependent on the accuracy of technological forecasts, is if flexibility is deliberately built into the alternatives considered. In the same way that Swedish bus operators, in anticipation of a possible switch from left- to right-hand driving demanded specifications permitting almost instantaneous conversion of passenger entrances, a manufacturer could, at some expense, deliberately over specify his requirements. He could design buildings to allow clearances greater than those required by any existing machinery, and lifting gear could be more powerful than is needed for any present tasks. In this way he has bought the capability of operating with new technologies to make new products.

Finally, a common response to technological uncertainty, particularly in the research and development area, is to pursue in parallel research programmes aimed to meet the same technological objectives by differing means. General Motors, for example, while still developing conventional internal combustion engines, are also researching into a range of alternatives — electric vehicles, steam power units, Stirling engines, gas turbines and so on, simply to protect themselves from the possibility that a technological change — perhaps a metallurgical breakthrough — will tend to make one of these alternatives dominant.

§ 10.8 Trend and envelope curves in technological forecasting

The simplest assumption that can be made in technological forecasting is that past experience provides the best guide to future developments. The forecaster is usually interested in relating technologically based improvements in performance to the historical passage of time enabling him to estimate the most probable level of performance at some future date.

Many researchers using extrapolation techniques have chosen to fit data on an exponential basis, although other relationships, ranging from logistic curves to probability density functions, have been used. (Different long-range forecasting curves were discussed in §7.7.) Whether an exponential function or some other form of relationship is assumed the basic procedure for constructing the trend curve is the same. In all cases the chosen form of relationship is fitted to existing observations by using least squares methods.

A common trend in technological development is the 'S' curve — where the trend in performance of the system under investigation develops over time in a characteristic S pattern (Fig. 10.2). It is suggested that the 'S' curve arises because when a new system is developed — for example the internal combustion engine in the 1890s; it is relatively simple to improve the original design so that rapid increases in performance are possible. After a time the scope for further development becomes less and the cost and time required to achieve it much larger. As a consequence development is no longer

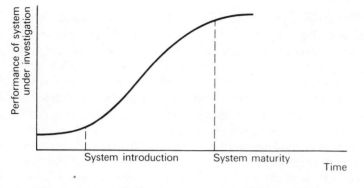

Fig. 10.2 *Generalized 'S'-shaped trend in technological development*

justified and the performance of the system tends to stabilize. Eventually a new system meeting the same set or a similar set of needs is discovered and the development process recommences.

As an example we might consider the development of passenger transport systems over the last two centuries (Fig. 10.3). It is noticeable that after a short period of explosive improvement in each mode, the pace of development slows as the technological constraints on the further development of that particular method are reached. However, if we use an envelope curve to connect the performance of successive technologies we have a more stable and therefore more reliable predictor of the overall rate of progress in achieving more rapid communication than would be possible if we

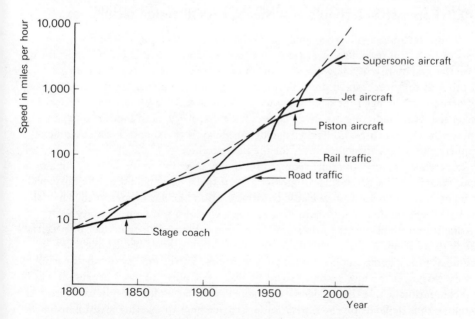

Fig. 10.3 *Passenger transport systems — the envelope curve*

projected the comparatively limited potential of any of the component technologies.

Identified trends in technology may also serve to make indirect forecasts of technological developments in other related areas. In order to use one trend to forecast another it is necessary of course to be convinced of a relationship. If this is satisfactorily established then the secondary trend can be projected from the primary trend on the basis of their known relationships. Typical situations in which such technological comparisons are possible are where technology performs similar tasks in two different environments. The pace of civil and military development of a technology would be similar, except that military applications would lead civilian applications by the several years of development required to meet the higher levels of reliability, economy and safety required for profitable civilian use. As an example vertical take-off for military aircraft is already available — although it may take a further 10—20 years before an effective non-military application can be introduced. It is unwise to rely on such a transfer automatically taking place however, because it does not necessarily follow that the establishment of a technological feasibility and the development of a military application will lead to subsequent non-military use. In many cases the difference between cultures — military and non-military, North American and European, may mean that transfer never takes place. For example the technology for supersonic flight is well established and has been used in military applications for several years. Its adoption for civilian transport will, however, require major technical developments in the area of cost reduction and social acceptability before it becomes a realistic alternative transport system.

§ 10.9 Forecasting technological change with diffusion techniques

The Delphi technique and trend analysis are basically concerned with defining the limits of technical feasibility over time. For business forecasts it is often important to relate the availability of a new process, product or technique to its subsequent adoption so that forecasts of demand for new capital equipment, raw material sources and perhaps of the need for skilled labour can be made. Diffusion analysis is basically concerned with predicting the delay between the discovery of an innovation and its widespread implementation. Knowledge of this delay is valuable to both equipment suppliers and prospective customers for the new product.

Research shows that the time required for a new invention to be adopted on a non-experimental basis is often surprisingly long — 10 to 15 years would not be untypical — and even longer periods may elapse before adoption becomes widespread. The delay can arise for a number of quite ordinary reasons. Questions of compatibility with existing support equipment for example is one important factor that can quite legitimately delay adoption. In re-equipping the telephone systems for example, the technology for a computer-controlled fully-automated electronic switching system already exists yet the new system cannot be instantaneously adopted because it would be incompatible with existing electro-mechanical routing. Full adoption of electronic switching thus depends on the separation or replacement of existing investment in the non-compatible technology. This inevitably takes time, so that before it is completed the new technology itself stands in danger of obsolescence from some as yet untried system – perhaps an optic-based system using laser transmissions down optic fibres.

This delay in adoption of new technology is thus as important to an existing or potential supplier or customer as the fact of the technological discovery itself. For this reason it becomes important to judge how long it will take before a given technological improvement will become widely exploited.

10.9.1 The diffusion of technology – an example

A research programme by the research division of a major steelmaker generated a new technique for oxygen enrichment during steelmaking. This process was adopted by the originating firm and subsequently by all the other firms in the industry, generating a rapidly rising demand for the supply of specialized equipment required for the new process. The problem is to forecast the future demand for this equipment as adoption of the new technology continues.

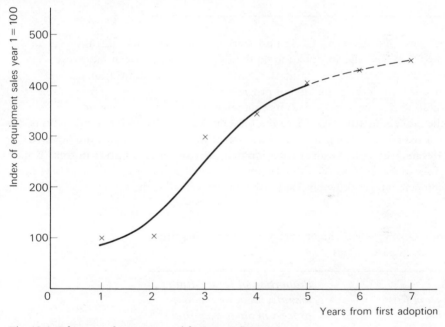

Fig. 10.4 Sales curve for oxygen enrichment equipment

The immediate reaction is to base projections on previous sales of the oxygen-enriching equipment. The direct extrapolation shown in Fig. 10.4 produces a forecast sales index of 420 for year 6 and 450 in year 7. The data on past and forecast sales are shown in Table 10.6.

However, the figures in Table 10.6 are the sum of the investment activities of all the firms in the industry, and each of those firms is likely to be at a separate stage in the adoption of the new process. To take account of this difference in development

Table 10.6

Index of past and forecast sales of oxygen enriching
equipment: projections in parentheses

Years from first adoption	Index of equipment sales
0	Year 1 = 100
1	100
2	103
3	300
4	348
5	402
6	(430)
7	(450)

between firms it is necessary to establish both a typical pattern of diffusion for an
individual firm, and also information on the time intervals between successive
adoptions by different firms within the industry. A pattern of diffusion can be
estimated by considering the kind of progress made in the pioneering firm (Table 10.7)
in integrating the new process into its equipment replacement programme.

If the pioneering firm (A) shared the total market equally with two other firms, one
of which (B) adopted the process 2 years after it was first introduced, the other (C)
after 3 years, we can make an assumption that the pattern of adoption in firms B and
C will follow that of firm A, with a lag of 2 years and 3 years respectively. Using the
diffusion percentages shown in Table 10.7 we can calculate the total industry adoption

Table 10.7

Diffusion of oxygen enrichment process in pioneering firm:
projections in parentheses

Years from first adoption	Proportion of total output manufactured by the new process in pioneering firm (%)
1	10
2	20
3	40
4	55
5	65
6	(72)
7	(78)
8	(80)

Table 10.8
Diffusion of oxygen enrichment process in all firms, together with forecast equipment sales

Years elapsed since process first adopted (t)	Output manufactured by the new process				Capacity switched to new process in year t (%)	Index of sales of the new equipment
	Firm A (%)	Firm B (%)	Firm C (%)	Industry Total (%)		
0	0	0	0	0	0	0
1	10	0	0	3.3	+3.3	100
2	20	0	0	6.7	+3.4	103
3 (Elapsed)	40	10	0	16.7	+10.0	300
4	55	20	10	28.3	+11.6	348
5	65	40	20	41.7	+13.4	402
6	72	55	40	55.7	+14.0	(420)
7	78	65	55	66.0	+10.3	(309)
8 (Forecast)	80	72	65	72.3	+6.3	(189)
9	80	78	72	76.7	+4.4	(132)
10	80	80	78	79.7	+3.0	(90)
11	80	80	80	80.0	+0.3	(9)

rate shown in Table 10.8, and thus calculated sales of the new equipment. By using the diffusion index (for an expanded discussion see Mansfield, 1961) as a basis for analysing the process of technology adoption it thus becomes possible to predict that the rate of growth in projected equipment sales would fall sharply in Year 6 and would decline rapidly after then, though this neglects possible replacement sales. A simple extrapolation of sales would fail to predict this turning point.

§ 10.10 Network methods in forecasting technological change

Frequently the PERT (Programme Evaluation Review Technique) network approach is used to forecast and control the progress of technology-based projects (Thornley, 1968). Network methods (see §3.5) allow a systematic approach to scheduling the large number of individual activities which all have to be completed successfully before a planned technological development becomes possible. For large projects the purely clerical aspects of the forecasting approach can easily be transferred to one of the many computer-based network packages. PERT methods are particularly suitable for forecasting the outcome of research activities because they can be specifically modified to reflect the uncertainty about the pattern and duration of activities which is characteristic of any new process.

The approach adopted is to collect not just single estimates on the likely duration of any component activity, but to collect sufficient information to establish a probability distribution for the duration of each activity. The PERT approach simplifies the task by assuming that the distribution of possible activity times can be represented by a beta distribution. The beta can be estimated using just three estimates of the time required to complete a given activity — pessimistic, most likely and optimistic. Once the parameters of the beta are fixed the distribution of possible outcomes is known.

If pessimistic, most likely and optimistic estimates of required time are defined as t_p, t_m and t_o, then expected duration (t_e) of the activity is calculated as follows:

$$t_e = 1/6 * (t_p + 4t_m + t_o),$$

and the standard deviation (s_e) of the distribution is given by:

$$s_e = 1/6 * (t_p - t_o).$$

For example, if, for a given activity, we have estimates of the possible completion time required, ranging from an optimistic estimate of 20 weeks through a most likely figure of 25 weeks to a pessimistic figure of 35 weeks then the expected completion time, together with the associated standard deviation can be calculated using the above formula:

$$t_e = 1/6 * (20 + 4 * 25 + 35) \text{ weeks}$$
$$= 25.83 \text{ weeks};$$
$$s_e = 1/6 * (35 - 20)$$
$$= 2.50 \text{ weeks}.$$

The effect of the PERT assumptions is to allow for more time for this activity (25.83 weeks) than would have been allocated on the basis of a single valued mean estimate (25 weeks). This reflects the forecaster's expectation that the delay in unfavourable circumstances is substantially greater than possible time-saving in favourable conditions. In addition, the standard deviation of 2.50 weeks associated with the forecast can be used as an indicator of the range of possible error.

If we are trying to forecast the completion date for a research project with many contributing activities (some of which may be parallel activities with the same objective) the information provided by the PERT estimates for each activity in the network allows us to predict a probability distribution for the expected completion of the project that takes into account not just the expected delay down the critical path but also the possibility that lengthy delays down ostensibly non-critical paths may extend overall project time. Further, once computer assistance is available it is possible to forecast the probability with which particular activities will become bottlenecks in achieving project completion. Once bottlenecks are identified it then becomes possible to reconsider the resources initially allocated to these activities to see if additional resources can be found to alleviate the blockage.

10.10.1 PERT in forecasting technology — an example
A car manufacturer in planning the models he wishes to sell 5 years ahead, has to take into account the need to meet the following anti-pollution requirements on any vehicle he offers for sale.

1. The vehicles will have to operate using lead-free fuel.
2. Exhaust components other than water vapour and carbon dioxide will have to be reduced by 80 per cent from existing levels.

To meet these requirements a research programme is initiated to produce suitably modified engines and to develop a suitable catalytic exhaust reactor within 4 years. While each of these tasks required the performance of a multitude of smaller activities the overall plan for the research project is shown in Fig. 10.5.

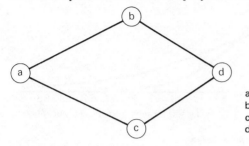

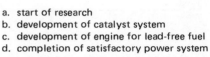

a. start of research
b. development of catalyst system
c. development of engine for lead-free fuel
d. completion of satisfactory power system

Fig. 10.5 Simplified pollution control research network

With optimistic, pessimistic and most likely estimates for each component activity in the network collected, the estimated time along path a → b → d is 41 months while along a → c → d it is 44 months. It therefore appears that developing a modified engine design to operate on lead-free fuel is the critical task, and that in any event it will take only 44 of the available 48 months. Because of the uncertainty, however, it is not sufficient just to consider the path with the highest expected duration. In order to find the expected completion date the possibility of overruns on a non-critical path to the point at which it becomes critical has to be considered. This can be done by using the PERT formula in §10.10 to calculate the standard deviation for each of the paths – suppose this was 7 months for path a → b → d and 3 months for path a → c → d. Because any path length is the sum of a series of randomly varying activity durations, the deviation round the total path length may be assumed to be normally distributed. (Though each activity length has a beta distribution the sum of activities is approximately normal.) This leads to a forecast of the probability that the research programme will overrun, since for a normal distribution we know that 50 per cent of the time an activity path will be completed at or before the expected time. Similarly 84 per cent of the time completion would occur at or before the expected completion date plus one standard deviation. Plotting out the whole distribution in Fig. 10.6 shows that far from worrying about the critical activity path a → c → d, if the project does overrun 48 months it would be much more likely to be because of activity path a → b → d. This conclusion is reached by calculating the probability of overrun for each of the two paths using the data graphed in Fig. 10.6.

Reading the probability of completion at 48 months from the graph it is 0.84 for a → b → d and 0.91 for a → c → d. The probability of overrun on path a → b → d at month 48 is:

1 − Prob (completion time, path a → b → d < 48) = 1 − 0.84 = 0.16

and similarly,

Prob (overrun on path a → c → d) = 1 − 0.91 = 0.09.

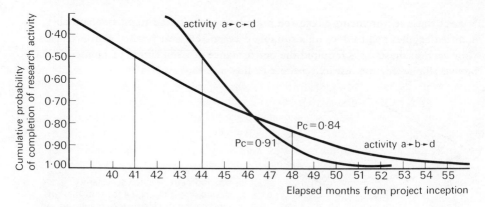

Fig. 10.6 Probability distribution of activity completion date

From these calculations it appears that overrun over 48 months is twice as likely for a → b → d as it is for a → c → d, so this is the activity that requires close monitoring. This conclusion, however, would have been different if the deadline was 45 months, because a → c → d has a higher overrun possibility than a → b → d. Since the overall success of the project depends on both a → b → d and a → c → d being complete the overall probability of completion for the project within the target of 48 months can be calculated. Overrun would take place if either a → b → d or a → c → d, or in fact both of them were not completed by the due date. The probability of both being complete is the product of the probabilities of each being complete, as long as we can assume the completion times independent of each other.

Prob (completion time, overall < 48) = Prob (completion time, a → b → d < 48)

$$* \text{ Prob (completion time, a → c → d < 48)}$$

$$= 0.84 * 0.91$$

$$= 0.7644$$

and the probability of failure to complete is then 1 − 0.7644, or 0.2356. In most projects this level of failure would be unacceptably high. Thus the example shows how unrealistic it is to base plans on the overall estimate of 48 months. Either the time allowed should be increased or else the resources available (particularly to path a → b → d) should be increased.

§ 10.11 Summary

Before we consider a change as likely we have to be satisfied that it is technically feasible, and that society regards it as desirable. Where forecasting is concerned with existing or known developments the feasibility of a solution that perhaps reduces costs or increases welfare may be taken for granted. Outside known applications however, feasibility is a constraint on change which has to be specifically recognized.

This chapter gives some indication of the forecasting methods employed when the required lead time of the forecasts and the relative newness of many of the techniques to be used means that no easy base of comparison between alternative methods exists. For this reason it seems preferable to make long-range and technological forecasts using more than one method since a comparison between their predicted outcomes provides both an indication of forecast errors and an improved insight on the plausibility of the underlying assumptions of alternative methods.

It is important to remember that technological forecasts attempt to define only what is feasible. The events they forecast have to be desirable as well as feasible to actually occur. Just as technological forecasts impose boundaries of feasibility on non-technological forecasts of what is desired, so desirability criteria equally limit the sensible projection of technically feasible developments. As an example space scientists can forecast a set of technological developments that would permit humans to live in self-sufficient units under the moon's crust, and assume this means that the moon will eventually become inhabited. On desirability grounds such a forecast could be dismissed because even if the technology was established as feasible it would make more sense to apply it in exploiting the earth's crust. Similarly, control of genetically inherited characteristics seem increasingly within our technical abilities. Its implications for society are considerable and it is only through a forecast of its likely effects that society can judge whether it can solve the problems genetic control raises, and decide whether this is a desirable or undesirable development.

References

CSO (1973) 'Input—output tables for the United Kingdom', *Studies in Official Statistics*, No. 22, HMSO, London.

Dunckel, E. B., Reed, W. K. and Wilson, I. H. (1970) *The Business Environment of the Seventies: a Trend Analysis for Business Planning*, McGraw-Hill, New York.

Esch, M. E. (1969) in Arnfield, R. V. (ed.) *Technological Forecasting*, Edinburgh University Press, Edinburgh.

Mansfield, E. (1961) 'Technical change and the rate of imitation', *Econometrica*, vol. 29.

Milkovich, G. J. Annoni, A. J. and Mahoney, J. A. (1973) 'The use of the Delphi procedure in manpower forecasting', *Management Science*, vol. 19, No. 4, Part 1.

North, H. Q. (1968) 'Technology the chicken, corporate goals the egg', in Bright (ed.), *Technological Forecasting for Industry and Government*, Prentice-Hall, New Jersey.

Parker, E. F. (1971) 'Forecasting future market profiles by the Delphi method', *The Business Economist*, vol. 3, No. 1.

Sigford, J. V. and Porvin, R. H. (1965) 'Project PATTERN: A methodology for determining relevance in complex decision making', *I.E.E.E. Transactions on Engineering Management*, vol. 12 : 1.

Stern, L. (1974) Contingency Planning: 'Why? How and Much?', *Datamation*, vol. 20.

Thornley, G. (ed.) (1968) *Critical Path Analysis in Practice: Collected Papers on Project Control*, Tavistock, London.

Additional references

Input—output
For a basic introduction:

Robinson, J. N. (1972) *Planning and Forecasting Techniques*, Weidenfield and Nicolson, London, Chs 1 and 2;
Chiou-Shuang, Y. (1969) *Introduction to Input—Output Economics*, Holt, Rinehart and Winston, New York.

A non-technical introduction is given by the originator of the method in:

Leontief, W. (1966) *Input—Output Economics*, Oxford University Press, New York,

while the latter part of the book becomes more difficult, requiring the use of matrix algebra. For a recent bibliography see:

Richardson, H. W. (1972) *Input—Output and Regional Economics*, Weidenfield and Nicolson, London.

A more advanced though older work is:

Chenery, H. B. and **Clark, P. G.** (1959) *Interindustry Economics*, Wiley, New York.

Planning under uncertainty

Mack, Ruth P. (1971) *Planning on Uncertainty*, Wiley, New York.

Delphi
For a full description of the Delphi technique see, for example:

Martino, J. P. (1972) *Technological Forecasting for Decision Making*, Elsevier, New York.

Technological forecasting
The choice of references is almost as large as the subject. An excellent book capturing the 'state of the art' in 1967 by one of its most eminent practitioners is:

Jantsch, E. (1967) *Technological Forecasting in Perspective*, OECD, Paris.
Ayres, R. V. (1969) *Technological Forecasting and Long-Range Planning*, McGraw-Hill, New York,

is also seminal. A more recent text, which aims, in its 750 pages, at completeness, is:

Martino, J. P. (1972) op. cit.

while

Bright, J. R. and **Schoeman, M. E. F.** (eds) (1973) *A Guide to Practical Technological Forecasting*, Prentice-Hall, Englewood Cliffs, New Jersey,

in about the same number of pages, offers us the latest ideas from practising experts in the field. At the other extreme, a brief survey is given by:

Gerstenfield, A. (1971) 'Technological forecasting', *The Journal of Business*, vol. 44.

On particular topics,

Helmer, O. (1966) *Social Technology*, Basic Books, New York,

is useful on Delphi, while for an expanded description of relevance trees, see:

Swager, W. L. (1973) *Technological Forecasting in Planning — a method using Relevance Trees*, Business Horizons.

We touch briefly on forecasting for new products in our discussion of diffusion techniques, a whole area we have been forced to neglect.

Kotler, P. (1971) *Marketing Decision Making: a Model Building Approach*, Holt, Rinehart and Winston, New York,

offers a survey and bibliography. The literature of new product modelling is filled with *ad hoc* solutions with no evaluative basis. The problems after all are similar to those discussed in this book except that the data base is small.

Fitzroy, P. (1975) *Analytical Methods in Marketing Management*, McGraw-Hill, New York,

discusses some of the better known models from a viewpoint close to our own. For a recent application with colour television see for example:

Mathur, S. S. and Padley, H. (1974) 'Forecasting first owner sales of consumer durables', *Industrial Marketing Management*, vol. 3.

More generally such books as:

Weber, E., Teal, G. K. and Schillinger, A. G. (1971) *Technology Forecast for 1980*, Van Rostrand Reinhold, New York,

or

Kahn, H. and Wiener, A. J. (1967) *The Year 2000*, Macmillan, New York,

offer us the authors' forecasts on both the technological and social front, while more current thoughts on long-range and technological forecasting are contained in the journals, *Futures* and *Long-Range Planning*.

Appendix 1 — Expectation

In a chance situation in which there is a total of n possible numerical outcomes, a_1, $a_2, \ldots a_n$ the expected value of the outcome is obtained by multiplying each possible outcome by the probability of it occurring and summing these products over all the possible outcomes. Since the outcomes are exhaustive (no other outcomes are possible) and mutually exclusive (only one of the specified outcomes can in fact occur) the probabilities $p(a_1)$, $p(a_2)$, $\ldots$, $p(a_n)$ of each of the outcomes used in the calculation above, must sum to 1. These probabilities form the probability distribution of the random variable X which represents the outcome of the chance situation and may therefore take on the value of each of the n possible outcomes.

Now if we made N repeat observations in the chance situation and outcome a_1 occurred with a frequency f_1, outcome a_2 with a frequency f_2, etc., then the observed average value of the chance outcomes, $\overline{X}$, would be:

$$\overline{X} = \frac{a_1 f_1 + a_2 f_2 + \cdots + a_n f_n}{N}.$$

In repeating the experiment N times we would expect the relative frequencies f_1/N, f_2/N, $\ldots f_n/N$ to approximate the underlying probability distribution of X, $p(a_1)$, $p(a_2)$, $\ldots p(a_n)$. We can use this result to interpret our earlier definition of the expected value of the outcome, EX. Now in the first paragraph we defined EX as:

$$EX = a_1 p(a_1) + a_2 p(a_2) + \cdots + a_n p(a_n).$$

The expected value of the random variable X is the value of the outcomes, weighted by their probabilities. By comparison with the formula for the observed average, $\overline{X}$, we may think of EX as the underlying average or expected outcome of the chance situation.

The definition of EX may be easily extended to include situations where the outcomes of the chance situation are continuous; for example the situation might be company sales next year. The possible outcomes might be all values of sales between £5 m. and £10 m. The interpretation of EX remains the same; it is the underlying average outcome.

Appendix 2 — Summation notation

Suppose we wish to add up a series of measurements $X_1, X_2 \ldots X_n$. This we would normally write as $(X_1 + X_2 + \cdots + X_n)$ the dots signifying the omission of measurements similar to those at both the beginning and end of the series. The summation notation is designed to simplify such expressions as well as make them more precise. We will write Σ (read sigma) to stand for 'sum'. The sum of the measurements may then be written $\sum_{i=1}^{n} X_i$ where X_i is the ith measurement, either $X_1, X_2 \ldots$ or X_n. This is read 'sum all elements X_i, as i takes integer values from 1 to n'. The lower subscript on the Σ is called the lower limit of the sum, the superscript the upper limit.

Explicitly, the summation tells us to take the first element X_i, with i = 1 substituted, add to it the second, X_i with i = 2 substituted, the third etc., and to stop when the final element, the nth has been added to the sum, i.e.:

$$\sum_{i=1}^{n} X_i = (X_1 + X_2 + \cdots + X_n).$$

Example 1.
Suppose $X_1 = 1$, $X_2 = -1$, $X_3 = 0$, $X_4 = 2$.

$$\sum_{i=1}^{4} X_i = (X_1 + X_2 + X_3 + X_4) = (1 + (-1) + 0 + 2) = 2.$$

There is no reason why the summation limits should start at 1 and finish at n. We may wish to express $(X_3 + X_4 + \cdots + X_{n-3})$ concisely. This may be written $\sum_{i=3}^{n-3} X_i$. The first element is identified by the lower limit to Σ, the last element by the upper limit.

Example 2.
Using the values of $[X_i]$ from example 1,

$$\sum_{i=2}^{3} X_i = (X_2 + X_3) = -1.$$

Appendix 2 — Summation notation

Example 3.

Suppose $X_i = 2$ for all n measurements;

$$\sum_{i=1}^{n} X_i = \sum_{i=1}^{n} 2 = (2 + 2 + \cdots + 2) = 2n.$$

Generally, we may note that $\sum_{i=1}^{n} c = nc$ when c is constant. A more general application
of summation is when the measurement is transformed in some way. For example, the
sample variance of n measurements is calculated using the formula:

$$s^2 = \left\{ \sum_{i=1}^{n} X_i^2 - n\bar{X}^2 \right\} \bigg/ (n - 1)$$

where $\bar{X}$ is the average of the observations $= (X_1 + X_2 + \cdots + X_n)/n = \dfrac{1}{n} \sum_{i=1}^{n} X_i$

'$\sum_{i=1}^{n} X_i^2$' stands for $(X_1^2 + X_2^2 + \cdots + X_n^2)$.

The typical measurement X_i is squared and these new values are summed.

Example 4.

Using the values of $[X_i]$ from example 1.

$$\sum_{i=1}^{4} X_i^2 = (X_1^2 + X_2^2 + X_3^2 + X_4^2) = 6.$$

It is worth noting that we have used i as an index, when we could as well have used j
or k. The sum does not depend on the index, only the values of the measurements.

Suppose we have n pairs of measurements (X_j, Y_j). As part of the calculation of the
correlation coefficient of Chapters 5 and 6, the quantity $\sum_{j=1}^{n} X_j Y_j$ is needed. Here the
jth element is $X_j Y_j$ and the summation stands for $(X_1 Y_1 + X_2 Y_2 + \cdots + X_n Y_n)$. As we
remarked above whether i or j is used as the summation index is unimportant.

Appendix 3 — An example of step-wise regression

The data and basic printout

Notes: Typically a multiple regression program allows the user to transform the raw variables in many different ways. We discussed some of the possibilities in §6.3 and §6.5. The user usually has the option of asking for a printout of either the raw data, the transformed data or a mixture of both. (The data are printed out to four significant figures although the raw data used in the calculations are more accurate.) Here we give just the transformed data. As there were no transformations made the raw and transformed data sets are identical. However, if we wished to include Y_{t-1} as an 'independent' variable in the model we would take the data in column 9 and make a lag transformation, placing the transformed values in a fresh column, column 10.† The number of new variables added using the available transformations is listed on page 1 of the printout (p. 268), as are the transformations made.

A variable may be transformed (say by squaring each value) and may be put in place of the original variable or alternatively may be added in a fresh column in the transformed data matrix. The summary information is, of course, sufficient to say which of the possibilities has occurred, and by reference to the data matrix the user is able to assure himself that he has been successful in carrying out his intentions.

Finally, the data format statement is a means of preparing the computer to read the raw data cards. At least one of the authors always has to consult a programmer to make sure his input instructions are correct.

Pages 4 and 5 of the printout give details of the provisionally selected models as first $X - 1$ is included, then $X - 7$, $X - 8$ and $X - 5$ while at STEP NUMBER 5, $X - 1$ is deleted. The final model is given at STEP NUMBER 6 when $X - 4$ enters. The residuals are also plotted.

---

† Note that because Y_t is transformed into Y_{t-1} the first observation is lost because there is no value in the transformed data set corresponding to Y_1 in the original set. In this example there would therefore be only nineteen data points remaining.

267

STEPWISE REGRESSION   FILDES-WOOD   PAGE 1

****

THE BASIC VARIABLES ARE:

X - 1 : TIME
X - 2 : INDEX REAL PER CAPITA EXPENDITURE ON CONSUMER DURABLES, 1955 = 100
X - 3 : X - 2 LAGGED ONE PERIOD
X - 4 : RELATIVE PRICE
X - 5 : PERCENTAGE PER CAPITA CHANGE IN REAL INCOME
X - 6 : AVAILABILITY OF CREDIT
X - 7 : REAL PER CAPITA EXPENDITURE ON PRODUCT ADVERTISING EXPENDITURE
X - 8 : INDEX NEW HOUSEHOLD FORMATIONS, 1956 = 100
X - 9 : SALES IN UNITS PER CAPITA * 100

PROBLEM NUMBER   1
NO OF OBSERVATION   20
NO OF VARIABLES (IN DATA)   9
NO OF VARIABLES (ADDED)   0
NO OF VARIABLES (IN PROBLEM)   9
DATA FORMAT USED
(9(F8.5,X))

               NO TRANSFORMATIONS

****

STEPWISE REGRESSION -   FILDFS-STFREO   **PAGE 2**

TRA	1	1.000	100.0	98.31	1.431	1.935	37.94	39.20	101.1	12.94
TRA	2	2.000	102.0	100.0	1.144	2.156	44.48	88.28	100.0	15.67
TRA	3	3.000	104.5	102.0	1.096	2.499	40.67	156.7	102.4	22.45
TRA	4	4.000	105.9	104.5	1.159	2.468	51.77	169.1	100.6	19.68
TRA	5	5.000	108.2	105.9	1.089	2.027	56.23	171.2	95.56	15.46
TRA	6	6.000	110.4	108.2	.8488	2.035	51.44	221.9	102.9	23.37
TRA	7	7.000	115.0	110.4	1.162	2.151	41.09	218.6	99.28	20.64
TRA	8	8.000	119.4	115.0	.9361	1.966	46.46	229.0	97.63	20.22
TRA	9	9.000	123.4	119.4	.8726	2.625	46.73	196.5	99.48	23.51
TRA	10	10.00	130.3	123.4	.9404	2.674	53.71	198.9	99.44	22.53
TRA	11	11.00	132.7	130.3	.9562	2.402	60.82	179.5	102.2	23.52
TRA	12	12.00	139.9	132.7	1.054	2.832	54.45	176.1	100.3	24.00
TRA	13	13.00	142.8	139.9	.9402	1.840	55.01	199.8	103.7	23.08
TRA	14	14.00	147.4	142.8	1.131	2.490	63.21	194.6	102.6	22.80
TRA	15	15.00	152.3	147.4	1.084	2.534	52.22	211.7	100.4	23.13
TRA	16	16.00	161.1	152.3	.9666	2.897	48.76	187.2	99.32	21.69
TRA	17	17.00	174.4	161.1	.9505	2.064	51.23	187.2	101.0	22.10
TRA	18	18.00	177.5	174.4	.9895	2.549	54.18	192.5	99.85	22.19
TRA	19	19.00	179.1	177.5	.9497	2.785	47.72	195.5	104.1	26.65
TRA	20	20.00	186.3	179.1	1.131	4.141	57.95	185.7	98.20	25.34

VARIABLE	MEAN	STANDARD DEVIATION	VARIANCE	**PAGE 3**
1	10.50000	5.916080	35.00000	
2	135.6353	28.44102	808.8914	
3	131.2378	26.96158	726.9267	
4	1.041524	.1343459	.1804883E-01	
5	2.453601	.5114951	.2616272	
6	50.90281	6.751874	45.58780	
7	179.9473	44.37207	1968.881	
8	100.5019	2.098313	4.402917	
9	21.54636	3.389122	11.48615	

CORRELATION MATRIX

VAR	2	.084							
VAR	3	.980 (1)	.996 (2)						
VAR	4	-.403 (1)	-.315 (2)	-.307 (3)					
VAR	5	.559 (1)	.575 (2)	.575 (3)	-.007 (4)				
VAR	6	.502 (1)	.428 (2)	.434 (3)	-.312 (4)	.287 (5)			
VAR	7	.508 (1)	.384 (2)	.375 (3)	-.730 (4)	.145 (5)	.402 (6)		
VAR	8	.124 (1)	.123 (2)	.154 (3)	-.128 (4)	-.153 (5)	-.017 (6)	-.028 (7)	
VAR	9	.719 (1)	.648 (2)	.653 (3)	-.636 (4)	.535 (5)	.388 (6)	.712 (7)	.404 (8)

PAGE

```
**************                                                    PAGE 4
PROBLEM NUMBER      1
SUBPROBLEM NUMBER   1
F TO ENTER        4.00000         -0.00000
F TO REMOVE       4.00000         -0.00000
TOLERANCE          .00001
MAXIMUM NO OF STEPS  8
DEPENDENT VARIABLE   9

STANDARD ERROR OF Y = 3.3891    , FOR DEGREES OF FREEDOM = 19.

**************
STEP NUMBER  1
VARIABLE ENTERING       1              ANALYSIS OF VARIANCE FOR REDUCTION IN SS DUE TO VARIABLE ENTERING
MULTIPLE R             .71950           SOURCE            DF      SS          MS              F
STD ERROR OF Y.X      2.41823          DUE REGRESSION      1    112.976     112.976         19.3193
R SQUARE               .51768          DEV. FROM REG.     18    105.261       5.84783
                                       TOTAL              19    218.237      11.4861
     MULTIPLE REGRESSION EQUATION
VARIABLE  COEFFICIENT  STD. ERROR  T VALUE  PARTIAL COR.  ELASTICITY†    PARTIAL COR. FOR VAR. NOT IN EQUATION
CONST.     17.219       1.233      15.328                                VARIABLE  COEFFICIENT  F FOR SELECTION
   X- 1     .41218      .53775E-01  4.3954    .71950        .20086   *     X- 2    -.48348       5.1860
                                                                          X- 3    -.37294       2.7465
                                                                          X- 4    -.54475       7.1735
                                                                          X- 5     .22992       .94880
                                                                          X- 6     .45047E-01   .34567E-01
                                                                          X- 7     .57893       4.5701
                                                                          X- 8     .45654       4.4782
**************
STEP NUMBER  2
VARIABLE ENTERING       7              ANALYSIS OF VARIANCE FOR REDUCTION IN SS DUE TO VARIABLE ENTERING
MULTIPLE R             .82422           SOURCE            DF      SS          MS              F
STD ERROR OF Y.X      2.02893          DUE REGRESSION      2    148.255      74.1277         18.0072
R SQUARE               .67933          DEV. FROM REG.     17     69.9815      4.11656
                                       TOTAL              19    218.237      11.4861
     MULTIPLE REGRESSION EQUATION
VARIABLE  COEFFICIENT  STD. ERROR  T VALUE  PARTIAL COR.  ELASTICITY     PARTIAL COR. FOR VAR. NOT IN EQUATION
CONST.     12.229       1.9475     6.2794                                VARIABLE  COEFFICIENT  F FOR SELECTION
   X- 1     .27634      .91341E-01  3.0254    .59159        .13467   *     X- 2    -.89503E-01   .12921
   X- 7     .35652E-01  .12178E-01  2.9275    .57893        .29775   *     X- 3    -.60835E-01   .59434E-01
                                                                          X- 4    -.20188       .71781
                                                                          X- 5     .42809       3.4200
                                                                          X- 6    -.86907E-01   .12176
                                                                          X- 8     .63964       11.079
```

† See §8.2 for an explanation of elasticity.

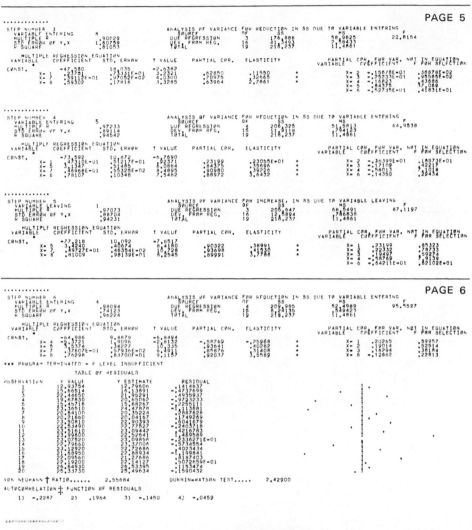

† A description of Von Neuman's Ratio is given in Johnston (1972), p. 250.
‡ The autocorrelation function is defined in §7.4 and is an estimate of the correlation between e_t and e_{t-k}, k = 1,2,3,4. For k = 1 this the 'ρ' of §6.6.1.

The forecasting printout

Using the same model as the previous section we give here a set of forecasts based on the extrapolation data which the program first reprints. Once the confidence level is specified (the degrees of freedom being known) the t value is fixed and we may use the previously estimated forecasting equation with the corresponding standard error to find the confidence limits for the next 5 years, contingent on our having the correct forecasts of the independent variables. The output is shown below.

FORECASTING: MODEL 2   FILDES–WOOD

****

NO. OF FORECASTS TO BE MADE 5

EXTRAPØLATIØN DATA

X–1	X–2	X–3	X–4	X–5	X–6	X–7	X–8
21.00000	180.00000	186.30000	1.15000	2.00000	60.00000	190.00000	95.00000
22.00000	182.00000	180.00000	1.10000	.20000	68.00000	180.00000	91.00000
23.00000	184.00000	182.00000	1.00000	.50000	68.00000	185.00000	95.00000
24.00000	189.00000	184.00000	.98000	2.00000	60.00000	200.00000	100.00000
25.00000	195.00000	189.00000	.95000	4.00000	50.00000	220.00000	108.00000

FØRECASTING EQUATIØN IS:–

$$X-9 = -64.9860 - 5.3721(X-4) + 3.5374(X-5) + .0376(X-7) + .7629(X-8)$$

STANDARD ERRØR= .74123   CØNFIDENCE LEVEL=90%

T–VALUE= 1.75300

FØRECAST NØ.	FØRECAST	RANGE
1	15.530385	1.621533
2	6.004070	2.448131
3	10.842100	2.014032
4	20.634142	1.373403
5	34.725305	2.027852

END ØF FØRECAST

The heading 'RANGE' defines the actual confidence interval through the formula:

CONFIDENCE INTERVAL = FORECAST ± RANGE.

It depends, as in the one dimensional case discussed in §5.4 as the standard error, the confidence level and the corresponding t value, as well as the extrapolation data.

References

Johnston, J. (1972) *Econometric Methods*, 2nd edn, McGraw-Hill, New York.

Appendix 4 — The construction of quality constant price indices

In validating causal models we have emphasized the expectation that the relationships between each explanatory variable and the dependent variable should be of the expected sign and magnitude and should also be 'significant'.

Consumers naturally do not respond to price changes resulting from quality changes in the same way as they do to pure price changes at constant quality. It follows that using unadjusted price observations which reflect both pure price changes and the transmitted costs of quality changes in a sales forecasting model will result in a parameter estimate which has no obvious interpretation and may well be of the wrong sign. However, this leaves us with the problem of deriving a pure price term with the effects of all quality changes netted out. To do this we need a working definition of product quality as perceived and valued by consumers.

If we were investigating car sales obvious measures of product quality are power, fuel economy, passenger and luggage space and measures of this sort were included by Cowling and Cubbin in their index for UK cars (Cowling and Cubbin, 1972). We could also justify further factors which are less easily measured but demonstrably generate consumer satisfaction, the advertised image of the car, the status it confers and so on.

Suppose we start with a list of N of these product attributes, $A_1 \ldots A_N$, each of which may measure some aspect of quality. We can then predict product price for the jth product variant in any given year as a function of its scores along these 'N' dimensions of product quality, using an additive model:

$$P_j = \beta_0 + \sum_{i=1}^{N} \beta_i a_{ij} + e_j \quad j = 1, 2, \ldots, n,$$

where P_j is the price of brand j, n is the number of brands and a_{ij} is the level of attribute i in the jth brand.

Since we are led to believe that for manufactured products all models of a given brand are homogeneous with respect to the attribute levels this means that each of the n brands only provides one data point whether it sold one unit or one million. To correct for this we use a technique called weighted least squares as our criterion in fitting the equation. This technique consists of multiplying each residual error in predicting brand price by a weighting to reflect the relative importance we wish to give the brand with which it is associated. In this case the appropriate weighting is the market share of the jth brand m_j and we seek to minimize the weighted squared error:

$$\sum_{j=1}^{n} m_j(P_j - \hat{P}_j)^2,$$

where n is the total number of brands and hence the total number of observations.

Using this criterion we may estimate the parameters of the brand pricing equation for each year separately, deriving estimates $\beta_0(t), \beta_1(t) \ldots, \beta_N(t)$, t denoting the year. These parameters, despite obvious problems of collinearity (power and speed for example are closely associated attributes in cars) can be interpreted as the average 'shadow' prices imputed to the various product characteristics in year $t = 0, 1 \ldots$ etc. Given these regression coefficients calculated for each year we can use them to estimate a price index for the tth year compared with the base year 0.

$$I_t = \frac{\sum\limits_{i=1}^{N} \hat{\beta}_i(t) * \overline{A}_i(0)}{\sum\limits_{i=1}^{N} \hat{\beta}_i(0) * \overline{A}_i(0)}$$

where $\overline{A}_i(0)$ is the average level of the ith attribute in year 0, so if brand j has attribute i in quantity $a_{ij}(0)$ and market share $m_j(0)$ the average level of attribute i across all brands is:

$$\overline{A}_i(0) = \sum_{j=1}^{n} a_{ij}(0)m_j(0).$$

The $\beta_i(t)$'s are the regression coefficients in year t and of course $\beta_i(0)$ are the coefficients in the base year 0.

In reported applications this index has been modified. Musgrove (1969) used dummy variables rather than continuous variables, so the base weighting $\overline{A}_i(0)$, applied to the estimated coefficients $\beta_i(t)$, is just the proportion of units sold possessing attributed A_i in the base year. A further modification is to use a chain index in which the value of I_t is relative to I_{t-1} rather than the I_0. This overcomes the problem that qualities which were thought desirable at one stage — perhaps a rear engine — became undesirable at a later date. The index formula then becomes:

$$= I_t/I_{t-1}.$$

However, the index is calculated it can be used in two ways. First it can be used to deflate a series of observed prices in a product market where quality changes occur. This deflation gives a quality adjusted price series from which we might expect consistent coefficients if we used it to forecast overall sales. The second use is in market share calculations where the price for a given brand can be replaced by the difference between market price and the estimated price, based on the 'shadow' attribute prices, of securing that particular brand's mix of attributes. So for example, Cowling and Cubbin (1971) estimate brand price through the model:

$$\hat{\log} P_j(t) = \hat{\beta}_0(t) + \sum_{i=1}^{N} \hat{\beta}_i(t) a_{ij}(t), \quad j = 1, 2, \ldots, n$$

where there are n brands and N product attributes and consequently the differential price, $\hat{U}_j(t) = \log P_j(t) - \hat{\log} P_j(t)$ represents the amount paid for brand j over and above what one might expect to pay for a product processing the characteristics $a_{1j}(t), a_{2j}(t) \ldots a_{Nj}(t)$. This differential is then incorporated into their market shares model directly as shown in §8.3.4. Of course where actual price is below estimated price the brand is competitive; if above it is uncompetitive. We would therefore expect the quality adjusted price $\hat{U}_j(t)$ to have a negative sign when included in a forecasting model.

References

Cowling, K. and Cubbin, J. (1971) 'Price, quality and advertising competition', *Economica*, vol. 38.

Cowling, K. and Cubbin, J. (1972) 'Hedonic price indices for U.K. cars', *The Economic Journal*, vol. 82.

Musgrove, J. C. (1969) 'The measurement of price changes in construction', *Journal of American Statistical Association*, vol. 64.

Index